# Bahamian Rhapsody

The Unofficial History
of Pro Wrestling's
Unofficial Territory
1960 to 2020

# Bahamian Rhapsody

## The Unofficial History of Pro Wrestling's Unofficial Territory

### 1960 to 2020

By

Ian C. Douglass

DARKSTREAM

Published by:

Darkstream Press

www.darkstreampress.com

This book is set in Garamond.

10 9 8 7 6 5 4 3 2 1

ISBN 979-8-218-06966-7

This book is dedicated to the memory of

# David Cecil Capron

December 3, 1938 – March 12, 2020

Thank you for taking me to see Dusty Rhodes
wrestle at Nassau Stadium.

# Table of Contents

# Foreword

People who never spent an evening inside of Nassau Stadium prior to 1991 will never understand what it was truly like to wrestle in the Bahamas.

It's hard for modern wrestlers and wrestling fans to imagine entertaining a crowd that believed everything we were doing was real with every fiber of their being. The Bahamian fans lived and died with every punch, kick and slam that transpired in front of them. They rushed to come to the aid of the wrestlers they liked, and they wished to inflict legitimate bodily harm on the wrestlers they despised. Considering how hard wrestlers have struggled to extract genuine emotion from fans over the years, I fondly recall nights in Nassau when getting the fans to love you or hate you was easy.

The Bahamas itself was paradise, and any time I was fortunate enough to wrestle there, it was like going on a three-day vacation with a little bit of wrestling thrown in for good measure. When I had the opportunity to bring the Florida wrestling territory back from the dead, there was no doubt in my mind that we were going to run shows in the Bahamas if we could. I wanted the new wrestlers I was teaching and training to also enjoy having an opportunity to wrestle in paradise as a reward for their efforts, and to gain the experience of wrestling in energetic environments where the responses of the people couldn't always be predicted.

In this book, you're going to hear stories about threatening situations that arose in the Bahamas, and that's because those stories were true. That's not because the Bahamian people are in any way more violent than any other group; they wanted to protect the good guys who were being unfairly harmed by the bad guys.

What the Bahamian people saw happening in the ring may not have been real, but it's one of the ultimate compliments to the performers who presented wrestling as a form of entertainment to the fans of the Bahamas that we were able to elicit that type of reaction from them. And if I was having my teeth kicked in by someone in real life, I know that any of those Bahamian fans in Nassau Stadium would have my back if I ever asked them for help.

I've wrestled all over the United States, and especially in the southern part of the country. It's true what they say about southern hospitality, but that absolutely pales in comparison to the love and kindness that I was shown by the Bahamian people every time I traveled to the Bahamas.

# Bahamian Rhapsody

So kick back, relax, and learn what it was like to eat, sleep and wrestle in one of the most unique settings in the history of the professional wrestling industry. In a world where so much is scripted, improvised, and inauthentic, there was no environment where pro wrestling's perils were any more real – or where the fans were any more passionate – than in the paradise provided by the Bahamas.

God bless,

Steve Keirn

# Prologue

I was born and raised in Southfield, Michigan, which is in Oakland County, just north of Detroit's northwest corner. Much to the immediate chagrin of my parents, I can confidently say that I became a professional wrestling fan from the very first moment I ever laid eyes on the product.

In 1987, the Oakland County municipality of Pontiac was the host for the legendary WrestleMania III event featuring a main-event match between Hulk Hogan and Andre the Giant, for which the World Wrestling Federation reported an attendance figure of 93,173. Every time I turned on the television on Saturday morning, the only wrestling-related programming I saw consisted of syndicated WWF programs that were held at major stadiums and large venues around the United States, and which were taped in front of large audiences.

To many educated wrestling fans who were alive at the time, this will sound like borderline sacrilege, but by 1989 I had barely even heard the name of "Nature Boy" Ric Flair, I had no concept of the National Wrestling Alliance as an entity comprising an alliance of anything at all, and I had no idea whatsoever for what a wrestling "territory" was.

As far as I was concerned, no wrestling existed outside of Vince McMahon's World Wrestling Federation. This remained true to such an extent that if a wrestler materialized inside of a WWF ring for the first time, I had no idea where they had emerged from, and when they disappeared from WWF programming, I had no clue where on earth they had departed to.

Nor did I care, necessarily. The only thing that mattered to me at the time – aside from the Detroit Pistons hopefully winning the NBA championship that year – was whether or not "Macho Man" Randy Savage could somehow regain the world championship from the wrestler who was the favorite of everyone else in my elementary school, Hulk Hogan.

4

In light of all this, when I traveled to my mother's native city of Nassau on New Providence Island in the Bahamas as a nine-year-old boy, the last thing I ever expected was for Uncle David to tell me he was taking me to see a professional wrestling show.

"Will the Macho Man be there?" I asked, hopefully.

"No," said Uncle David. "You're going to see Dusty Rhodes!"

"*Who* is Dusty Rhodes?" I asked him.

"You'll see," smiled my uncle.

We picked up Mr. Willard Johnson in my uncle's car, drove east along Bay Street, passed Mackey Street (where my mother grew up) and parked close to The Poop Deck restaurant. From there, we climbed out of the vehicle and walked along the dimly lit road as my eyes searched through the dark for the vast arena where the show would certainly be held in, and which had somehow escaped my notice during all of my prior trips to the island. Instead, I followed my uncle up Fowler Street to a one-story, lime-green building with an arched roof and a concrete exterior.

**The Fowler Street entrance to Nassau Stadium**

# Bahamian Rhapsody

We walked in through one set of doors – just long enough for me to glance to the left at people seated at the bar countertop of what appeared to be a restaurant – and immediately out through another doorway. From there, I could see a wrestling ring was set up in plain view in the middle of a courtyard surrounded by rows of wooden chairs, beyond which were wooden bleachers that had been erected on three sides. Two wrestlers who I had never seen before were already in the ring. I would later learn that one of them was Mike Graham, son of legendary wrestler and promoter Eddie Graham.

The three of us found seats on the bleachers off to our right, which faced south. The surroundings I found myself in were a far cry from anything my young mind had ever associated with professional wrestling. The tops of the cement walls contained the piercing presence of glass shards from broken beer bottles permanently embedded in them. Above one of the restaurant entrances was a tunnel of chicken-wire fencing with debris stuck to the top of it, and I couldn't imagine how all of that trash could possibly have become lodged there. Why wouldn't someone come to clean it off?

When the participants for the next bout made their way out to the ring, I quickly learned how all that debris came to rest at the top of the wire structure. Bottles and trash soared through the air from all over the stadium in the direction of the latest bad guy to walk to the ring. From that moment until the conclusion of the evening, everything I thought I had known about professional wrestling steadily dissipated into the haze of the Nassau evening sky.

As the night progressed, The Nasty Boys – a team I might have known something about if I'd ever watched the American Wrestling Association's programming on ESPN – won the PWF Florida Tag Team Championship, and the Bahamian crowd erupted in approval at the conclusion of that match. It was the loudest sustained applause I'd ever heard in person up until that point of my young life. However, the tolerance level of my ears was about to be tested twice more.

When it was time for the main event, the largest human being I'd ever seen sauntered out to the ring, and trash rained down upon him from all angles. Then, the cheers from the crowd crescendoed as a round, bleach-blonde man hustled out to the ring, stood on the ring apron, and turned to salute us all.

This was the first time I ever laid eyes on "The American Dream" Dusty Rhodes. It wasn't on the TBS or TNT cable networks, and it wasn't being supplied by local Florida programming and beamed onto my uncle's television set at his Soldier Road home. It was live in Nassau Stadium with 2,000 people surrounding me, and screaming their collective heads off.

Rhodes won a last-man-standing match with Big Steel Man that night to conclude the event and send us all home happy. The atmosphere in the stadium was electric, and I couldn't have been any more pleased with my first experience at a live wrestling event.

"You had a good time?" asked Uncle David through a wide grin as we walked back to the car.

"Yes!" I replied, although I was confused by how this altogether different and comparatively bizarre world of wrestling could somehow have existed without my knowledge.

Nearly 30 years later, I made a casual allusion to Bahamian wrestling during an exchange with my Bahamian wife, and I was struck with a question that abruptly halted the flow of the conversation.

"There was *wrestling* in the Bahamas?" she asked me.

"Yes!" I responded, in disbelief. "Dusty Rhodes… Barry Windham… Tyree Pride… There was wrestling there all the time!"

"If you say so," she shrugged. "I've *never* heard of any wrestling in the Bahamas."

On one hand, I couldn't blame my wife for not knowing anything about pro wrestling in the Bahamas. No wrestling promotion had consistently held wrestling events in the Bahamas since 1990. On the other hand, it was simply unacceptable for her to *not* know this. After all, this was *Dusty*

*Rhodes* I was talking about, and he used to perform every four to six weeks in a building which stood only 400 meters from the Starbucks that I met her in... just a few doors down from her father's medical clinic!

It just so happened I had recently begun working with Florida wrestling legend Mike "Buggsy McGraw" Davis on his autobiography, and I formulated a plan to educate my wife about what a major attraction professional wrestling used to be in her homeland. In the process, I would educate myself, and I would learn everything I had ever missed out on prior to what turned out to be Dusty Rhodes' final show at Nassau Stadium as he entered the twilight of his legendary in-ring career.

Prior to one of our recording sessions for his autobiography, I informed Buggsy about the Bahamas wrestling book I intended to write, and he generously offered to answer questions for me for that book as well.

"Thanks, Buggsy," I told him. "Can you tell me what it was like seeing Nassau Stadium for the very first time?"

"Nassau Stadium?" Buggsy asked, quizzically. "Nassau *Stadium?* Now, when you say 'Nassau Stadium'... I want to make sure we're talking about the same thing... Is that the little restaurant with the concrete walls in the back?"

"It certainly is," I chuckled.

From that moment on, I knew working on this book was going to be thoroughly enjoyable.

## One: The Oakes Field Incident

The first mention of a professional wrestling show taking place anywhere in the Bahamas was embedded on page 16 of *The Nassau Guardian* on September 15, 1960. In the article, Douglas Carey, the "manager and promoter of the Bahamas Boxing Stadium," announced a September 23rd event which would feature three matches.

This announcement may have seemed benign and uncomplicated on its surface, but the 109,000 residents of what was then formally known as the British Crown Colony of the Bahamas had no idea what sort of complexity lay in store for them by inviting the colorful world of professional wrestling onto its attractive, sandy shores.

Still relatively isolated from the nearby United States in certain matters of entertainment, which assuredly included the world of pro wrestling out of the need of the latter to preserve its trade secrets, Bahamians would have had no way of knowing they weren't simply welcoming an isolated hand-to-hand combat event into their country, but were instead rolling out the proverbial red carpet for the Florida-based representatives of a worldwide entertainment empire.

Far from being a nefarious wrestling network – at least with respect to the intentionality of its structural design – the development of the National Wrestling Alliance had been a natural byproduct of the progression of a sport possessing elements that were simultaneously legitimate and rooted in carnival theatricality.

At its core, professional wrestling is an offshoot of activities that customarily took place regularly at late-19th-century county fairs and in similar public spaces, where promoters would challenge anyone in the crowd to last a predetermined number of minutes inside of a traditional boxing ring with the appointed strongman of the fair.

When an onlooker would accept the challenge of the promoter and step forth to square off against the strongman, the promoter's champion would often carry his unskilled opponent close to the time limit to build the excitement of the viewers in attendance – and also to maximize the number of bets being placed in favor of the gutsy opponent – before abruptly finishing the contest with any number of painful holds, and boosting the amount of cash that landed in the pockets of the promoter's waistcoat.

Naturally, interest would build toward the idea of having the capable champions of individual promoters compete against one another in legitimate wrestling contests until things evolved to the point where an authentic sport emerged from these events.

From there, it didn't take very long at all for promoters and wrestlers alike to conclude that there was ultimately more money to be made if the grapplers colluded with one another and produced exciting contests with predetermined outcomes, replete with lucrative rematches in the future if the events appeared highly competitive to the onlookers, but the outcomes left enough doubt that a different ending to a subsequent bout might be possible. All the while, the in-ring action remained controlled, and all combatants stayed safe.

Out of this ecosystem that blended sport, performance and business emerged a territorial system that defined the geographic lines within which the individual promoters could organize and oversee wrestling shows, whereby enough revenue could be generated to support everyone involved in these efforts. The individual owners and operators of the NWA's territories could elevate their own champions, dictate who should win and lose matches at the most monetarily advantageous moments, and also guarantee a stable inflow and outflow of wrestling talent so that fans never grew bored with wrestling acts that might otherwise grow stale through repeated viewing.

Within the NWA's uniquely sketched map of the planet, the state of Florida was its own self-contained wrestling territory. By 1960, it contained four of the most populous cities in the United States, and had only that year managed to surpass Indiana to become the 10th most populous state in the nation with just under five million residents. When paired with a warm, snow-free climate that invited families outdoors throughout the year in search of entertainment, this combination of features made Florida one of the most highly attractive territories of the U.S. in which to stage pro wrestling events.

Not to be outdone, possessing a population of just under 80,000 residents by 1960, the island of New Providence and its one true city, Nassau, probably seemed to be a location worth gambling on for the founder of Florida's wrestling territory, Clarence "Cowboy" Luttrall. Even with the myriad inconveniences of air travel factored in, a plane trip to Nassau from most locations in Florida was still shorter in duration than a cramped car ride from Tampa to Jacksonville.

'KILLER' AUSTIN          HANS SCHMIDT          CHIEF BIG EAGLE

# Tag Wrestling Tonight At Bahamas Boxing Stadium

Furthermore, there were other intrinsic factors that made the Bahamian public an ideal target for professional wrestling, beginning with the isolated nature of New Providence, an island only 21 miles long and seven miles wide, which contained a population that was overwhelmingly concentrated within a six-square-mile area in the island's northeastern quadrant, where the actual city of Nassau was situated.

Moreover, the average Bahamian now had even fewer options for casual exploration of the local environment, at least for the sake of entertainment. The closest outlying island – Hog Island – was no longer a suitable location for post-church picnics. It had been purchased the prior year and had its name changed to "Paradise Island," and development was well underway to transform it into a playground for wealthy tourists.

If any new entertainment diversions introduced into this environment presented themselves as sufficiently unique, then any venues hosting such events could be readily filled to capacity by Nassauvians, the majority of whom could easily reach the hosting location within the span of a 30-minute stroll. Further, any such events that were successful in attracting a crowd of even 2,000 onlookers could make a rational claim to have gathered a respectable chunk of New Providence Island's adult population.

Speaking of the venues, there were already several locations in Nassau that were optimally arranged for the viewing of professional wrestling matches. By 1960, Nassau had morphed into a boxing-mad community. Bahamian boxer William "Yama Bahama" Butler had provided Black Bahamians – who represented the overwhelming majority of the nation's residents, but wielded political and financial power that was wholly incommensurate with their numbers – with their first sustained taste of representative professional sporting success on the world stage.

Butler was ranked as one of the 10 best middleweight boxers in the world, having amassed a professional record of 60 wins against 10 defeats and three draws. In the process, he had won fights in several of the sport's most esteemed venues, including Madison Square Garden in New York City.

Owed in part to Butler's pugilistic success, interest in the Bahamian national boxing scene intensified, with many young Bahamian men flooding to local gyms in the hope of being fashioned into the next Yama Bahama. Throughout the compact Nassau region in particular, boxing matches and exhibitions were plentiful, and there was no shortage of promoters willing to arrange fights between many of the young, hungry, up-and-coming Bahamian fighters.

Amazingly, the very first organized wrestling bout in Bahamian history would be a women's match pitting Ella Waldek against Bonnie Watson. The night would then continue with a bout between Chief Big Eagle and Tony Altomare, and conclude with a main-event matchup between Eddie Graham and a wrestler who was named as Johnny Austin. Understandably new to the names and personalities of the wrestlers, the writer of the article misidentified 31-year-old "Killer" Buddy Austin.

Also of note is the fundraising component to the festivities, as Carey, who also owned the boxing venue on Wulff Road in addition to being the event's promoter, added that proceeds from the event would benefit the Crippled Children's Fund.

Several of the wrestlers on Nassau's inaugural match card had also achieved great notoriety in the sport of wrestling, albeit under circumstances far less than pleasant in some cases. Nine years prior to this event, Ella Waldek had actually been arrested and nearly charged with manslaughter for allegedly killing another wrestler, Janet Boyer Wolfe, during a wrestling match in East Liverpool, Ohio.

Although Waldek was not at fault, her popularity and drawing power grew as a result of the attention garnered by this incident, and by 1960 she and Watson were embroiled in a feud that involved the Florida promotion's two women's championships: the NWA Florida Women's Championship and the NWA Southern Women's Championship, which, despite its name, was exclusively a Florida-based wrestling title.

On the other end of the match listing, Edward Gossett had acquired the surname of "Graham" after teaming with Dr. Jerry Graham to form a legendary tag team tandem for Capitol Sports in the northeastern United States, which would eventually change its name to the World Wide Wrestling Federation, the World Wrestling Federation, and finally to World Wrestling Entertainment. In comparison to Eddie, Jerry Graham came by the Graham name more honestly, having legally changed his surname to match his stepfather's.

By the time he reached Nassau, Eddie had stepped away from working in a regular tag team pairing and was in his first year in Florida as a singles competitor. His September match with Buddy Austin represented just one in a series of matches Graham would have against the villainous Austin to establish himself amongst the most popular fan-favorite – or "babyface" wrestlers – operating in Florida.

The first wrestling event in Bahamian history was obviously successful enough to warrant a repeat engagement, because three weeks later, Carey appeared in the pages of *The Nassau Guardian* yet again, promoting a three-match card featuring a grand total of four wrestlers. It is possible that Carey and Luttrall were collectively testing the Bahamian waters with a bare-bones approach to island-based promotion, or perhaps they were relying on the novelty of wrestling in the Bahamas to be a sufficient attraction all on its own.

The order of the matches consisted of Buddy Austin facing off against Chief Big Eagle in a one-on-one match, followed by a tag match pitting the teams of Austin and Harry Smith against Big Eagle and Hans Schmidt, then concluding with Smith facing Schmidt one-on-one, in a best-two-out-of-three-falls match.

In November, Graham and Austin returned to Nassau once again to compete on the undercard of a blended boxing and wrestling show involving another popular Bahamian fighter who was rapidly blazing a path to stardom with a record of 36 wins, three defeats and three draws, the 21-year-old Gomeo Brennan.

Without any prior exposure to the spectacle of professional wrestling, one can only imagine what this first wave of Bahamian witnesses to such events thought of the world that was now being displayed before them. While boxing was plentiful in the Bahamas, and the islands were certainly a tourist destination visited by guests from all over the globe, Nassau was not exactly a location where champions from other sports competed with regularity.

Oddly enough, the most land-based popular sporting showcase in the Bahamas that was contested amongst the world's best with any regularity was the annual Nassau Speed Week road-racing event. The idea that international wrestling representatives and holders of prestigious championships were now competing live before their very eyes on a monthly basis must have seemed like an unfathomable turn of events for the Bahamians in the audience.

Of course, professional wrestling is misleading at its very core. Despite packaging and presenting himself as a villainous, post-World-War-II Nazi sympathizer, the 250-pound Hans Schmidt was actually Guy Larose, a French Canadian from Joliette, Quebec, Canada.

Similarly, Chief Big Eagle was George Dahmer of Ohio, and was certainly not the headdress-wearing American Indian from Cherokee, North Carolina that he was depicted to be in the ring. It has been a frequent routine for wrestlers to adorn themselves in spurious gimmicks for the sake of broadening their appeal to the audiences they engage with, exoticizing elements of the show, and capitalizing on pop-cultural imagery. However, it was a reliance on this classic wrestling trope that arguably touched off the first riot in Bahamian wrestling history.

By January of 1961, wrestling had moved to the Oakes Field Hangar, which was literally an old aircraft hangar and a remnant of the former Oakes Field Airport on Thompson Boulevard. At the peak of its operation, Oakes Field consisted of three runways of 6,000 feet or longer, and the location had been utilized for the training of thousands of Royal Air Force personnel. Pan American Airways became the first commercial carrier to begin the regular transportation of people to and from Nassau via Oakes Field in 1941.

The repurposed Oakes Field facilities had previously been the chief point of attraction for another sport. In 1957, it was remodeled to become the host of Nassau Speed Week after the prior hosting grounds at Windsor Field were rearranged to manage the bulk of Bahamian air travel.

The January 11th edition of *The Nassau Guardian* announced the pairing of "Sweet Daddy" Siki and "Killer" Buddy Austin as the main event of a forthcoming show on January 18th. To add to the allure of the match, Siki was declared to be the reigning World Eastern Champion, an uncommon name for a wrestling championship, and certainly not an official championship sanctioned by the NWA's Florida-based territory.

# WRESTLING

## OAKES FIELD HANGAR

*TONIGHT*
**8:30 P.M.**

RESERVATIONS
CALL 4121
OR
OLYMPIA HOTEL
LOBBY

SWEET DADDY SIKI vs. KILLER AUSTIN

Midgets
LORD LITTLEBROOK
vs.
BILL BRUMMEL

CHIEF BIG HEART
vs.
COWBOY LEN HUGHES

RINGSIDE: £2 and £1-0-0 ★ GENERAL ADMISSION: 10/-

SWEET DADDY SIKI    *Part Proceeds in aid of Crippled Children's Fund*

Surprisingly, no mention was made of the fact that Siki was a 20-year-old African American wrestler from Texas. This was one element of the pairing that would be fittingly corrected, and a full body shot of Siki – with his dark brown skin and bleach-blonde hair, was printed in *The Guardian* just six days later.

Despite the novelty of a Black wrestler performing in Nassau for the first time, there was no obvious special effort undertaken to bring Siki to the Bahamas on that night. In fact, Siki and Austin had wrestled one another in Miami just four nights prior on the undercard to an event headlined by Johnny Valentine and Antonino Rocca – two of the most popular stars in all of wrestling at the time.

On January 20th, *The Nassau Guardian* reported the fallout of Siki's Nassau debut under the headline "Wrestling Matches Incite Fans," and for the first time, the reporting of the results of the wrestling matches warranted more than the typical short blurb.

Apparently, Siki was introduced as hailing from "Kingston, Jamaica" at the outset of the event, as if to further the sense of British West Indian or Anglophone Caribbean kinship between himself and the overwhelmingly Black Bahamian audience.

For what it's worth, when asked about this incident for this book, Siki had absolutely no recollection of the event, but does remember occasions in which he asked the ring announcer to modify his place of origin for the sake of eliciting a desired response from the crowd.

Twenty-eight minutes into their best-of-three-falls match, Buddy Austin pinned Siki with a body press. Within six minutes, Siki evened the score by pinning Austin after a flurry of dropkicks. For context, Black Bahamians living in the pre-Majority-Rule era were now on the verge of witnessing the heretofore unfathomable sight of a fellow British West Indian vanquishing a White American wrestler and retaining his hard-won championship in the process.

Ultimately, Austin got himself disqualified, which was a cowardly move that made the fans irate at an unsatisfying finish, but also allowed them to breathe a sigh of relief that Siki had won the bout, and his status as a champion remained secure. However, Austin had no way of knowing the sort of historical satisfaction he had just deprived the Bahamian fans of witnessing, and as he and Siki brawled on the outside of the ring, Austin grabbed and brandished a steel chair with the clear intention of striking Siki with it.

At this point, many of the fans in attendance decided they'd had enough of seeing their fellow West Indian mistreated by a cheating White miscreant, and they surged toward Austin, who retreated into the dressing room to escape from the justice of the Bahamian mob. Police were later summoned to disperse the crowd, and to enable Austin to flee from the Oakes Field Hangar with his life.

The full fallout from the Siki incident would take some time to manifest itself, although a follow-up mention in *The Guardian* stated, "The crowd participation was so enthusiastic that unscheduled boxing took place with one or two bodies and the odd chair hurtling through space." In the meantime, the shows continued, and the very next wrestling event on the island featured another wrestling attraction on the undercard of a boxing event at the Bahamas Boxing Stadium on Wulff Road.

This time, legendary Bahamian fighter William "Yama Bahama" Butler headlined the event, but the wrestlers on the undercard were Henry Roach and George "Killer" Maury.

Both of these wrestlers were probably wrestling without the official approval of any organizations sanctioned by the National Wrestling Alliance, and were likely performing under pseudonyms. This is strongly hinted at by the fact that "Henry Roach" is the real name of Florida-based professional wrestler Billy Sandow, the grandson of legendary strongman and bodybuilder Eugen Sandow. Roach had died at home of a self-inflicted gunshot wound several years prior, in April of 1953.

A few days later, Bahamian authorities weighed in on the curiosity known as professional wrestling and what was to be done with it. Partially as a result of the riot induced during Siki's match with Austin at Oakes Field, Spurgeon Bethel petitioned his fellow members of the House of Assembly to create the Bahamas Boxing and Wrestling Commission in order for the sports to be "cleaned up."

Although boxing was cited in the formation of the commission, special emphasis was plainly given to the wrestling side of the pairing. Bethel's most direct reference was to the bout between Austin and Siki, to which he proclaimed, "A couple of nights ago there was a wrestling match at Oakes Field, at the end of which there was a free for all. We don't want anything like that here."

With that proclamation, the connection between boxing and wrestling in the Bahamas was codified, and the implications were such that it became a near impossibility for wrestling organizations headquartered in the United States to operate in the Bahamas without oversight from Bahamians heavily involved in the national boxing scene. This likely gave tremendous pause to Cowboy Luttrall, as too much direct interaction between American wrestling promoters and improperly vetted Bahamian boxing promoters ran the risk of exposing the true nature of wrestling and permanently spoiling the money-making potential of the Bahamas as a pro wrestling mecca.

Pausing briefly, it is worth taking the time to scrutinize a few things about the overall presentation of Sweet Daddy Siki, aside from calling attention to the fact that he never wrestled in the Bahamas again. The practice of Siki branding himself as West Indian was nothing new to him, nor was it new to any number of Black wrestlers traversing the United States in that era. "Bearcat" Wright – arguably the first Black wrestler to win a recognized and respected world wrestling championship without the word "negro" affixed to it – was also regularly billed as "Jamaican" despite actually hailing from Nebraska.

In the absence of television programs by which the race or ethnicity of a wrestler could be readily seen or communicated to a viewing audience, newspaper advertisements were commonly the means by which fans learned about wrestling events taking place in their nearby gathering places, and the names of wrestlers were often the only clue as to the area of the world they represented or emerged from.

Sometimes the race of a Black wrestler was communicated through his name, like "Mr. Ebony" Tom Jones, "Soulman" Rocky Johnson, or much later, Sweet Brown Sugar. In the absence of a nickname, this could be accomplished by supplying a Black wrestler with a hometown or country identified with Black people. "Jamaica," in a sense, became a code word for "Black."

## Colored Wrestling

**BUD Richardson** VS **WILLIE Love**

"Bahamian" professional wrestlers Richardson and Love

Given the demand for exoticized blackness in American pro wrestling, it shouldn't come as much of a surprise that African American wrestlers also used "Bahamas" as a code word for "Black" on multiple occasions during tours of the United States. While wrestling on the very same card in Casper, Wyoming, "Sweet" Willie Love and Bud Richardson were both identified as Bahamian wrestlers, ostensibly for the sake of exoticizing their unique brand of Blackness to rural Wyomingites, many of whom had little chance of ever taking a flight to the Bahamas. In fact, during a 1965 tour of Montana, Willie Love seemed to vacillate between the use of Jamaica and the Bahamas as his preferred birthplaces depending on whether the show was held in Billings or Great Falls.

Ironically, these two "Bahamian wrestlers" appear to have been booked as a package deal during periods of their careers, often competing against one another for regional, national, or world "Negro" championships in different states. During one Texas show, Willie Love was billed as hailing from Wichita while Bud Richardson was advertised as a Detroiter. While on a Virginia card, Love was declared to be from Dallas and Richardson from Memphis.

Presumably, neither Love nor Richardson expected any "true-true" Bahamians to be present in Montana or Wyoming to ask them which islands of the Bahamas they were actually from, or more specifically, "Who ya people is?" Regardless, they are each worthy of honorable mention as the first professional wrestlers to outwardly represent Bahamian faces to American wrestling fans, albeit in a fictitious capacity.

Back in 1960s Nassau, true Bahamians were still reeling from their first taste of professional wrestling turmoil. The bureaucratic fallout that ensued would cause considerable time to elapse before Florida's accomplished wrestling stars would return to the Bahamas or resume a sustained pattern of holding shows there. Notwithstanding the tumultuous first phase of their relationship, the Florida wrestling organization and the Bahama Islands were far from finished with one another.

## Two: Freeport's Adopted Son

The Florida territory of the National Wrestling Alliance –
now commonly identified by the name of its television
program "Championship Wrestling from Florida" –
made its return to the Bahamas in 1962, after the colonial
British territory had enjoyed back-to-back years of growth
exceeding 20 percent in its tourism-based economy. During
that time, wrestler Eddie Graham had acquired a share of the
ownership in the company, and when he returned to Nassau
with additional wrestlers in tow, he did so under the clear and
public guidance of local event promoter Charles Major.

The tall, slender Charlie Major was by no means a
stranger to athletics as either a promoter or a participant. He
was among the first wave of Bahamian athletic stars to venture
to the U.S. and compete in track-and-field events. He had been
a world-class high jumper at St. Bonaventure University in
New York during the 1920s, preceding Bahamian greats like
four-time Olympian Thomas Robinson with his success in
American collegiate athletics by multiple decades. Since that
time, Major had settled into a role as perhaps the most
respected and prominent local boxing promoter in Nassau.

To maximize his chances of success, Major erected an
open-air building of his own design on Fowler Street, just 100
meters south of East Bay Street, and upon the very spot that
had previously been occupied by the house he had been raised
in. The cement-walled building's configurations were based on
a scaled-down interpretation of the shape of Butler Memorial
Gymnasium on the campus of St. Bonaventure University,
where Major had experienced such transcendent Bahamian
success.

In his first attempt at directly promoting NWA
wrestling to a Bahamian audience, Major took over the
management of events at the Oakes Field Hangar on October
24th of 1962, for what was billed locally as "The Wrestling
Spectacular." In his *Nassau Guardian* interview promoting the
show, Major urged fans to arrive early to avoid a last-minute

rush at the gate to see an event headlined by a tag team bout involving Tony Baillargeon and Maurice LaPointe – collectively known as "The Flying Frenchmen." The tandem was advertised as being famous for its "flying dropkick attack."

The pair of French-Canadians was slated to wage war against the Russian Crusher and "Rowdy" Red Roberts. Also on the card of note was The Great Malenko, billed as "the roughest, toughest wrestler on television." He would eventually become a regular sight at Bahamian wrestling events.

"Malenko is arguably the greatest heel – or bad guy – to ever work in the state of Florida, and that covers a lot of ground, because at one point nearly *every* top heel wrestled in the state of Florida," declared Florida wrestling historian Barry Rose. "The feud between Eddie Graham and the Great Malenko really put CWF on the map. They were drawing huge houses and getting the fans invested into what CWF was. Malenko was able to keep fans riled up for an entire decade. He made people believe, and that translated into ticket sales."

It would be a further three years before the stars of Championship Wrestling from Florida would be invited to the Bahamas to battle in front of Bahamian fans on May 6th of 1965, within a nation that was now internally self-governing, but not completely independent of Great Britain.

Nassau was also at the tail end of four months of motion-picture excitement; production was about to wrap on the film *Thunderball* – the fourth in the James Bond film series. Bahamian actor Sidney Poitier had also singlehandedly elevated the international profile of the Bahamas by winning the Academy Award for Best Actor during the prior year.

This time, the wrestling would take place inside of the structure Charlie Major had christened "Nassau Stadium." In effect, Nassau Stadium was the very same facility that Charlie Major had designed as a dual-purpose restaurant and athletic facility, but which he had also once leased to a metro cab company during his early, lean years. The open-air section of the venue had now been fully optimized as a multipurpose athletic facility capable of hosting events ranging from roller skating to basketball, but which was primarily used throughout the week for the training of fighters, and boxing competitions.

This time, "El Gran" Lothario, better known to most wrestling fans as Jose Lothario, would make his debut in Nassau, touted as "the magnificent master of the Mexican leglock from Mexico City." Lothario would baptize Nassau Stadium as a wrestling venue along with his opponent Sputnik Monroe in a best-of-three-falls main event with a one-hour time limit. Other wrestlers appearing on the card included Jesse James and Duke Keomuka, while Lester Welch competed against Tony Nero in the opening bout.

By this time, Lester Welch had also fully bought into the ownership of Championship Wrestling from Florida, and he hadn't arrived in the Sunshine State alone. Accompanying him for the journey was his longtime girlfriend Marlene Belkas, popularly known by her ring name "Sherri Lee."

"I started working for Lester in Kingsport, Tennessee," explained Lee. "He was partners with Nick Gulas in Nashville and in Kingsport. He sold out to Nick, got away from Nick, and then bought in with Cowboy Luttrall and Eddie Graham in Florida. When that happened, Cowboy told me that I'd be welcome to come to Florida to get a job as secretary in the office in Tampa, and they would use me to wrestle whenever they used girls on the wrestling cards."

Lee accepted that job as a secretary in the office at 106 N. Albany in Tampa, and she and Welch remained in a relationship for 13 years, making Lee a frequent companion of Welch's during trips to and from the Bahamas. However, the Bahamas wasn't the first place that Lee had gained experience working in a tropical environment.

"I got hurt badly when I was in Bermuda of all places," laughed Lee. "We were working out of Montreal when they sent us over there. The guys didn't tighten the ring ropes up as much as they were supposed to. Vivian Vachon threw me into the ropes, and they just gave out. I went right on through and ended up hurt out on the cement."

Working in the Bahamas had become a far more convenient endeavor with the addition of Lester Welch to the Florida territory's management team. Welch was an accomplished pilot and could easily ferry members of the CWF roster over to the islands for wrestling engagements.

"I flew with Lester on almost every flight to Nassau during that time," said Lee. "When he would take the guys to Nassau, Freeport, or anywhere, he would bring them on one of the planes he owned; there were a few different-sized planes; one seated seven passengers and some were nine-seaters. I would end up being the hostess. I would make sure there were drinks and sandwiches if the guys wanted something. Lester did the flying, and I just kind of took care of the rest of the passengers on the plane."

Lee was obliged to work at the gate and collect money from the fans seeking entry to the venues. During the earliest of such shows at Nassau Stadium, she was keenly aware of the fact that several young Bahamians boosted themselves up over the relatively low wall of the Stadium to try to get into the events for free.

"They had to put in protection," said Lee. "Almost all of the fans paid their way into the events and bought their tickets from me at the ticket booth. Most of the people who jumped the fence were either older teenagers or people in their early 20s. That's why they installed glass along the edge of the cement wall sometime in 1965, and also had dogs running along there. The dogs were there first, and I remember the fans being absolutely scared to death of them."

The glass consisted of shards from broken beer bottles that were permanently embedded into the cement atop the walls that surrounded the venue. It would become one of the signature features of Nassau Stadium, especially to the wrestlers who had never seen anything like it before.

"The first time I saw that wall with the glass sticking out of it, I thought the whole place looked like a fortress," remarked wrestler Brian Knobbs.

Bahamian Rhapsody

Major held a year-end wrestling event at Nassau Stadium in December of 1965. On that occasion, the local fans from Nassau took a strong liking to the young, handsome Hawaiian wrestler Sam Steamboat. Despite not necessarily being a top headliner in Florida at the time, Steamboat was cheered wildly by the Bahamian crowd, suggesting that the Bahamian penchant for supporting non-White wrestlers with darker shades of skin against paler-faced opposition extended even to non-Black wrestlers of Hawaiian descent.

"Sam Steamboat got over *really* big with the people in the Bahamas," said Michael Davis, who wrestled in the Bahamas under multiple names, but most frequently as Buggsy McGraw. "He was a very good wrestler who was very adept in the ring. He mixed his wrestling with the kicking and punching during his comebacks against the heels. He had a memorable way of starting his comebacks with what I referred to as a 'Hawaiian dance.'"

Back-to-back shows lauding the return of Steamboat to Nassau were hastily arranged for January 7th and 14th of 1966, regardless of the fact that the announcement was seemingly outshined by publicity for a future appearance by midget wrestlers Lord Littlebrook and Frenchy Lamont, which was scheduled for January 28th.

Major trumpeted the international appeal of the show during his interview with *The Nassau Guardian*, noting that four of the five continents would be represented by wrestlers booked for the event.

"Sam Steamboat, one of the world's best, is the Hawaiian champion," stated Major. "In his last bout here, which was just over a month ago, he gained many admirers with his flawless style. I have been asked by many fans to bring him back to Nassau. Steamboat will be matched against Jungle Jim Starr, a roughneck South African."

Clearly, in a nation with a majority Black population that routinely felt oppressed by the White merchants who ran the United Bahamian Party, having their somewhat dark-skinned favorite wrestle against the symbolic representative of a South African regime noted for its system of codified racial segregation known as apartheid made for an unprecedented attraction.

This announced main event was plainly meant to attract fans anxious to have their bloodlust sated by the public flogging of a presumed racist. Furthermore, it was strongly suggested by the wording of the article's introduction, which plainly stated, "More seating accommodation and greater supervision of the crowd between matches are planned for Friday night's wrestling show at the Nassau Stadium," that things may have gotten characteristically unruly during Steamboat's prior appearance on the island.

"Sam got a great push when he wrestled in the state of Florida; he got that number-two babyface slot right behind Eddie Graham," said Florida wresting historian Barry Rose. "Sam wasn't being pushed in main events, but he was certainly in the semi-main event. Even the great champion Lou Thesz thought that Sam Steamboat was one of the best wrestlers in the world. Sam even got a couple world title shots against Thesz while he was working in Florida, and I believe that was at Thesz's urging. He was thought of as a truly solid worker inside the ring."

The January show at Nassau Stadium were also noteworthy as the final wrestling event for which British Pounds were accepted as currency at the gate. Bahamian minister of finance Sir Stafford Sands declared that the shift in currency would ease Bahamian accounting processes in handling the high volume of American tourists' dollars, which now represented the overwhelming bulk of foreign currency changing hands in the Bahamas.

**WRESTLING**
SATURDAY
DEC. 10 — 8:30
NASSAU STADIUM

HIRO MATSUDA
DUKE KEOMUKA
vs
EDDIE GRAHAM
SAM STEAMBOAT

SPUTNIK MONROE
vs
SILENTO RODRIGUEZ

LES WELCH
vs
CORSICA JEAN

ADMISSION PRICES
RING SIDE .... $3.00
GEN. ADM. $2.00
CHILDREN .. $1.00

The Bahamas made the transition from pounds to dollars on May 25th of 1966, and fixed the value of Bahamian currency to that of its larger neighbor to the north, making American currency attractive to acquire, easy to exchange with Bahamian dollars on a one-to-one basis, and acceptable on the spot by Bahamian vendors in lieu of Bahamian currency.

By the time of the late-August Nassau Stadium show, which was headlined by the team of Don McClarity and "Freeport's Adopted Son" Sputnik Monroe competing against Les Welch and Jose Lothario, the price of general admission had been set at $3.00, while ringside seats were $4.00 apiece.

World's Greatest Professional Wrestling

# WRESTLING
## NASSAU STADIUM

SATURDAY, SEPT. 3rd — 8.30 P.M.

### TAG TEAM MATCH
**DON McCLARITY and**
**Freeport's Adopted Son SPUDNIK MONROE**

vs

**LES WELCH and**
**JOSE LOTHARIO**

**SAM STEAMBOAT**

vs

**(Spain) PEDRO AMESSA**

**ARGENTINE ZUMA**

vs

**JIM AUSBORNE**

## RINGSIDE $4.00
## GEN. ADMISSION $3.00

It just so happens that the city of Freeport on Grand Bahama Island was in the midst of explosive growth that would eventually see it become the second most populous area of the Bahamas during that era. It was viewed among many Bahamians – and particularly by supporters of the Progressive

28

Liberal Party, which was already threatening to wrench power away from White elites and into the hands of the island chain's Black majority during the next election – as a location where wealthy, White businessmen did entirely as they pleased.

Common criticisms leveled against the de facto rulers of Freeport included claims of preferentially employing White foreign workers at the expense of Black Bahamians, and also not paying adequately toward the public funding of Bahamian government operations. Referring to himself as a representative of Freeport was a surefire way for a vilified heel like Monroe to attract volcanic levels of heat from an incensed Nassau crowd.

"Sputnik had a great run as a main-event heel," explained Rose. "Everybody will tell you that Sputnik's greatest strength was his psychology; he knew exactly what to do to connect with an audience as both a babyface and a heel. He gave the impression that he was a real badass, and psychologically he was one of the best we've ever seen in the wrestling business."

By the time of the year-ending shows, which offered tag team affairs involving Eddie Graham rotating between partners Don Curtis and Sam Steamboat to do battle with the villainous tandem of Hiro Matsuda and Sputnik Monroe, prices for wrestling events had settled at a lowered level of $1.00 for children, $2.00 for general admission, and $3.00 for ringside seats. For reference, these ticket prices were almost perfectly aligned with those paid by Florida wrestling fans for seating in Tampa's Fort Homer Hester Armory during that exact same time period.

"Sam Steamboat teamed up with Eddie Graham a lot," recalled McGraw. "They were constantly tagging together. Eddie actually enjoyed working with guys who could actually wrestle during their matches, which is probably one of the reasons why he enjoyed partnering with Sam Steamboat so much."

By 1967, both Nassau and Freeport were functioning as fully integrated sites within the Florida wrestling territory, marking one of the rare occasions when a British Crown colony would be fully absorbed as an offshore domain within an American wrestling territory. However, this status was tenuous, as the Bahamas was hurtling rapidly toward outright independence from Great Britain following the election of PLP representative Lynden Pindling to the position of Bahamian Premier, making him the first Black Bahamian to hold such a powerful and influential office.

The year began with the wrestlers regularly flying to the islands for Saturday evening shows, which were often followed by matches involving the same participants the following night in Freeport.

"Lester would fly all of us over to Freeport right from Nassau," said Lee. "We would stay at a place called the Freeport Inn. The city of Freeport had a nice outdoor stadium called the Tropical Sports Arena. It was away from the small building set aside from the stadium that we had an office in. Other than that, the stadium area was just land, with a place to park and nothing else around it. I would do work out of the nice office we had fixed up in there. I would take all the money we made in Nassau and handle the banking over at the Freeport office."

The fact that Championship Wrestling from Florida maintained an office in Freeport and conducted banking there during this era cannot be carelessly glossed over.

In essence, Freeport had been founded to be exactly what its name implied; it was a city that was established as a free-trade zone under the Hawksbill Creek Agreement of 1955, and was governed by the Grand Bahama Port Authority. Companies that established a presence in Freeport were required to pay no taxes on property, inventories, income, capital gains or profits until 1990.

With respect to Championship Wrestling from Florida, any cash proceeds taken in during Bahamian shows after paying the wrestlers would not have been subjected to any form of taxation. It also would have provided the office with a fantastic opportunity for the NWA's Florida territory to shelter money earned during U.S. shows in what amounted to a convenient tax haven, especially if it was reported as income earned in the Bahamas. As such, CWF was just one of a growing list of foreign-based Freeport businesses deemed problematic by the inbound Progressive Liberal Party of the Bahamas.

To be clear, Lester Welch was not the only pilot on the CWF ownership team.

"I was best friends with Mike Graham back then, and Eddie Graham would fly us down there on his own plane to watch the shows in the Bahamas as kids," said Steve Keirn, who would eventually become a mainstay of the Florida territory.

Of note during the early stages of 1967 was the overlapping of the February 11th show at Nassau Stadium with a two-week tour of the Florida territory by Lou Thesz. During that tour, the pioneering wrestler spent most of the latter week dueling with Sputnik Monroe. As the longest reigning NWA World Heavyweight Champion in the history of that particular championship, Thesz was tantamount to wrestling royalty. After first capturing the title in 1949, Thesz had been a central figure in the absorption and unification of lesser world championships into the NWA's version of the title.

Far from simply being a showman, Thesz was widely reputed to be a legitimate shooter and "hooker," capable of locking painful holds onto opponents and securing authentic submissions if his opponent was entertaining any fantasies about not complying with the agreed-upon conclusions to their matches.

By 1967, Thesz was now two years removed from his final reign as the recognized world champion of the NWA. Still, his presence in Nassau was significant inasmuch as he was the first former holder of the most prominent championship sanctioned by the most respected governing body in the wrestling world to appear in Nassau.

Speaking of world championships, the holders of Florida's version of the world tag team championship – the masked team known as "The Infernos" – defended their championship against Graham and Steamboat on the exact same show. This marked the first time that the participants in any of the pro wrestling contests held in the Bahamas were advertised with one of the sanctioned championships of the Florida territory up for grabs.

Although the National Wrestling Alliance took great pains to maintain the legitimacy of a single world heavyweight championship held by a sole individual that was approved by a majority of the member territories, each territory was relatively free to create and promote whatever championships they liked as long as they did not appear to dispute the exclusivity claim of a lone world heavyweight champion.

As such, the majority of the major singles championships defended within the NWA's member territories usually featured the name of a state, like the Florida Heavyweight Championship – the name of a region, like the Southern Heavyweight Championship – or the name of a country or a collection of countries.

With respect to tag team wrestling, several of the NWA's governed territories promoted their tag team championship titles as "world" tag team championships. Therefore, even as the Infernos defended their world tag titles in Nassau, there were at least half a dozen versions of titles declared to be "NWA World Tag Team Championships" being defended elsewhere during 1967.

Despite this appearance by the tag titles, the active holders of the Florida territory's championship belts – consisting of the Florida Heavyweight Championship, the Southern Heavyweight Championship, the Southern Tag Team Championship and the World Tag Team Championship – seldom made trips to the Bahamas.

Those belts were fixtures at wrestling events held in Florida, and were used to attract crowds at the regular weekly events at locations like Tampa, Miami, Fort Lauderdale, Jacksonville and Orlando. Fans in those locales were accustomed to seeing titles defended every week, while wrestling was viewed as such a novelty in the Bahamas that no championship belts were required to attract a rabid crowd.

In April of 1967, the shows made the shift to Thursday nights, which would endure as the customary night for semi-regular wrestling events for the remainder of the year. One particular bout pitting Lester Welch and Sam Steamboat against The Garvins – Ronnie and Terry – was deemed worthy of a rare, post-event write-up in *The Nassau Guardian*.

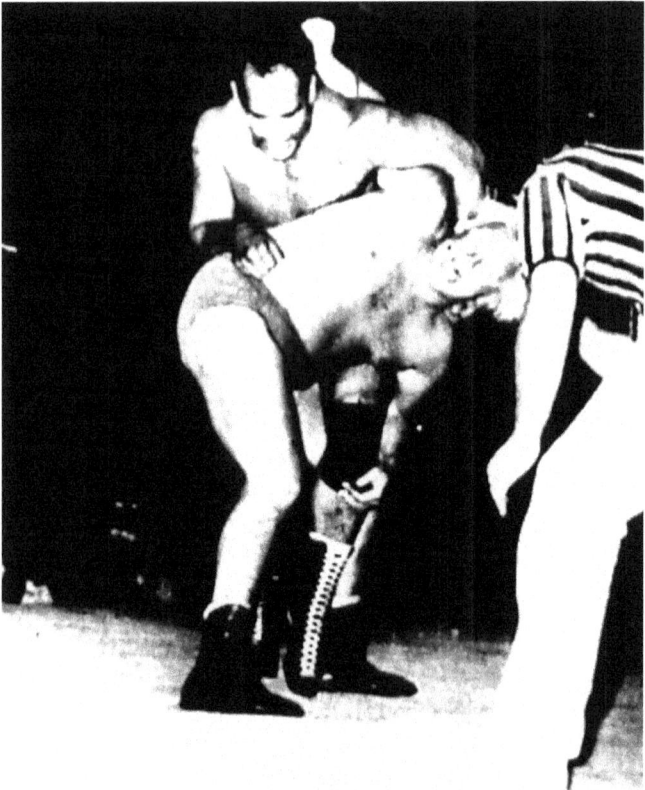

**Sam Steamboat forces Terry Garvin to submit**
**(Nassau Guardian)**

Welch and Steamboat won the first fall in the best-of-three-falls contest by securing a disqualification victory in the first fall, and then they captured their second consecutive fall when Steamboat locked Terry Garvin in an abdominal stretch.

Still showing the unmistakable signs of unfamiliarity with professional wrestling, the assigned writer from *The Guardian* referred to the victory in each fall as a "pin," even though neither fall was actually recorded via a three-count pinfall.

Earlier in that same show, fans at Nassau Stadium were treated to an appearance by a very young Terry Funk, just a few months shy of his 23rd birthday. The young Funk was in the midst of his first major, multi-month tour outside of his family's NWA territory based in Amarillo, Texas, and his elder brother Dory Funk Jr. was well on his way to being groomed to hold the top prize in all of wrestling.

The younger of the two Funk brothers was in the opening stages of a stellar career that would see him capture multiple world heavyweight championships on the road to international stardom. He pinned Phil Brummett in the 12-minute opening contest.

As the summer drew to a close, August presented a rare opportunity for Bahamian fans to see "Sailor" Art Thomas during his very first tour with Championship Wrestling from Florida. Thomas was a massive man by the standards of any wrestling generation, billed at 6'6" and 255 pounds. He also sported the unmistakable frame of a disciplined bodybuilder.

Equally as significant was the localized advertising of Thomas, who was a pioneer for Black wrestlers in the United States. Even in 1967, advertisements for his appearances in Florida towns referred to him as a "Negro giant," and also as the "Negro World Champion," which wasn't always merely a descriptive term.

WRESTLING

THURSDAY
AUG. 24 — 8:30 P.M.
Nassau Stadium

SAILOR ART THOMAS
AND SAM STEAMBOAT
—vs—
KURT AND SKULL
Von STROHEIM

BRONCO KELLY
—vs—
HIRO MATSUDA

LES WELCH
—vs—
RICK NEAL

ADMISSION
RINGSIDE ........
GEN. ADM. ........
CHILDREN ........ $1.00

Throughout the 1950s and 1960s, Black wrestlers like Thomas and Siki joined fellow pioneers like Bobo Brazil and Bearcat Wright in competing for Negro heavyweight titles across the United States, and especially in territories where Black wrestlers were not permitted to wrestle in the same rings against their White counterparts.

According to another Black wrestler who was getting his start during that time, "Soulman" Rocky Johnson, the booking of Black wrestlers that were top attractions had to be handled with greater precision than most people realized.

"There were only three or four true Black stars in the business back then," explained Johnson. "I was the only one in California for a while, and naturally I was attracting all the Black fans. I went there for six months and wound up staying for five years because they wouldn't let me go. They also had Earl Maynard up there in San Francisco, and he had just won the Mr. Universe bodybuilding contest. I was in Los Angeles, and they were going to switch us for six months, but Earl didn't get over with the fans because he had that accent. He's from Barbados in the West Indies and the American Blacks couldn't identify with him. That's when they came up with the name 'Soulman' for me."

On August 24th and September 7th, Thomas headlined back-to-back shows in Nassau, with the August 24th promotional advertisement capitalizing on the very first opportunity since the appearance of Siki seven years prior to convey the unmistakable Black heritage of the inbound Wright.

WRESTLING

**THURSDAY**
NOV. 30 – 8:30 P.M.
Nassau Stadium

**9 MAN**
OVER-THE-TOP
BATTLE
ROYAL

Klondike Bill
Red Demons #1 & 2
Omar Atlas
Crusher Karlsson
Bronco Kelly
Hiro Matsuda
Duke Keomuka
Sam Steamboat

– WINNER GETS –
$300 BONUS!

– ALSO –
4 SINGLE MATCHES

ADMISSION PRICES
RINGSIDE ............... $3
GEN. ADM. ............... $2
CHILDREN ............... $1

October was also a month of firsts. In this case, it was the occasion of the first over-the-top-rope battle royale ever staged in the Bahamas. The nine-man battle royale – suspiciously the exact number of men Lester Welch was capable of squeezing into one of his planes – was deemed to be so noteworthy that an entire page of *The Nassau Guardian* was dedicated to advertising it.

"Competing in this amazing event will be the massive Klondike Bill, Les Welch, Karl Von Brauner, Sputnik Monroe, 'Gentleman' Saul Weingeroff, Silento Rodriguez, the Ox, and the two Japanese grapplers, Hiro Matsuda and Duke Keomuka," wrote *The Guardian*'s sportswriter. "All these men are top-name wrestlers who are ranked highly in world ratings. They have all seen a lot of action here in Nassau, and most of them are very popular with the local wrestling fans."

A unique feature to the evening was the fact that the battle royale was scheduled to happen first, with the winner allegedly receiving a $100 bonus, and the losers all being required to compete in singles contests later in the evening, as determined by the order in which they were eliminated.

This atypical battle royale concept was so popular that it was repeated once again on November 30th, and this time with Klondike Bill, Red Demons #1 and #2, Omar Atlas, Krusher Karlsson, Bronco Kelly, Hiro Matsuda, Duke Keomuka and Sam Steamboat as participants, and with the winner's bonus tripled to $300.

As much as the wrestling rings of the Bahamas had heated up during the mid-1960s, the frequency of the shows and the craziness of the competitors was about to escalate as the decade drew closer to its conclusion.

## Three: A Cyclone Strikes

J anuary of 1968 marked the first time Wahoo McDaniel made the eastward journey from Florida over to the Bahamas, at least in his capacity as a wrestler. McDaniel had enjoyed undeniable success as a professional football player, having been a member of the American Football League's championship-winning Houston Oilers in 1960. During his tenure in Texas, McDaniel – who was of legitimate Choctaw-Chickasaw descent – trained to become a professional wrestler under the tutelage of Dory Funk Sr., the father of the accomplished Funk brothers.

The participation of McDaniel in professional wrestling contests was representative of an era in which professional athletes routinely found off-season work to sustain themselves and continue earning income. It just so happened that McDaniel's off-season employment enabled him to acquire fame as another sort of athlete, and magnified his notoriety in both endeavors.

The territories for which McDaniel appeared were understandably dependent upon the football team he was competing for at the time; a relocation to play on behalf of the New York Jets resulted in the first appearances by McDaniel for the World Wide Wrestling Federation in the Northeast.

**WRESTLING**

**THURSDAY**
MARCH 21 – 8:30 P.M.
NASSAU STADIUM

WAHOO
**McDANIEL**
vs
JOHNNY
**VALENTINE**

THE BLUE DEMONS
– vs –
RED      JOE
BASTIEN   &   SCARPA

BUTCHER VACHON
– vs –
SAM STEAMBOAT

ADMISSION PRICES
RINGSIDE .................. $3
GEN. ADM. .................. $2
CHILDREN ................... $1

McDaniel subsequently played two seasons for the Miami Dolphins prior to his retirement, which made him a double attraction for Bahamian fans interested in football, as the majority of Bahamians who frequented Miami and followed the American sport supported the nearby Dolphins at the time.

"Wahoo McDaniel, the sensational defensive linebacker for the Miami Dolphins, teams with popular Jose 'El Gran' Lothario to face the rugged and capable combination of Aldo Bogni and Bronko Lubich," stated *The Guardian*'s unnamed writer, apparently not realizing that referring to McDaniel as a "defensive linebacker" was redundant. "Wahoo and Lothario are former world tag team champions and are seeking a win over Bogni and Lubich in hopes of gaining a shot at the current world champions, Ronnie and Terry Garvin."

McDaniel made three further appearances in Nassau during February, and during the second of those appearances, Nassau also hosted Seiji Sakaguchi of Japan, who was in the midst of an overseas grooming tour in the United States.

As was a common practice in Japan during that era, future stars were often targeted and selected from amongst the ranks of successful combat sport athletes. In a maneuver that preceded the selection of future Japanese superstars Jumbo Tsuruta and Riki Choshu, both of whom were standouts and Olympians in Greco-Roman wrestling, the Japanese Pro Wrestling organization recruited Sakaguchi – who was an elite judoka on the world level – and sent him overseas to gain experience before unveiling him before the discerning eyes of Japanese wrestling fans.

Sakaguchi would soon return to Japan where he would spend the better part of a decade as the number two native wrestler in New Japan Pro Wrestling behind the company's founder and top-drawing star, Antonio Inoki. His opponent in Nassau was Koa Tiki – real name Roy Kamaka – a Hawaiian wrestler of Japanese descent whose brother Tor Kamata would become a major star in several territories, and also in Japan.

Wahoo McDaniel continued to headline Bahamian shows against Johnny Valentine, with two of those events bookending several months of inactivity. This was likely dictated by pending renovations at Nassau Stadium. During that intermission between wrestling events, Lynden Pindling and the Progressive Liberal Party won a smashing victory over the United Bahamian Power that granted them nearly total government control for all intents and purposes.

In the aftermath of his victory, Pindling publicly stated that outright Bahamian independence from Great Britain was not a priority, but owners of overseas businesses who had invested in enterprises on Bahamian soil were quoted in the American press as saying they were monitoring the situation in the island chain very closely.

**WRESTLING**
SATURDAY
AUG. 31
8:30 P.M.
**OAKES FIELD HANGAR**

Jose LOTHARIO
vs
JOHNNY **VALENTINE**

EDUARDO PEREZ
& LOUIE TILLET
vs
SPUTNIK MONROE
& TOM JONES

**JACK BRISCO**
vs
**JIM DALTON**

ADMISSION PRICES
RINGSIDE ............... $4.00
GEN, ADM. ............... $3.00
CHILDREN ............... $1.00

After a multi-month hiatus following a mid-March event, wrestling returned to the Bahamas at the end of June, but this time it was once again staged at the old airplane hangar at Oakes Field – charitably referred to in promotional materials as the "Sports Centre." Despite no wrestling events being held there for years, the Hangar had continued to be one of Nassau's most popular boxing venues.

After another two month-break, wrestling returned to the Stadium yet again at the end of August, with Jose Lothario headlining against Johnny Valentine, and Tom Jones featured prominently in the advertising.

The young Jones, who was a relative newcomer to professional wrestling in general, was brand new to the Florida territory. Despite still being in a state of his career where he was paying his dues, Jones was touted in *The Nassau Guardian* as a "negro star" who would be teaming with the reformed Sputnik Monroe.

Rounding out the card would be Jack Brisco, the first Native American to have ever won an individual national championship as an NCAA wrestler, which he captured in

1965 for Oklahoma State University. Brisco would make Florida his home territory for years, and would eventually spend more than two years as the NWA World Heavyweight Champion.

Meanwhile, Lothario was beginning to appear in the Bahamas with increasing regularity.

"I think wrestling Valentine will be something like bullfighting," Lothario told Bahamian reporters. "The opponent is dangerous and doesn't care about the rules. He is also not quite so much in the brain department, and you can tell 'El Toro' Valentine I said so!"

One of the reasons for the elevated frequency of Lothario's presence in Nassau was the penetration of Championship Wrestling from Florida into Puerto Rico, which represented a much larger market than Nassau. Cowboy Luttrall and Eddie Graham – doing business as L&G Promotions – had begun offering regular events in San Juan, which had a population exceeding 900,000, and which reportedly drew crowds that easily topped 5,000 fans. This dwarfed what was capable of being squeezed into the largest Bahamian sports venues that Charlie Major had access to even under the most exigent circumstances.

As a Latin American star – albeit one of Mexican descent – Lothario was relied upon to cater to Puerto Rican wrestling fans. While Lothario was by all accounts a tremendous wrestler, he could also employ a bloodletting style that was often displayed in "brass knuckles" matches, during which both participants entered the ring with their fists taped, and then spent the bulk of their time pummeling one another's foreheads.

"Jose was a top worker in the state of Florida for years," opined Barry Rose. "If he wasn't in the top program on the card, he was usually in the semi-main event. Jose was an excellent brawler and wrestler who was a master at getting the audience behind him."

This fists-of-fury style of wrestling perpetuated by Lothario played a role in shaping the punch-heavy, blood-drenched brand of professional wrestling that predominated in Puerto Rico for decades. Lothario accomplished all of this while defending his Caribbean Heavyweight Championship, which is a championship that Luttrall and Graham introduced specifically for Lothario's matches in Puerto Rico.

"Jose Lothario used a decent number of wrestling moves, but as the matches progressed, he would usually lose his temper and then make a comeback," observed Buggsy McGraw. "When that happened, a lot of the wrestling went away, and he threw even more punches. Then again, most of the babyface comebacks back then had a lot more kicks and punches than wrestling moves. When the babyfaces got angry, they tended to show it by punching more."

Lothario lost his Caribbean title in a match against Johnny Valentine in San Juan, and then reportedly recaptured it from him during a match in Freeport, Grand Bahama Island on October 24th of 1968. If true, this was likely done so that Valentine could lose the championship in a location that would care about it before he departed for Georgia. This occasion also marks the first reported instance of a professional wrestling championship changing hands on Bahamian soil.

Speaking of Bahamian soil, that was a concept that was becoming an increasing point of government contention. By the end of 1968, Lynden Pindling – whose title had since been upgraded to Prime Minister of the Bahamas – had visited Miami and submitted to an interview with *The Miami Herald*, during which time he made it clear that the Bahamas would be seeking full independence from Great Britain.

41

While not providing a clear timeline for the transition, Pindling declared that the Bahamas was "one stage off independence" from its longstanding proprietor. It was only a matter of time.

Wrestling action in 1969 commenced on January 9th with another nine-man, over-the-top battle royale. This time the list of participants included The Gladiator, Koa Tiki, Eduardo Perez, Joe Scarpa, Duke Keomuka, Tarzan Tyler, The Outcast, Bobby Hart and Mac McFarland, with the winner receiving a $200 bonus. Once again, this event followed the pattern of the winner of the battle royale getting to relax for the remainder of the evening, while the other eight combatants were then paired off in singles contests.

In retrospect, the early part of 1969 was marked by the ascension of Jack Brisco to main-event prominence. The collegiate star headlined back-to-back cards in late January and early February, with *The Nassau Guardian* running a special feature on February 6th to evaluate his teaming with Nick Kozak to battle the masked tag team of The Medics.

"Brisco, a former collegiate wrestling champion and the younger member of his team, has made greater progress in less time than just about any fledgling professional since the great Lou Thesz, who won the world heavyweight championship at the age of 19," submitted *The Guardian*'s writer.

This was a stretch of both Thesz's credentials and the definition of the term "world championship" as Bahamians had been educated to understand it. The National Wrestling Alliance had not formed until 1948, and

**WRESTLING**
**THURSDAY**
JAN. 23 – 8:30 P.M.
**Nassau Stadium**

JACK BRISCO
& NICK KOZAK
— vs —
TARZAN TYLER
& KING LOUIE
TILLET

| EDUARDO' | | BOBBY |
| PEREZ | — vs — | HART |

| THE' | — vs — | KOA |
| OUTCAST | | TIKI |

ADMISSION PRICES
Ringside ...................... $4.00
Gen. Adm. ...................... $3.00
Children ...................... $1.00

Thesz began his initial reign as the NWA World Heavyweight Champion in 1949 when he was already 33 years old.

To his credit, Thesz *did* capture multiple world heavyweight championships of a lesser vintage prior to 1949, but the first advertised world championship to fall into his lap belonged to the American Wrestling Association of Boston, and Thesz was 21 years of age at the time he acquired it.

"This, of course, occurred before wrestling had grown to the major sport it has become in recent years," continued the writer, "and even at that, Thesz is such an outstanding competitor that he has won the championship no less than six times in the course of his illustrious career. Considering the difference in their ages, Brisco's achievements as a pro grappler seem readily comparable to those of Thesz."

Speaking of the world heavyweight championship, it would make its very first appearance in Nassau on the very next show. Gene Kiniski would make the initial defense of the NWA World Heavyweight Championship in the Bahamas on Thursday, February 13th by waging war against Kurt Von Stroheim.

Lurking on the undercard of that event was the man who would soon dethrone Kiniski, the young Dory Funk Jr. Partnered with Bobby Duncum, the grappler being groomed for NWA dominance would square off against Louie Tillet and Bobby Hart.

In the leadup to the same show, the CWF office filtered an excuse through *The Nassau Guardian* as to why so few of the Florida territory's championships were defended in Bahamian wrestling rings: "The Medics currently hold the Florida tag team championship; the title cannot be defended outside the state, however."

"It was a pleasure to go there. I always had a good time," stated Funk in reference to the Bahamas. "And I enjoyed teaming with Bobby. He was a football player from West Texas University – where I went to school. I recall looking around the stadium and up into the trees surrounding it, and it seemed like the trees were full of people even to the point where some of the branches might break."

The follow-up event at the end of February is notable for its inclusion of Cyclone Soto and Roberto Soto on the undercard. The two men were native Puerto Rican wrestlers who would both eventually wrestle for long stretches in the World Wrestling Federation. Roberto Soto would don a mask later in his career and form one half of The Invaders, the flagship tag team of the company that would eventually supplant the CWF in Puerto Rico, the World Wrestling Council.

The March 5th show at Nassau Stadium was a noteworthy affair for two reasons. First, the newly christened NWA World Heavyweight Champion Dory Funk Jr. appeared in the Bahamas to make his first defense of the NWA's flagship title in the islands. On this occasion, Funk defended against Hans Mortier – erroneously named in advertisements as "Hans Mortimer" – who was billed as the European Champion despite holding no sanctioned titles to speak of.

"Mortier was a wrestler's wrestler," said Barry Rose. "There weren't a lot of *pure* wrestling heels. Mortier could go out and have a great wrestling match with anybody, using a scientific wrestling style, and *still* be the heel during the match. He also had a very imposing look, even into his later years. He was in great shape, was able to have great matches, and he had the respect of everyone he worked with."

Second, this show marked the first Bahamian contest engaged in by Cyclone Negro, a former boxer from Venezuela

WRESTLING
SATURDAY
MARCH 8th......8:30
NASSAU
STADIUM
★ WORLD ★
HEAVYWEIGHT
TITLE MATCH

WORLD CHAMPION.
Dory Funk, Jr.
vs.
European Champion
Hans Mortimer
THE MEDICS
Joe vs. The
Scarpa & Gladiator
Cyclone vs. Kurt
Negro Von Stroheim
ADMISSION PRICES
RINGSIDE ............$4.50
GEN. ADM. ........$3.50
CHILDREN ..........$1.00

44

with a reputation for being a hard puncher, but who could also capably mix some impressive acrobatics into his routine. Although his name would endure through several alternate spellings – including Cyclon, Ciclon and Ciclone – Negro would eventually become one of the most popular wrestlers in the history of the Bahamas.

"Cyclone brawled a lot, but he was also excellent when it came to using actual wrestling moves," said Buggsy McGraw. "He knew how to work a crowd and do high spots as well as anyone. I wrestled him a lot in San Francisco after I left Florida, and he was excellent in the ring."

By April, Negro was already receiving the picture-box slot in advertisements for wrestling events held on the island, and a six-man tag team match that month was partially sold through The Great Malenko's threats that he and his European teammates – Hans Mortier and Kurt von Stroheim – would trim Cyclone Negro's beard if they managed to defeat Negro and his teammates, Joe Scarpa and The Gladiator.

WRESTLING
SATURDAY
APRIL 26 – 8:30 P.M.
NASSAU STADIUM

Hans          Cyclon
Mortier - vs - Negro
The Medics
— vs —
Joe               The
Scarpa & Gladiator
Jack              "The Good
BRISCO – vs – DOCTOR"
DR. "X" –vs – JOHN HEATH
RINGSIDE ................ $4.00
GEN. ADM. ..... ....... $3.00
CHILDREN .. .... ...... $1.00

"One of the strengths of Cyclone Negro was his ability to connect with a crowd," said Rose. "He really had the people on his side. You would see every so often a hint of a Mexican, lucha-libre-style move from him, but he was usually a rough-and-tumble wrestler and didn't use a ton of finesse. He could go through all the mechanics of being a really good professional wrestler, but he was a *really* great brawler."

Negro would headline the next few shows, including a show that marked the first appearance in Nassau of Beautiful Brutus, who would later gain tremendous fame on the west

coast of the United States as "The Brute" before returning for
Florida roughly a decade later as Buggsy McGraw.

Although his name has been listed as "Bugsy," "Buggsy," "Bugsie," and "Buggsie," the spelling with two Gs followed by a Y remains the wrestler's preferred spelling.

"I remember flying in for one of those early Nassau shows through some inclement weather," remembered McGraw. "I was nervous about it, but we all figured if Lester Welch was willing to fly, then we should *all* be willing to fly. He was trying to land us in Nassau, and he radioed into the airport to try to get clearance to land the plane. They answered back and said, 'Don't worry about it; you're the *only* plane in the sky. You can land whenever you want!'"

Positioned as a protege of The Great Malenko, Brutus fought against Joe Scarpa during his first trip to Nassau, then competed against Cyclone Negro on the undercard of the June 21st show, headlined by the return of Lou Thesz to Nassau in a clash with Han Mortier. Thesz would subsequently headline the next show in April in a $1,000 challenge match against Dale Lewis.

It was a matchup between gifted wrestlers with authentic credentials, as Thesz was regarded among the most dangerous shooters in the world, while Lewis had competed for the United States in two separate Olympic Games, and also won a gold medal at the 1959 Pan American Games in Chicago. Lewis was a fairly fresh arrival in Florida at the time, and was playing the role of villain, which was a rarity for American wrestlers with legitimate Olympic experience.

**WRESTLING**
**SATURDAY**
JUNE 21 – 8:30 P.M.
**NASSAU STADIUM**

**LOU THESZ**
– vs –
**BARON HANS MORTIER**

| Jack BRISCO | – vs – | Dale LEWIS |
| Beautiful BRUTUS | – vs – | Cyclone NEGRO |
| Joe SCARFA | | The Good DOCTOR |

| RINGSIDE | ............... | $4.00 |
| GEN. ADM. | ............... | $3.00 |
| CHILDREN | ............... | $1.00 |

46

# Bahamian Rhapsody

Occurring in the background of this in-ring activity, and probably escaping the notice of many of the wrestlers, were the efforts of Bahamian Prime Minister Lynden Pindling to rein in Bahamian businesses seen to be discriminating against native Bahamian workers.

This was especially true of the businesses viewed as operating with impunity in Freeport. As part of an effort referred to as the "Bahamianization" of the Bahamas and its workforce, the Pindling administration initiated a freeze on the issuing of work permits to many foreigners, which enraged many business owners operating in Freeport, while often crippling their businesses depending on the degree of specialized education and training require by their respective employees.

The situation for several Freeport business owners and investors became even less tenable in July when Pindling issued his famous bend-or-be-broken decree to the Freeport merchants, stating, "Bahamians are nevertheless still victims of an unbending social order which, if it now refuses to bend, must now be broken."

Pindling's statement painted a clear picture that businesses located in the Bahamas would not be able to persist without some form of oversight from the Bahamian government, and actions by business owners that were perceived as discriminatory against Bahamian people would be dealt with harshly.

For many businesses headquartered in Freeport, the Bahamian boomtown had instantly become a far less attractive place to conduct business in the aftermath of the actions leveled against it by the Pindling administration. These decrees were lauded as essential by many who felt discriminated against within their own homeland, but they were also rebuked as oppressive by several outsiders with Bahamian business interests, and particularly those individuals who had bought into the dream of a land offering total financial freedom, minimal taxation, and virtually nonexistent government oversight.

Meanwhile, back in the ring, the return to Nassau of NWA World Heavyweight Champion Dory Funk Jr. in August for a title defense against Dale Lewis was sufficient to command increased coverage by *The Nassau Guardian.*

"It was always a privilege to work against amateur wrestlers with the skill of someone like Dale Lewis," said Funk reflecting on his wrestling career.

The same article trumpeted the debut of "negro mat star" Sonny King, who was brand new to the wrestling business, and who was spending the summer of that year sharpening his skills by working his way through Florida. He was immediately thrust into a headlining position in Nassau as the tag team partner of Sputnik Monroe against the villainous tandem of Hiro Matsuda and the Missouri Mauler. For their return to Nassau in late August, the pair were dubbed as "Big Cat" King and "Sweet Man" Monroe, with King receiving prominent placement in the event's advertisements.

**WRESTLING**
**SATURDAY**
SEPT. 13  8.30 P.M.
**Oakesfield Hangar**

CYCLON
NEGRO
& SAM
STEAMBOAT

- vs -

HANS
MORTIER
& THE
GREAT
MALENKO

Sweet Man                    Eduardo
**MONROE  vs  PEREZ**

SONNY
"BIG
CAT"
KING

- vs -

EL
MONGOL

RINGSIDE ........ $4.00
GEN. ADM. ....... $3.00
CHILDREN ........ $1.00

In early September, professional wrestling events were moved back to the Oakes Field Hangar, with promoter Nelson "Chippie" Chipman – a former boxer and frequent organizer of local boxing events – claiming that the sizes of the Nassau Stadium crowds had led the organizers of the events to seek larger and more suitable accommodations.

"Because of our concern for the safety of the public and the overflow crowds at the stadium, we are forced to transfer the wrestling to the Hangar in Oakes Field," declared

Chipman. "There we will have room to accommodate more fans and cars."

Wrestling events continued at Oakes Field unabated until early October, which included a Brass Knuckles championship match between Beautiful Brutus and Dale Lewis. That's when a scheduling conflict with a national championship boxing match between Bert Perry and Leonard "Boston Blackie" Miller forced wrestling to move back to Nassau Stadium.

Unfortunately, the wrestling and boxing events had been double booked at Oakes Field for October 10th. The newspapers also included some elaboration as to the rationale behind the initial decision to once again stage professional wrestling events inside of the timeworn airport hangar.

"The stands in the Stadium are not good," Chipman told *The Guardian*. "They keep breaking under the weight of the spectators, and before someone gets hurt seriously, I decided to move down to the Hangar. But since the Hangar is booked out for that night, I have no other alternative but to move back to the Stadium."

The writer of the article posed this as a problem that would cause financial strife for the backers of the boxing match, including the statement: "It is a known fact that wrestling draws much more fans than any other local action."

The same article mentioned that the match participation of the

**WRESTLING**

SATURDAY Nov. 22
8:30 p.m.

**OAKES FIELD**

HANGAR – NASSAU

TEXAS
DEATH
MATCH

CYCLON
NEGRO
& SAM
STEAMBOAT
vs
BRONKO
LUBICH
& CHRIS
MARKOFF

DORY
DIXON
vs
BLUE
DEMON
#1

DANNY   vs   BLUE
MILLER     DEMON #2

RINGSIDE .............. $4.00
GEN. ADM. ............ $3.00
CHILDREN ............. $1.00

Missouri Mauler in Nassau was a means of sidestepping his suspension by the NWA, which supposedly had "no jurisdiction in the Bahama Islands." There was some mild storyline validity to that statement, as the Mauler was banned from wrestling in Florida according to CWF storylines, and had been relegated to managing Hiro Matsuda and El Mongol for most matches.

Events promptly returned to the Oakes Field Hangar in November in time for a tag team match pitting local favorites Cyclone Negro and Sam Steamboat against Bronko Lubich and Chris Markoff. *The Nassau Guardian* noted that "Texas death match rules will be in effect, making it a totally wide-open contest."

Receiving picture space alongside Negro for the advertising of the event was newcomer Dorrel "Dory" Dixon, an authentic West Indian wrestler from Kingston, Jamaica, who got his start in the wrestling business by working for several years in the EMLL wrestling promotion in Mexico, which would be rebranded much later as CMLL.

Dixon's tenure in Mexico included a long reign as the NWA World Light Heavyweight Champion, a title that was essentially owned and controlled by EMLL, and was not subject to the same scrutiny and approval by the board members of the National Wrestling Alliance as the organization's heavyweight championship.

Despite being touted as "one of the mat sport's outstanding young athletes," the 34-year-old Dixon had already been wrestling steadily for 14 years, and was superbly skilled.

The path taken by wrestlers to and from the Bahamas from Tampa had become well-worn by the time 1969 reached its conclusion. It's unlikely that Eddie Graham and the performers on his roster realized as they raced into a new decade that policies set in place by the Bahamian government would soon place such travel plans on an indefinite hold.

# Four: The Hangar, The Club and The Stadium

The beginning of 1970 opened with the Oakes Field Hangar continuing to serve as the home of Bahamian professional wrestling action. Famous Black wrestler "Thunderbolt" Patterson immediately usurped the headlining slot for his very first card in Nassau, teaming with Sam Steamboat against Chris Markoff and Bronko Lubich. Sailor Art Thomas also made his return to Nassau in a bid to defeat Thomas Bogni. It was the first time that two distinctively Black wrestlers would appear on the card of a Bahamian wrestling event, but it would be far from the last.

The team of Steamboat and Patterson returned the following month to compete against the combination of Hiro Matsuda and Mr. Saito. Saito was an accomplished amateur wrestler, simultaneously winning Japan's freestyle and Greco-Roman wrestling championships in 1963. Saito then advanced to the third round of the freestyle wrestling competition in the 1964 Olympic Games.

Like Seiji Sakaguchi before him, Saito had been recruited to the ring by the Japan Pro Wrestling Alliance after his Olympic appearance. Unlike Sakaguchi, Saito defected to join the upstart Tokyo Pro Wrestling organization in 1966, and when it folded, he spent a year wrestling for the International Wrestling Enterprise company in Japan before ultimately departing to wrestle in the United States.

Not wanting to be limited by the truth, but certainly not wishing for the credentials of legitimate wrestlers to go to waste, the article promoting the March 12th show at the Hangar stated, "Saito is an Olympic gold medal winner. Roop, the youngest member of the opposing team, is also an Olympic champion."

While Roop had certainly fared better than Saito during his Olympic participation – finishing seventh in Greco-Roman wrestling during the 1968 Olympic Games – he was also *not* an Olympic gold medalist. Local wrestling promoters clearly weren't expecting Bahamians to have closely tracked the results of Olympic wrestling contests held during the prior decade.

Unbeknownst to all Bahamian wrestling fans, the show pitting two "Olympic gold medalists" against one another would never take place – at least not within the decaying walls of Oakes Field Hangar. The dilapidated venue was deemed too dangerous for continued operation, and was unexpectedly earmarked for demolition.

END OF THE LINE FOR THE OAKES FIELD HANGAR
...'in the interest of public safety'

## Hangar Closed; To Be Demolished
Oakes Field Hangar closure announcement (Nassau Guardian)

"The official announcement said that the Ministry of Education and Culture had been advised by the Ministry of Works that 'in the interests of public safety' the hangar should not be used for 'public assembly' and 'the entire structure will be demolished as soon as possible,'" declared the statement reported through *The Nassau Guardian*. "'The public is therefore advised that as of March 10 the hangar will be closed to public use and any engagements previously made must regretfully be canceled. The Ministry regrets any inconvenience this may cause, but it is felt that the safety of the public is of paramount importance.'"

Any confusion felt by Bahamian wrestling fans would certainly have been justified, as *The Guardian* still ran an unaltered advertisement calling attention to the show at the Oakes Field Hangar on the very same day that the front page of the paper reported the venue's permanent closure.

The Cat & Fiddle Club was hastily acquired as a suitable substitute location for professional wrestling on New Providence Island. It was an attractive alternative for several reasons, not the least of which was owed to the fact that it was a very brief drive down Nassau Street from Oakes Field.

A popular local attraction, the Cat & Fiddle Club was advertised as being Nassau's largest open-air nightclub, providing plenty of space for a ring to be erected and for matches to take place. It also closed at 8:00 p.m. on most weeknights, providing just enough time for the venue to be converted into a site suitable for accommodating professional wrestling events, replete with a chicken-wire fence for additional protection against lobbed projectiles.

Unfortunately for the fans, the move to the club was accompanied by a one-dollar increase in ticket prices. Unfortunately for the wrestlers themselves, the absence of a roof and the capability of onlookers wandering by on the street to monitor the in-ring action transpiring within the club created opportunities for malfeasance.

WRESTLING

The BLUE DEMONS
- - - vs - - -
SAM STEAMBOAT
& THUNDERBOLT
PATTERSON

HIRO      DANNY
MATSUDA -vs- MILLER

*MIDGET GIRLS*
DARLING -vs- DIAMOND
DAGMAR      LIL

BOB -vs- MR.
ROOP      SAITO

THURSDAY
8.30 p.m.   CAT & FIDDLE
            CLUB

$5 – $3.50 – $1.50 (kids)

"The Ministry has come under some severe criticism from this column for the lousy facilities that were available at the Hangar," stated a March 21st editorial in *The Nassau Guardian*. "Even though the Hangar was in such a dilapidated state, the announcement came as a surprise to many. The reason being that the place had been booked heavily for future events. Now many of the former patrons face a dilemma. Nelson Chipman had to take his wrestling to the Cat

& Fiddle. But he found that it is very easy for idle persons to throw missiles and injure spectators since there is no roof."

This was perhaps the first public acknowledgement of what would one day become an oft-recalled hallmark of wrestling in the Bahamas – rocks and other debris being hurled toward the ring and the participating wrestlers within it by persons situated both inside and outside of the venues.

The flinging of stones drastically elevated the harshness of the environment for the wrestlers, who needed to successfully execute their matches while also dodging objects being hurled by mischievous fans. This was also apparently in direct response to a very specific incident that occurred during a singles match between Bob Roop and Masa Saito on March 19th.

"Saito and I were supposed to wrestle for 20 minutes, and all of a sudden we heard this boing, boing sound," said Roop. "We looked up and saw this discus-sized rock. It looked like it was four inches thick and might have weighed 20 pounds. Somehow this rock had been lobbed over to the ring. Whatever chicken wire protection had been around the ring had been worn down, and no one had bothered to climb up there and patch it up. Saito was on his back, and I was sitting on my butt with a headlock on him. So, we were both looking up watching this rock. It bounces across the chicken wire, reaches one of the holes, teeters back and forth on the edge of the hole for a moment, and then slid down to the ring and landed three feet from Saito's head."

Understandably, this alarmed both wrestlers.

"We were two minutes into what was supposed to be a 20-minute match," continued Roop, "but Saito immediately said to me, 'We go home!' which meant we were going to go straight to the finish of the match without hesitation. I don't remember how we finished the match, but we got out of there. The people were pissed that the match only had two minutes' worth of action and started storming the ring. We had to call for security to clear a path for us to leave. It took about 20 minutes for us to get out of the ring and back to the locker room. The Bahamian police had to show up in their white uniforms to help us get out of there."

Even without suitable protection from fan-propelled objects, wrestling events continued to be held and the Cat & Fiddle Club until a suitable replacement venue could be found. Eddie Graham's former tag team partner Bob Orton would get an opportunity to headline a show at the club in April, and later that same month, Graham himself returned to wrestle in Nassau for the first time in years.

In May, world champion Dory Funk Jr. once again arrived in Nassau to face the Missouri Mauler, but the champ's title would not be on the line as he made his Cat & Fiddle Club debut. The Mauler provided an interview to the press that helped to turn the absence of a sanctioned world-title bout into a harbinger of the night's unpredictability.

"There is only one reason why Funk has refused to put his title up against me," the Mauler told the Bahamian press. "That reason is he knows that he's going to get the beating of his life! I'll give Funk credit for knowing when he's met his match, but he doesn't need to think I'm going any easier on him because of this little bit of trickery. If it were a title match, I'd have to watch myself – I'd have to be careful not to get disqualified; as it is, my only concern is to prove to everybody watching that I can give Dory Funk Jr. the beating of his life, and that's exactly what I'm going to do Thursday night!"

Once his plane touched down in Nassau, the champion issued a prepared response to the Mauler's threats.

WRESTLING

DORY FUNK JR. –VS– THE MISSOURI MAULER

ARGENTINA APOLLO & JOSE LOTHARIO –VS– EL LOBO & DALE LEWIS

JACK BRISCO –VS– THE GLADIATOR

THURSDAY – 8:30 P.M.

CAT & FIDDLE
CLUB – NASSAU

$5.00 - $4.00 - $1.00

55

"The Missouri Mauler has made some rather derogatory remarks about me," replied Funk. "I know that he specializes in backwoods brawling, and I feel that I have a fight – as opposed to a scientific wrestling match – on my hands Thursday night. This being the case, I don't want my hands tied by having the world heavyweight title up for grabs. I want to be able to use some of the rough tactics myself against people like the Mauler. The Mauler has asked for a fight, and that's what he's going to get – and if he thinks his Missouri mule-headedness makes him tough, then it's about time he tangled with a Texan!"

In essence, Funk had implied to the fans that his bout with the Mauler would be a wilder, faster-paced affair than the customary, hour-long matches synonymous with NWA title defenses. For fans accustomed to seeing rapid-fire wrestling on a routine basis, the distended, methodical structure of world-title matches was dismissed by some fans as being comparatively boring.

"You weren't going to get a great scientific match out of the Missouri Mauler," said Barry Rose. "When he got in the ring, a lot of his matches involved brawling, with an armlock or a headlock thrown in sometimes. He was an old-school cowboy in a lot of ways. Mauler would bleed a lot, he had great interviews, and knew how to get everyone riled up, but was *not* a great ring tactician."

Moving quickly in the background of these events, the Bahamian government was making preparations for full independence, while opening diplomatic offices in both New York and London as three centuries of designation as a British colony appeared to be drawing to a rapid close. As the march to independence continued, reports soon materialized in U.S. newspapers about Black Bahamian workers who were no longer behaving as contented servants to groups of predominantly White tourists, and who occasionally adopted an openly resentful and hostile disposition toward them.

Meanwhile, an article by William Montalbano of *The Miami Herald* stated that the continued Americanization of the culture of the Bahamas, and fears that it might be transformed into "a distant county of Florida," factored into the Bahamian government's efforts to curtail foreign influence on its many islands.

While walking through the Nassau airport, the Missouri Mauler experienced an ordeal that some might cite as a reflection of the changing attitudes amongst Bahamians.

"Mauler got kicked out of customs one time because of the way he called the customs agent 'man,'" laughed Roop. "The Bahamian at customs was questioning him about where he was from and what he had with him, and Mauler just kept calling the guy 'man.' Mauler resented the fact that he even had to talk to this guy. The guy said, 'Why do you keep calling me 'man' like that? Mauler said, 'What do you want me to do; call you *boy*?' Mauler was immediately told to get the hell out of there, and he had to sit on Lester Welch's private plane the entire time we were wrestling. Racism can *definitely* come back to bite your ass."

Following a three-month hiatus, the roster of Championship Wrestling from Florida resumed its activity at Nassau Stadium. It is unknown whether the Cat & Fiddle Club's owners decided wrestling resulted in too many stone-throwing incidents than they were comfortable with, or if it simply took that long for Charlie Major and Eddie Graham to reshuffle the schedule in a way that would enable wrestling to once again shift from Thursday nights to the preferred Saturday nights.

Whatever the reason was, a show headlined by Hiro Matsuda facing El Lobo headlined an August 29th show that marked the return of wrestling to Nassau Stadium for the first time in a year, and wrestling shows would continue to be held within the green-walled enclosure for the foreseeable future.

Of all the wrestling venues, Nassau Stadium was the most advantageous to the wrestlers for logistical reasons. Its western wall abutted the property of the Pilot House, a hotel owned by the Lightbourn family. The Pilot House also sat just across Bay Street from the Poop Deck, a popular waterfront restaurant that was also owned by the Lightbourns. This layout contributed to an easy eat-rest-wrestle arrangement for the wrestlers performing in Nassau.

For what it's worth, the increase in ticket prices that had accompanied the move from the Hangar to the Cat & Fiddle Club remained in effect at Nassau Stadium.

A new crop of wrestlers was inbound to Nassau during this time, including Jake the Kentuckian, a mammoth-sized wrestler attired in blue jeans who first appeared in September for a main event match against Dale Lewis.

"Lewis is a sleeper hold specialist and wins most of his matches in that method," stated the writeup in *The Nassau Guardian*. "Jake, 7 feet tall and weighing 358 pounds, is a special target for Lewis. Jake has never been defeated by the sleeper and Lewis boasts he will prove to the big man that he is not immune to the sleeper hold danger."

During his career, Jake the Kentuckian achieved his greatest fame wrestling as "Grizzly" Smith, and three of his children all went on to wrestle in front of national audiences in the United States: Sam Houston, Rockin' Robin, and Jake "The Snake" Roberts.

The influx of new wrestling talent would continue in early October when the young "Texas Outlaws" invaded Nassau for the first time to clash with Hiro Matsuda and Dale Lewis. Consisting of Dick Murdoch and Dusty Rhodes, the pair had a reputation for being outspoken and controversial.

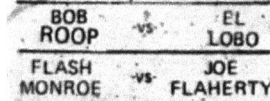

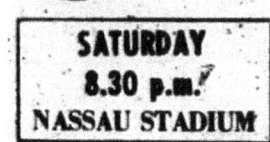

WRESTLING

BIG JAKE
-vs-
DALE LEWIS

BOB ROOP -vs- EL LOBO

FLASH MONROE -vs- JOE FLAHERTY

HIRO MATSUDA
-vs-
MR. SAITO

SATURDAY
8.30 p.m.
NASSAU STADIUM

$5.00 - $4.00 - $1.00 (kids)

58

"Nobody from Oklahoma – not Dale Lewis or anybody else – stands a chance against a Texan," boasted Rhodes.

"Lewis has to face not one, but two Texans, with nobody to help him but that skinny, slanty-eyed Jap," added Murdoch.

Murdoch maintained his cantankerous attitude when he returned to the Stadium in late October to challenge Jose Lothario for his Brass Knuckles championship.

"There ain't never been a Mexican that a big, tough Texan like me couldn't beat!" sneered Murdoch.

The Outlaws collectively took center stage again in November when they main-evented against both Lothario and Jake the Kentuckian. Once again, they provided plenty of creative promotional quips for the press to print.

"We gonna malign them two Mexicans!" said Rhodes.

"We call Jake a Mexican because when my ancestors and Dusty's was fightin' for freedom at the Alamo, Big Jake's ancestors, if he had any, were probably fightin' for the Mexicans," added Murdoch. "Anyway, he still is today!"

On the same card, Ron Fuller made his Bahamas debut in a battle with The Great Mephisto. Any Bahamian basketball fans who visited Miami may have recognized Fuller as Ron Welch, the 6'9" forward who had recently worn number five as a reserve on the University of Miami's basketball team.

**WRESTLING**

JACK BRISCO
-vs-
The GREAT MEPHISTO

DICK MURDOCK & DUSTY RHOADES
-vs-
DALE LEWIS & HIRO MATSUDA

GIRLS!
SHERRI LEE
-vs-
KATHY O'DAY

PAT VALENTINO -vs- JOE FLAHERTY

SATURDAY OCT. 10, 8:30 p.m.
NASSAU STADIUM
$5–$4–KIDS $1

Fuller was a member of the dynastic Fuller family of wrestlers and wrestling promoters, and was the son of Buddy Fuller and the grandnephew of Lester Welch. Also booked to wrestle on the same show was the 68-year-old Roy Welch – the much older brother of Lester and the grandfather of Ron Fuller.

In November, the newest member of the Fuller dynasty participated in a main-event match alongside Danny Miller against the two Outlaws, Rhodes and Murdoch. A rumor has emerged that Rhodes and Murdoch executed a stunt during this match that effectively discredited wrestling as a staged affair in a deliberate attempt to eliminate the Bahamas as a viable territory so that performers would no longer have to travel there.

Sherri Lee worked on the undercard of the show that night and recalls no such incident taking place.

"All the wrestlers I knew who came to the Bahamas wanted to come there and made plenty of money working there," said Lee. "Most of the people who came to Florida *asked* to come to the Bahamas. There would be no reason to try to kill the territory."

Little other evidence supports the idea that any individual stunts performed by Rhodes and Murdoch in the ring somehow killed the Bahamas as a viable territory, not the least of which is the makeup of the very next show in Nassau, which took place on December 5th.

It strains credulity to believe that as a punishment for attempting to expose the wrestling business as phony in Nassau, Murdoch would be rewarded with an NWA World Heavyweight Championship match against Dory Funk Jr. just

60

two weeks later, at the exact same venue, with Rhodes similarly being granted a slot in the semi-main event against Jose Lothario.

However, there were certainly bureaucratic processes in the works that *did* threaten to kill the Bahamas as a viable wrestling territory. By the end of 1970, syndicated columnist Howard Whitman had reported how the activities of Pindling's administration had resulted in a mass exodus of many business owners and residents from Freeport, Grand Bahama Island. The population of Freeport – which had grown to 40,000 in 1969 – retracted back to 25,000 in 1970.

According to Whitman's reporting, hundreds of British and American workers residing in Freeport had been expelled, with some only given 24-hour's notice. Any company with a business presence in Freeport was regarding their occupation of office buildings there as tenuous at best, and that certainly would have included the Florida wrestling territory with its office in Freeport.

CHAMPIONSHIP WRESTLING

WORLD
Heavyweight
TITLE
MATCH

| Dory FUNK Jr. Champion | vs | Dick MURDOCK Challenger |
| Jose Lotharia | vs | Dusty Rhodes |
| The Great Mephisto | vs | Danny Miller |

TARZAN TYLER
vs
JOHN HEATH

| Ron Fuller | vs | Lajardo Perez |

SATURDAY
Dec. 5 – 8:30 p.m.
— NASSAU STADIUM —
$5.00–$4.00–KIDS $1.00

This is where the clash of reality and "kayfabe" – the system of protecting the secrets of professional wrestling from outsiders – would have come into direct conflict with one another in the center of the Bahamas Immigration Office. The Bahamian system of granting work permits, which was now being aggressively restricted, required that any positions of employment being offered could only be filled with foreign workers if no sufficiently skilled Bahamians could be found within the general populace to fill the available positions.

In its early, pre-independence stage of enforcement, the work-permit disbursement policy was often enforced as one where work permits were more likely to be declined than granted or renewed whenever there was a doubt about a native Bahamian's potential to adequately execute the task in question.

In the United States, the austere fashion with which Bahamian officials now presided over the issuance of work permits was ridiculed to such an extent that an Associated Press report lampooned Bahamas deputy prime minister and minister of Home Affairs Arthur Hanna.

In a fictional response to an imaginary request from Jesus Christ himself for a Bahamian work permit – in a land often credited with possessing more churches per capita than any other – it was stated that Hanna would have replied, "Give him a two-week permit. We'll have a Bahamian trained to take his job by then."

To Bahamians responsible for issuing work permits, and who believed wrestling to be an authentic sport, the matter became a simple one: Why would we allow foreigners to fly in, fight one another for Bahamian money, and abscond with thousands of dollars of Bahamian cash if Bahamians could just as easily learn to wrestle and compete for the same money themselves?

When viewed through this pragmatic lens where wrestling is treated as a legitimate sports event, the act of continuing to import foreign wrestlers would be seen as flagrant discrimination against any Bahamians who wished to wrestle, but were never offered opportunities to break into the professional wrestling industry.

From the standpoint of Championship Wrestling from Florida, to expose that wrestlers required a specific level of specialized training in order to cooperatively execute their matches with the assistance of their opponents would have guaranteed the exposure of the business, and probably on the front pages of all major Bahamian newspapers. And even so, in a political climate that tilted toward nationalism, it may not have mattered one iota.

In January of 1971, Dory Funk Jr. returned to the Bahamas once again to defend the world title against Danny Miller, and the Bahamian press was gushing about Funk in an appraisal of his long championship reign.

"Funk has held the title for nearly two years since winning it from Gene Kiniski in Tampa, Florida in February of 1969," stated *The Guardian*. "Dory has been one of the most successful champions in the history of professional wrestling."

On the undercard of the event, Ron Fuller was joined by Jack Welch and Roy Welch in a six-man tag-team match against the masked tag team known as the Infernos and their manager J.C. Dykes, with both Fuller and Jack Welch slated to work double duty that night by first facing the respective Infernos in singles competition. This would have been a remarkable exertion for Jack Welch considering that he was only a few years younger than his brother Roy, and was seeing ring action into his mid-sixties.

The next show in February of 1971 began with the largest battle royale to date – an 11-man skirmish including Danny Miller, Bob Roop, Hiro Matsuda, Eduardo Perez, Oki Shikina, Ken Lusk, Cisco Grimaldo, Les Thatcher, both Infernos, and also manager J.C. Dykes. Aside from Dykes, all participants in the battle royale were distributed into singles or tag matches during the remainder of the evening.

Three more shows were held by Championship Wrestling from Florida in Nassau Stadium during the early portion of 1971, with the final event occurring on April 22$^{nd}$, and once again headlined by Dick Murdoch as he faced Jose Lothario.

"Murdock [sic] tips the scales at a solid 270 pounds, and has gained much fame as one of the roughest brawlers in the sport of wrestling today," stated *The Guardian*. "Lothario prefers a more scientific approach to mat competition, but as a former professional boxer who once held the brass knuckles championship, he can take care of himself against any style."

The match by familiar and popular wrestlers came and went with little fanfare. Wrestling fans of the Bahamas had little reason to suspect that their beloved international wrestling stars would soon be replaced in an abrupt and unforgettable fashion that would blur the boundaries between fandom and nationalism in the most remarkable of ways.

**A front-to-back, aerial view of Nassau Stadium with the east-facing Fowler Street entrance at the bottom (Courtesy of Google Maps)**

## Five: The Last Totally Foreign Show

Less than two weeks after a showdown between Jose Lothario and Dick Murdoch had Nassau Stadium rocking and reeling, a figurative bombshell was dropped on Bahamian wrestling fans. A professional wrestling product consisting exclusively of Bahamian wrestlers was suddenly being substituted for the stars of Championship Wrestling from Florida.

"Taking the place of the Lotharios, Grahams, Malenkos, Briscos and others will be Alex Hall, Curtis Cartwright, Tommy Burrows, the Bruiser, Rugged Gubber, Edward Penn, and many more," stated the article in *The Nassau Guardian*.

The description of the event publicly revealed that the first organized group of Bahamian professional wrestlers had been training behind the scenes for more than three months in preparation for the big reveal that had taken place on May 4th of 1971.

"These guys are good," stated an onlooker interviewed by *The Guardian*. "If I didn't know they were Bahamians, I would think they were some Americans practicing."

The full advertised card featured a main event of Joe Goose and Bradley Johnson meeting "The Hulk" and "The Grappler" in a best-of-three-falls tag team match, with "Big" Edward Penn meeting "Rugged Gubber" in singles competition. Matches involving Alex Hall, Curtis Cartwright, Tommy Burrows and "The Bruiser" provided the preliminary action.

**WRESTLING**
*"SPECIAL"*
PRA-PRA (DASH DOWN)...

ALEX HALL
VS
CURTIS CARTWRIGHT

TOMMY BURROWS
VS
THE BRUISER

★★★★★★★★
EDWARD PENN
VS
RUGGED GUBBER
★★★★★★★★
TAG TEAM EVENT
JOE GOOSE   BRADLEY JOHN
VS
THE HULK • GRAPPLER
★★★★★★★★★★★★★★
SATURDAY May 8th.
NASSAU STADIUM
ADM. $3.00, $2.00, .50c

Charlie Major, who was openly promoting and backing the event at Nassau Stadium, stated, "This is good for the Bahamas and I think that these boys should be encouraged. I don't really know how well the wrestling public will take it when they hear about the show, but I'm sure that if they were to see the show, they would forever support these youngsters."

Ticket prices for the event were substantially reduced to three dollars for ringside seats and two dollars for general admission, while the price of admission for children was cut in half to 50 cents.

Behind the scenes, Arnsel Tyrone Johnson and the members of his Bahamas Wrestling Club had been training in the style of their American heroes for months.

"I got into wrestling by watching Jack Brisco and all of those fellows who used to come in here and wrestle at the Nassau Stadium," said Johnson.

Johnson had a strong desire to emulate the wrestlers he had been watching on Saturday evenings, but was unable to do so due to the physical limitations imposed on him by an asthma affliction.

"I went to Mr. Wong's gym, and he taught me how to lift weights and stuff like that," continued Johnson. "I built up my strength, and I found that the asthma started to leave me, and my breath started to get a little longer. Mr. Wong told me the more I worked out, the better it would be for me."

Once his body filled out with muscles and his endurance improved, Johnson built his own wrestling ring on Balfour Avenue, with only a plywood mat. Within his rudimentary wrestling ring, Johnson would train with his brother Bradley, along with his friends Alex Hall and Joe Wildgoose.

"We would go through 'the format' together," explained Johnson. "Joe would put me in a hold, and I'd have to work my way out of the hold. I'd put him in a hold, and he'd have to try to do the same thing. We worked through all the holds that we had known about, and we'd practice falling by throwing ourselves down on the mat. We also did jogging and conditioning exercises around R.M. Bailey Park for about an hour every morning."

Before too long, the group of friends was joined by others, like Ed Penn from Freeport, and Andy Ifil. Their daily activities were certainly out of the ordinary, and the group was quickly discovered by a local promoter named Marty Goldstein.

"Marty Goldstein saw me, and he liked the way that I was moving around with my team," said Johnson. "He came there, and he saw who all was there, and how we were working out and stuff. I didn't know he was a promoter. He told me that I must get my boys all together, and we could do a little island hopping."

With Goldstein providing the financial backing, Johnson and his neighborhood wrestling club became what was known as the "Bahamas Wrestling Association." They also just happened to have been a few months into their training during the precise moment when the work permits of Championship Wrestling from Florida's wrestlers were no longer renewed.

Without being able to legally acquire permits for their workers, the CWF office in the Bahamas became just another Freeport business that closed as a result of being unable to supply legal jobs on Bahamian soil for its specialized personnel. As a going concern that held shows with regularity, the National Wrestling Alliance had been ousted from the Bahama Islands.

While CWF and its wrestlers wouldn't disappear for good, the mass exodus of foreign workers from the Bahamas had momentarily swept away the enduring presence of one of the NWA's most successful territories along with it.

Tax shelters and work permits notwithstanding, Florida was also not the same state it had been when its stars began making appearances in Nassau just over one decade prior. The state of Florida was in the midst of the most explosive population boom of any U.S. state, with a resident base that had grown by more than 37 percent from the previous decade.

While the population of the Bahamas had grown by roughly 60 percent to upwards of 160,000 during that same period, Florida also now boasted five cities ranked within America's 100 most heavily populated, with four of those cities – Jacksonville, Miami, Tampa and St. Petersburg – each possessing populations significantly larger than the Bahamas. All things considered, it remained to be seen whether or not the Bahamas would miss NWA wrestling more than NWA wrestling would miss the Bahamas.

While reviews for the first all-Bahamian wrestling event are difficult to come by, there are reasons to suspect that it was not as successful as its backers had initially hoped. When wrestling did make an eventual return to Nassau Stadium on Saturday, August 28th of 1971, the spots on the card were not filled with competitors from the Bahamas Wrestling Association, but were instead occupied by wrestlers from the Miami-based outlaw promotion known as the International Wrestling Association, which had also been operating in open opposition to Championship Wrestling from Florida within the Sunshine State.

The bulk of the matches that evening featured IWA wrestlers like the Golden Gladiator, also known as CWF veteran Ronnie Hill. He was joined by Dr. Mike Gordon and The Mummy, while one match was advertised as a special Bahamian undercard contest between "The Grappler" Arnsel Johnson and Joe Goose, the two founding members of the Bahamas Wrestling Club.

Goose and The Grappler therefore became the first authentic Bahamian wrestlers to appear at a wrestling event hosted by an American wrestling company, and certainly the first to do so in the Bahamas.

Johnson remembers having an animated exchange with one of the American wrestlers at the Stadium.

"I went in the back, and one of the wrestlers came to me and said, 'Show me a hold; they say you're a wrestler,'" recalled Johnson. "I put him in a hold with my hands around his neck, and I flipped over him. They said, 'No, no, no, no, no! You can't use that! You can't use that! That's too dangerous!' But all of them liked the way I was moving around."

In the meantime, nearly a year passed before Championship Wrestling from Florida finally returned to the Bahamas for one show in 1972, which took place in Highbury High School on Robinson Road on Thursday, May 11th. Still the world champion in his fourth uninterrupted year, Dory Funk Jr. headlined the card against Tim Woods, while Bob Roop, Bearcat Wright, Paul Jones, Louie Tillet, Ronnie Garvin and Johnny Gray filled out the undercard.

The odd date and location of the event lend to the unlikelihood that the show had any involvement from Charlie Major, Nelson Chipman, or any of the other experienced boxing and wrestling promoters of the Bahamas.

The arrival and inclusion of Wright trumpeted the participation of another Black wrestling pioneer who was also routinely billed as hailing from Kingston, Jamaica, even though he was actually born in Omaha, Nebraska. Like Sweet Daddy Siki and Sailor Art Thomas who preceded him, Wright was another frequent holder of "negro" heavyweight championships in various wrestling territories.

The absence of the customary fanfare for a Black wrestling pioneer like Wright, along with the omission of his photo from the newspaper, seems to indicate the promotional inexperience of whomever was handling the event's marketing. It may also have stemmed from a lack of enthusiasm for a wrestling event that was unassociated with Charlie Major, who was very well connected with members of the Bahamian press.

Regardless as to the cause of the venue change and comparative downturn in event coverage, this show held in an atypical setting would be Championship Wrestling from Florida's sole appearance in the Bahamas during the year.

In late July of 1972, an article published in *The Nassau Tribune* accentuated the looming problems faced by wrestlers seeking to work in the Bahamas as the country neared full-blown independence. A wrestler going by Manuel "Manny" Gonzales, who also claimed to have been the world light heavyweight wrestling champion, sat for an interview in which he claimed he was seeking employment as an instructor to the young wrestlers of the "Bahamas Wrestling Alliance."

"I investigated the matter to find out whether I could be of some help," said Gonzales. "I got Mr. G.R. Brennan to write the immigration department on my behalf, but a few complications have stopped me from instructing the boys."

In all likelihood, the wrestler being interviewed was "Speedy Gonzales," the active IWA Caribbean Heavyweight Champion. It was explained to him that the BWA would need to advertise an opening for a wrestling instructor, and if no qualified professional wrestling trainers came forward from amongst the Bahamian populace, the BWA would have to seek permission from the immigration department to hire a dedicated wrestling instructor from outside of the country.

"I guess I should be angry about the whole thing, but I'm not," continued Gonzales. "Actually, the matter was clearly explained, and laws are laws. I've been here (Nassau) since June 30, and I was only able to see the local wrestlers in a short workout, and I must admit that there is a lot of talent here in the wrestling field. I would like to be the one to bring out the better part of this raw talent."

**Manuel Gonzales (Nassau Tribune)**

With the Championship Wrestling from Florida promotion effectively booted from the Bahamas, the Miami-based IWA, which was entirely devoid of recognizable stars, and which was of a dramatically reduced level of in-ring quality compared with CWF, established a true foothold in the Bahamas in 1973, during the year national independence descended upon the Bahamas in its truest form.

Instead of providing Bahamian fans with international stars like Jose Lothario, Jack Brisco, Sam Steamboat and Cyclone Negro, the IWA, which operated under a variety of alternative names including the "Florida Wrestling Association," imported local Florida wrestlers to the Bahamas like Black Angel, Speedy Gonzales, "Lil" Abner Collins and "Wild" Bill Williams. The complicity of these wrestlers in working for an outlaw organization meant they had little hope of ever acquiring gainful employment anywhere else that the NWA held sway, and certainly not in the state of Florida.

**IWA wrestlers Speedy Gonzales and The Black Angel**

Elsewhere on the island, the Bahamas Wrestling Association began 1973 with some early exhibitions at events like boxing matches at Nassau Stadium, and the Mr. Bahamas International bodybuilding contest. Then in May, Bahamian pro wrestlers like heavyweight Ed Penn, The Sensational Bahamian Grappler, Super Plus, Black Eagle, Chris Rolle, Little

Bugs and The Question – who was *also* Arnsel Johnson working under a mask – made a major comeback to the local wrestling scene with a show at the Arawak Auditorium at Oakes Field.

A promotional excerpt taken from *The Nassau Tribune* on May 31st reveals one of the ways in which the wrestlers of the BWA suffered from the comparison to the Florida-based stars who had both inspired and preceded them. The weights of several of the Bahamian wrestlers were disclosed, and Edward Penn, who had been previously listed at 240 pounds, was the only identifiable competitor on the BWA roster to clear the heavyweight limit.

The excerpt from *The Tribune* also listed Chris Rolle at 135 pounds, Sydney Stuart at 145 pounds, Super Plus at 175 pounds, and Joe Goose at 200 pounds. To a public used to seeing powerhouses like Bob Roop, who easily topped 270 pounds, or Ron Fuller, who legitimately stood at least 6'8", most of the Bahamian newcomers would have looked downright diminutive in the eyes of their countrymen, with perhaps a few exceptions like Penn and Johnson.

In late June, the IWA held a show at the 1,200-seat Birdland Arena – a local boxing gym – with a show featuring the

Black Angel against Count Von Hess in the main event, and an undercard that included Speedy Gonzales, Prince Kukukaya, Miguel Serrano, the Black Panther and the Golden Gladiator. Not to be overlooked, reigning Bahamas heavyweight boxing champion Leonard "Boston Blackie" Miller was the special guest referee for the show. In addition to training at Birdland, Miller also directed the fighting events there, so the IWA's affair at the Birdland arena capitalized on Miller's influence to attract Nassau residents.

"Birdland couldn't hold the people that Nassau Stadium could," said Johnson. "Nassau Stadium was also a more famous name. Everyone used to go there for boxing, wrestling, and any kind of sports. Birdland was a much smaller venue."

Apparently, the local Bahamian wrestlers had difficulty competing against their Floridian counterparts for the hearts and dollars of Nassau's wrestling fans. Just one week prior to the realization of total national independence by the Bahamas, promoter Leslie Fox lashed out against "totally foreign wrestling shows" in an article published by *The Nassau Tribune* on July 3rd.

In that article, Fox threatened to lodge a formal complaint with the Immigration Department, the Ministry of Education, and the Ministry of Finance in an effort to motivate the government "... to do something to protect the sport of wrestling in the country." It was an indication of precisely how politicized the hosting of professional wrestling events had become in the Bahamas, with fans who turned up in support of shows featuring foreign talent committing what might have been equated to treason in the eyes of Fox.

"If there was no competition from foreign wrestlers then the Bahamians would support the local talent," Fox told *Tribune* reporter Gladstone Thurston, clearly blaming the IWA, and possibly the departed specter of the NWA, for the comparative inability of the BWA to attract

**ALL STAR PROFESSIONAL WRESTLING**

**BIRDLAND**

MT. ROYAL & CAREW

**SAT. JUNE 23RD. 8:30 P.M.**

BOSTON BLACKIE
*SPECIAL REFEREE*

Tag Team Match
— 2 Out of 3 Falls —

COUNT VON HESS
– VS –
BLACK ANGEL

BUDDY TAYLOR
– VS –
SPEEDY GONZALES

PRINCE KUKUKAYA – VS – THE TURK

MIGUEL SERRANO – VS – THE BLACK PANTHER

GOLDEN GLADIATOR – VS – THE RAIDER

GEN. ADM. $4.00
CHILDREN UNDER 12 $2.00
RES. RINGSIDE $6.00

fans. "I hope that the last wrestling show that was put on will be the last totally foreign show."

Fox went on to say that most of the proceeds from foreign wrestling shows had left the country without many Bahamians reaping any sort of financial benefit. He also demanded that all wrestling cards should be mandated to feature Bahamian performers, and offered a final parting shot: "If foreigners don't want to compete with the Bahamian wrestlers, then the Government should not grant them their work permit."

Since Fox's gripe was owed to the fact that foreign-run wrestling events had been indirectly competing with Bahamian wrestling shows by holding events weeks removed from BWA events – as opposed to head-to-head on the same evenings – his accusation that foreigners didn't wish to compete with Bahamian wrestlers implied that they didn't wish to *physically* compete with those wrestlers inside of a wrestling ring.

**Ed Penn and The Question of the Bahamas Wrestling Association**

If Fox knew that wrestling matches were predetermined affairs as opposed to legitimate sports contests, that would have made his protectionist appeal to fairness –

filtered through a lens of nationalism – simultaneously brilliant and decidedly underhanded.

What no one connected with the Bahamian Wrestling Association could have had the experience to know during the 1970s, in an era when many wrestling fans believed everything they were watching inside of a ring to be legitimate, is that the idea of running consistent professional wrestling events in which the majority of the participants came from the same small island would have been problematic for a whole host of reasons, even if the shows had been financially successful at the outset.

The fact that so many safety measures had been built into its system is just one of the many reasons why the National Wrestling Alliance had functioned so efficiently. Chief among those safety measures was the fact that wrestlers who did not grow up within the territories they performed were able to craft their own identities, character traits and backstories without having them questioned by hometown fans who knew them on a first-name basis, and who would be able to immediately question the veracity of any new claims or characterizations that were inconsistent with reality.

In general, the successful exceptions to this rule fell into a few different categories. For example, professional athletes with reputations for toughness could easily transition to wrestling professionally in their home cities. Dick "The Bruiser" Afflis was well known to be Richard Afflis of Delphi, Indiana, a professional football player who was better known for his altercations with people off the football field than he was for his very competent play on it.

When the Bruiser began his wrestling career and eventually owned and operated his own World Wrestling Association promotion based out of Indianapolis, people from his home state came in droves to see the Bruiser pummel his adversaries.

Similarly, professional wrestlers with legitimate amateur wrestling credentials could become box office attractions in their hometowns. There is no better example of this than

Verne Gagne, the owner and usually the world champion of the American Wrestling Association. Not only was Gagne an All-Big-Ten football player at the University of Minnesota, but he was also a multi-time NCAA wrestling champion and an alternate on the 1948 U.S. Olympic Wrestling Team. No one in Minnesota questioned Gagne's credibility when he founded the AWA in Minneapolis and quickly received recognition as its world champion.

As uncertain as the road ahead may have been, the first crop of Bahamian professional wrestlers had now been produced. Simultaneous to this, new symbols of Bahamian identity had also been established. The red, white and blue colonial ensign bearing the Union Jack that had flown over the Bahama Islands for more than a century had been replaced by a tricolored flag of black, aquamarine and gold. Likewise, the coat of arms that had eulogized the expulsion of pirates from the Bahamas in the early 18th century had been replaced by the slogan "Forward, Upward, Onward, Together."

It would remain to be seen exactly how much togetherness would be demonstrated, along with how accepted a group of home-grown Bahamian grapplers would be by a public that yearned to establish a collective sense of national identity, yet one that had also been irreversibly spoiled by frequent visits from many of the best active professional wrestlers on the planet.

## Six: The Elisha Obed of Wrestling

No matter how misguided Leslie Fox's efforts to regulate professional wrestling may have been, apparently they were not in vain. Eleven days after the promoter's demands were made public, the wrestling card for the Birdland Arena announced the debut of "The Bahamian Grappler" Arnsel Johnson within that facility, as he teamed with Speedy Gonzales and Jan Marsch to take on the Raiders and the Interns.

Thus, Arnsel Johnson became the first Bahamian to directly participate in a match with and against non-Bahamian wrestlers.

A few weeks later, Bahamas Heavyweight Wrestling Champion Ed Penn was also fully integrated into the IWA's shows. The August 4th edition of *The Tribune* described how he kept his hometown Freeport fans on the edge of their seats at Independence Arena while demonstrating a fine array of body slams.

During the same event, Speedy Gonzales defeated the Cave Man, and Black Angel teamed with Florida Heavyweight Champion Lil Abner Collins in a losing effort. The joint IWA/BWA shows seemed primed to replicate and replace Championship Wrestling from Florida's scheduling pattern right down to the consecutive nightly performances on the newly independent nation's two most populous islands.

No professional wrestling events were prominently promoted in the Bahamas during the remainder of 1973. Then, when advertisements appeared in the newspapers revealing a February 2nd wrestling event at Birdland Arena in 1974, it probably caused both a great deal of excitement and confusion for any Bahamians with prior experience watching wrestling in their homeland.

Unmistakably, the promotional materials advertised the presence of the wrestling stars Bahamians were accustomed to seeing; the advertisement plainly said "Florida T.V. Stars

Wrestling" at the very top, and had no fewer than three photos of the popular NWA wrestler Cyclone Negro printed on it.

Curiously, Negro was not mentioned by name, while several of the listed wrestlers were easily recognizable as performers who had previously appeared on IWA wrestling cards promoted in the area, and no fewer than three of the wrestlers were members of the Bahamas Wrestling Association, including the Bahamian Grappler.

As it turns out, "Florida T.V. Stars Wrestling" merely alluded to the stars of the IWA, who had acquired a local television deal limited to Miami. The advertisement may have used a bit of misdirection to dupe the Bahamian public, but it also seemed to indicate the full-fledged partnership between the BWA and the IWA.

With all due respect, none of the IWA wrestlers involved in the presentation were heralded as stars anywhere in the United States, let alone throughout the broader wrestling world. Moreover, the tactic of labeling wrestlers as "Bahamian" in the advertising of the shows is a clear indication that Leslie Fox and others had successfully pressured the IWA and Birdland crews into acting out his dream by hosting wrestling events with a nearly 50 percent rate of Bahamian representation.

In spite of the cooperation of the IWA with his wishes, Fox's desires had evidently not been made mandatory, nor were they adhered to by everyone. Just two weeks later, Charlie Major would announce an appearance by Florida's *real* television wrestling stars. Championship Wrestling from Florida made its return to Nassau Stadium on March 16th, boasting a main-event match between Dusty Rhodes and Joe LeDuc, and an undercard of The Alaskans against Louie Tillet and Paul LeDuc, "Cowboy" Bill Watts and The Texan, and one other "All-Star match" to be named.

Back in Florida, Dusty Rhodes had just completed a babyface turn, and was in the process of rebranding himself as "The American Dream." Swept up in the swell of Rhodes' booming popularity, Championship Wrestling from Florida would be carried to loftier heights than the organization had ever realized before.

CWF's return to the Bahamas was momentary, but its seeming reemergence may have startled its unwary and ill-equipped opposition into an immediate retreat. The next wrestling show to take place at the Birdland Arena featured no involvement from the IWA, and the roster was composed entirely of Bahamian wrestlers.

Less than one year after his public appeal to impose limitations on wrestling companies with rosters composed entirely of non-Bahamians, Leslie Fox was about to realize his dream. A wrestling company with a talent roster formed exclusively of Bahamians would now be permitted to conduct business without any regular competition from outside companies.

Birdland had renamed itself as the "House of Champions" just prior to April of 1974, and its all-Bahamian show would feature Bahamas Heavyweight Champion Ed Penn in a contest with Joe Wild Goose, who had recently defeated Bahamian Grappler for the middleweight title.

**AT LAST!**

**WRESTLING**

RETURNS TO THE

**NASSAU STADIUM**

**SAT. MARCH 16TH**

Main Feature

**JOE LEDUCE**
—vs—
**DUSTY RHODES**

also THE ALASKANS
—vs—
LOUIE TILLET and PAUL LEDUCE

COWBOY BILL WATTS
—vs—
THE TEXAN

Plus One Other
ALL-STAR Match

By the next month, another obstacle to running a local wrestling company in a place as small as Nassau became glaringly obvious. Without also having a television program as a conduit through which rivalries and fan interest could be cultivated, the shows became extremely repetitive, with the same wrestlers competing against one another every week without being driven by storylines, and also bereft of any allusions to influences like local, regional or world rankings.

**The competitors of the Bahamas Wrestling Association
(Nassau Tribune)**

In the world of legitimate Bahamian athletics, sports fans were consistently apprised of the progress of boxers like Leonard Miller and Elisha Obed on the world stage. In particular, Obed was in the process of smashing through every American who dared step in the ring with him en route to the North American Boxing Federation Light Middleweight Championship. Fittingly, the local Nassau newspapers were rife with coverage of the progression of the first Bahamian boxer to so much as sniff world championship gold as he ascended the ranks of world-class boxing.

By comparison, the Bahamas Wrestling Association was not connected to any reputable governing bodies that could lend credence or legitimacy to its championships, nor could it dangle additional forms of motivation in front of the BWA's wrestlers. There were no Caribbean or Pan American championships for Bahamian Heavyweight Wrestling Champion Ed Penn to aspire to win since his local wrestling promotion was cut off from any of the established wrestling organizations of North America that offered championships with greater prestige.

**Iron Man Destroyer, Sensational Bahamian Grappler, Philip Pinder, "Wild" Joe Goose and "The Terror" Alec Hall at the House of Champions (Nassau Tribune)**

As unconventional as the presentation of the Bahamas Wrestling Association may have been, they did manage to extend the reach of professional wrestling to previously untouched islands of the Bahamas, including Great Exuma and

Inagua, which were islands with population totals that numbered in the hundreds at the time.

Beginning in late May, the standard Bahamian practice of selling naming rights to local sponsors was evident during at least one of the BWA's outings. At the May 25th event, the Bahamas Beverage Company offered up the "Pepsi-Q Trophy" to the winner of the tag team encounter pitting the Bahamian Grappler and Iron Man Destroyer against Joe Goose and Alec Hall.

ALL STAR
**WRESTLING**

**House of Champions**
MT. ROYAL AVE. & CAREW ST.
Door Opens 7:45 p.m.

Captain of Hells

Captain of Baby Faces
The
BAHAMIAN
GRAPPLER

**4 SINGLE BOUTS**
**2-4 MAN TAG MATCHES**

ALEC HALL
"The Terror"

Children with discount coupon 75c
Teenagers ............................... $2.00
General Admission ............. $4.00

BECK'S the BIG one will be there ... will YOU?

In June, the newcomer "Coca-Cola" Flash debuted, which is a name choice that would certainly be legally actionable in many other nations, and which would be likely to baffle many outsiders to the Bahamas who are unfamiliar with the sponsored naming practices in organized Bahamian sports.

The acquisition of Bahamian sports sponsors on a local level has led to some naming practices that would shock non-Bahamians, which is perhaps best exemplified by the "Kentucky" basketball team of the 1970s. Playing in the top division of the Bahamian Amateur Basketball Association, the Kentucky team was sponsored by the local Kentucky Fried Chicken affiliate.

**WRESTLING**

Saturday February 1st.

**AT THE HOUSE OF CHAMPIONS**
(formerly Birdland) Mt. Royal & Carew

**DOOR OPENS 7:45P.M.**

Children............$2.00
Adults..............$4.00
Reserved...........$6.00

Five Single Matches
Plus 1 Championship
4 Man Tag Match

**Special Features**

RETURN OF BAHAMIAN
HEAVYWEIGHT
CHAMPION
**ED PENN**
Plus
• WILD ONE EGOR
• IRON MAN DESTROYER
• DYNAMITE FUSE
• NASTY GERMAN

**BECK'S the BIG one will be there...will you?**

Their emergence directly overlapped with the existence of two popular U.S. basketball teams from Kentucky: The Wildcats of the University of Kentucky, and the highly successful Kentucky Colonels basketball organization—a team that actively played in the American Basketball Association, and which was on the cusp of winning its second championship in four seasons.

On June 18th, Bahamas Wrestling Club director Marty Goldstein made a public plea in the pages of *The Nassau Tribune* in which he all but begged Bahamians to support the all-Bahamian wrestling cards hosted at the House of Champions, all while accusing Bahamians of being "unfair to the local wrestlers."

"At present, six amateurs are hard at training, trying to join the pro ranks," Goldstein told *The Tribune*. "However, if the fans don't realize what they are missing and lend their support, the fellows will just have to quit."

It was a frustration that Arnsel "The Bahamian Grappler" Johnson and the rest of his team were forced to contend with constantly.

"At that time, people didn't pay much attention or concern about the Bahamian wrestlers," said Arnsel Johnson. "They thought we just didn't have *it*. There *were* some people who used to be there all the time. Sometimes you had to tell them, 'Ain't nothin' happenin' today.' The children around the time *really* enjoyed the shows. The mothers and fathers used to come around us and tell them it was time to come home because we would be up wrestling and training until 11:00 p.m. or midnight."

In fact, Johnson had hoped to teach children how to wrestle, at least in the legitimate Greco-Roman fashion.

"I was asking the big officials in government if I could teach wrestling in the schools after 3:00 p.m.," said Johnson. The people told me straight and plain, 'That is too dangerous, and you shouldn't be doing it because you could break somebody's arm or break somebody's leg!' After they told me they couldn't do it because it was too dangerous, I lost all interest in it."

Johnson was also eternally grateful for everything Goldstein had done for him and the rest of his friends in the Bahamas Wrestling Club.

"Marty Goldstein was one of the best and nicest men I've ever met," said Johnson. "If you wanted something and he had it, he was going to give it to you. He would come to you and ask you questions, and he would sit down and actually listen to you. He would do everything he possibly could to look out for you."

By the time the middle of July had rolled around, Goldstein and his crew had apparently made an effort to address one of the perceptible shortcomings with their presentation. In a July 13th *Tribune* article that hailed the Bahamian Grappler as "the Elisha Obed of wrestling," it was announced that the Grappler would become the first Bahamian to compete for an international wrestling title when he challenged "the United States Middleweight Wrestling Champion."

**The athletes of the Bahamas Wrestling Association in action**

The Grappler, the article went on to say, had waited "five years" for this opportunity, which likely starts the clock at the time when Johnson had first been inspired by the presence

**"The Sensational Bahamian Grappler" Arnsel Johnson
BWA Bahamas Middleweight Champion**

of Jack Brisco in Nassau Stadium. Unsurprisingly, the identity of the U.S. middleweight champion that the Grappler would be challenging went undisclosed, as middleweight championships in pro wrestling were virtually unheard of outside of Mexico and Great Britain.

Wrestling at the House of Champions continued sporadically beyond 1975, but most of the active participants of the Bahamas Wrestling Club gradually began to develop other interests, and their events began to achieve less notoriety.

All things considered, for a neighborhood wrestling club that sprouted spontaneously in the middle of Nassau to have blossomed into an inter-island touring organization was a remarkable achievement. Johnson and his team had done an admirable job of keeping the spirit of professional wrestling alive after performances by major American wrestling companies had essentially ceased.

"We did the best we could at the time," Johnson stated. "The most important thing I think you should take away from a person who was trying to do the best they could at the time is to continue it."

The only other wrestling event from that year to attain any significant press attention was a December event marking a visit by the stars of the CWF, whose appearances in the Bahamas had likewise become far more sporadic.

December's CWF show featured the promotional debut of Charlie Major's son – Charlie Major Jr. – with respect to the management of professional wrestling events. The event was headlined by Bob Roop and Rocky Johnson, and was propped up by an undercard that included Cyclone Negro, Omar Negro, Roger Kirby, Rip Hawk, Karl Von Steiger and Ron Starr.

Speaking about this event to the press, Major Jr. simply stated, "It will be a night to remember."

It was undeniably a night to remember for Rocky Johnson because of the antics of the Bahamian fans.

"I really don't think the Bahamian fans were educated to wrestling, and I mean that in a good way," said Johnson.

"They honestly believed that wrestlers were either bad guys or good guys. They would buy halves of chickens, and if you were a bad guy, then they would throw the bones at you while you were in the ring."

Fortunately, there were other sports distractions for Bahamians to gravitate toward in the absence of regular pro wrestling shows, and particularly in boxing and baseball. In the process of securing a stellar record of 59 wins, one draw and two losses, Elisha Obed achieved a resounding TKO victory over Miguel de Oliveira in Paris, France to capture the light middleweight world championship of the World Boxing Council in November of 1975. Obed therefore became the first Bahamian to reign as a world champion in boxing.

Earlier in the year, Bahamian Ed Armbrister broke new ground as a member of the Cincinnati Reds, collecting his first of back-to-back World Series Championships with "The Big Red Machine." This made Armbrister the first Bahamian to win a world championship in a major international team-based sport.

The successes of Obed and Armbrister were emblematic of Bahamians who were beginning to excel in a wider variety of sports, and on the most elite levels of play. Moreover, it underscored some elements of the Americanization of the Bahamas. Just one generation prior, Armbrister's skills with a bat and ball were far more likely to have been displayed on a cricket pitch.

Sustained Bahamian success at the highest levels of both sports would be fleeting. Luckily for the Bahamian public, a local pro wrestling resurgence was just around the corner.

## Seven: Sweet Like Sugar

C hampionship Wrestling from Florida stars would continue to make irregular appearances in the Bahama Islands during the remainder of the 1970s, although the days of automatically following Nassau trips with immediate flights to Freeport had become a thing of the past. As an example of this, a Nassau Stadium show from May 23rd of 1979 headlined by Jack Brisco and Buggsy McGraw – with Eddie Graham, Thor the Viking, Cyclone Negro, Hiro Matsuda, Bud Sawyer, Don Serrano, Gordon Nelson and Ben Alexander filling out the undercard – advertised that the company would be making a separate trip to Freeport on June 1st.

During one of those trips to Freeport, Buggsy McGraw would wrestle Ox Baker.

"That match against Ox was one of the proudest moments of my career," stated McGraw. "Ox had an incredible persona and look, but I'd already had a match with Ox in Detroit while wrestling for the Sheik's company, and that's when I learned that Ox sometimes had serious difficulty getting back up if he fell on his back. When they booked me to work with him in Freeport, I had to tell him to stand in the center of the ring and let me do everything during the match, because I didn't want a repeat of what happened in Detroit. It went fine; Ox stood in the middle of the ring, and I just bumped around him. The Freeport crowd was with us the entire time."

It wasn't until 1982, when restrictions on foreign investment and partnerships between Bahamian businesses and foreign companies began to loosen, that Championship Wrestling from Florida was able to make a sustained return to the Bahamas. And when they did return, they were instantly followed by other promoters interested in catering to Bahamian wrestling fans.

The return to Nassau was orchestrated by Dory Funk Jr., who had recently acquired booking control of the CWF, and who had received clear instructions from Eddie Graham on what he was expected to accomplish in his new role.

"Eddie talked me into coming to Florida to book the territory because they were in need of heroes – 'babyfaces' as we call them in the wrestling business," said Funk. "They were shy on that end."

When the restrictions that had stymied foreign involvement in the Bahamas were eased somewhat, Funk quickly seized the opportunity.

"In the eyes of Eddie Graham and I, the Bahamas was historically a part of the Florida territory, and it was a very good market for wrestling – not on a weekly basis by any means – but to go in there every six weeks, we could go in there with attractive shows," said Funk. "Our television was in the Bahamas, and the fans were terrific and receptive to professional wrestling. For me, it was just a fun place to go."

It was true: Television had become widely available in the Bahamas beginning in 1977, and in the early stages of 1982, Funk was able to re-ingratiate the CWF with Bahamian fans by featuring African American stars Butch Reed and "Sweet Brown Sugar" Skip Young as the company's headliners.

"I got over really great down there," offered Reed. "The Bahamian fans really showed up for us."

As for why he chose to feature Reed and Sugar as the top attractions, Funk said it was an easy decision based on their established track records in the state of Florida.

"Butch Reed and Sweet Brown Sugar were my superstars throughout the Florida territory," explained Funk. "I was the one who brought them into Florida, and I booked them in the Bahamas, too. They just did a *fabulous* job. Sweet Brown Sugar and 'Hacksaw' Butch Reed were personal friends of mine *and* business friends of mine in the wrestling business. I brought them into the Florida territory, and they did one *hell* of a job for us."

The Major family was certainly welcoming of the full-scale return of the CWF stars, as they had just been linked with a sporting event that amassed for them their greatest notoriety to date, but not without a degree of controversy.

Charlie Major Sr. served as the promoter for the infamous "Drama in Bahama" boxing event in Nassau on December 11th of 1981, which was held in the remodeled, 25,000-seat Queen Elizabeth Sport Centre. Embarrassingly, a misplaced key to the venue resulted in a two-hour delay to the start of the evenings fights.

When the event finally unfolded, the 39-year-old boxing legend Muhammad Ali, who was potentially suffering from the early signs of Parkinson's disease, was battered by Trevor Berbick for 10 rounds in what would be the final fight of Ali's career. In the fight's aftermath, Charles Major Jr. was questioned by the media – most notably *Time Magazine* – after both Ali and Berbick complained that they had still not been paid everything they were owed for the fight one month later.

Shortly after the successful return of Championship Wrestling from Florida to the Bahamas in the early months of 1982, a new pair of Bahamians entered the fray and spawned a fresh era of concurrent wrestling promotional activities. On April 17th, boxing promoters Charlie Thompson and Kevin Smith, known collectively through their company TK Promotions, announced that a wrestling show would be held in their home building – the Poinciana Sporting Arena – for the first time ever.

The Poinciana Sporting Arena was housed within the Poinciana Inn, which was a building that had been originally constructed on Bernard Road by Ortland Bodie Jr. to serve as a skating rink. However, the building was never used for that purpose prior to its purchase by Thompson.

Seemingly in an effort to find a competitive advantage to wield against the Major family and Championship Wrestling from Florida, Thompson and Smith introduced the Bahamian public to the NWA World Women's Champion, the Fabulous Moolah.

In promoting the event, Smith stated at a press conference that he and Thompson were proud to bring

women's wrestling to the Bahamas "for the first time," which
was either a statement uttered out of presumptive ignorance, or
a blatant untruth. Not only had women been involved in
several matches contested in Bahamian wrestling rings over the
years, but the very first wrestling match in the history of
Bahamian professional wrestling was waged between Ella
Waldek and Bonnie Watson.

"It is now a reality," said Smith. "The Fabulous Moolah
will defend her world championship title at the Poinciana
Sporting Arena tomorrow night."

The other women advertised on the card were Donna
Christanello and Princess Victoria. The featured male attraction
was the 500-pound Man Mountain Mike, not to be confused
with the far more famous *600*-pound Man Mountain Mike.

**Princess Victoria, Kevin Smith, Donna Christanello, Rocky Starr,
Fabulous Moolah, Mountain Mike and Charles Thompson at the
Poinciana Sports Arena (Nassau Guardian)**

"I feel great coming to the Bahamas to defend my title,
and I'm confident I will have a successful defense," the 59-
year-old Moolah told the press. "I'm ready, willing and able,
and there is no stopping now."

Unbeknownst to the Bahamian people, the Fabulous
Moolah was truly in a position to guarantee the success of her
title defense because it was quite literally *her* championship. She
had purchased the personal right to control the NWA women's
championship years prior. Further, the other women on the

show, Princess Victoria and Donna Christanello, had both been trained at Moolah's personal estate in South Carolina, and their careers and finances were directly controlled by Moolah, who was the de facto queenpin of women's wrestling.

"Moolah booked us there and told me I was going at the last minute," said Princess Victoria. "Going to Nassau was the first and last time that I ever rode with a live band on the back of a flatbed truck. All of the other wrestlers were up there with me, and we went riding through the streets telling people about the matches that night. We had a line of cars riding behind us; you couldn't see the end of it. They literally followed us to where the matches were, and it was a good show with a full house."

When the inaugural wrestling event at the Poinciana Arena ultimately took place, it included several Bahamian wrestlers who had gone unadvertised: Former Bahamas heavyweight champion Edward Penn, and the Destroyer, and the Sensational Bahamian Grappler. All of the men competed in a battle royale that was won by Man Mountain Mike. The mountainous one also toppled the team of Rocky Starr and The Bruiser in a two-on-one contest, and then defeated The Bruiser in a one-on-one match, apparently because he had not been pinned in the prior encounter.

In singles competition, the Grappler defeated the Destroyer in a match that enabled him to emulate his hero Jack Brisco right down to the use of the figure-four leglock to collect the submission victory.

The event appears to have been successful, but Moolah and the rest of her crew wouldn't be making a return to wrestle at the Poinciana Sports Arena ever again.

"Moolah had great relationships with all of the major wrestling promoters, from Vince McMahon Sr. to the Crocketts, to Verne Gagne and everyone else," explained Victoria. "She must have booked that show before she realized Championship Wrestling from Florida had started running in Nassau again. She never wanted to get on the bad side of any of the major promoters."

Aside from the wrestling she did at the Poinciana Sports Arena, Victoria did have one other memorable moment in Nassau when she decided to hang out with one of the other wrestlers at the Hilton Hotel.

"We had sat down on the dock, and I was just sitting there twiddling with my sterling silver agate ring," said Victoria. "I dropped it down into the crystal-clear water. I was just about to hop in after it, but then a tiger shark swam underneath me literally right where I was about to jump. I said, 'Well, I guess *that* ring is gone!'"

Events transpiring far off in Japan may have played a crucial role in the way future wrestling events would be booked in the Bahamas, and also may have determined the top prize CWF wrestlers would fight for during future Bahamas trips.

On April 21st, Dory Funk Jr. lost his NWA International Heavyweight Championship to Bruiser Brody, and he would not be winning the title back. All Japan Pro Wrestling owner Giant Baba clearly wished to give Brody a lengthy reign as the international champion in order to cement his own homegrown star Jumbo Tsuruta as the new ace of AJPW once Tsuruta captured the title from Brody.

Although it was represented in Florida by an altogether different belt, the NWA international title controlled by All Japan was the prize Funk defended in main-event matches in Nassau. A suitable replacement would have to be crafted.

In the meantime, Sweet Brown Sugar would wrestle in the main event of a show at Nassau Stadium on June 12th against Les Thornton, who was substituting for reigning NWA Florida Heavyweight Champion Jimmy Garvin. Butch Reed tangled with Kendo Nagasaki on the undercard, Brian Blair wrestled Derek Draper, and Terry Allen fought Hiro Matsuda.

*The Nassau Guardian* concluded its coverage by promoting a paid afternoon appearance by Sugar and Reed at the Bristol Club in Golden Gate Plaza, with funds from the meet-and-greet going to benefit the Bahamas Disabled Association.

Then on July 3rd, Nassau Stadium held its independence show, and *The Nassau Guardian* advertised the main event match as "Sweet Brown Sugar battles Dory Funk Jr. for the Bahama Island Championship." As the man who had recently defended the NWA International Heavyweight Championship in Nassau, Dory Funk Jr. anointed himself as the appropriate man for Sugar to beat to become the first Bahamas Heavyweight Champion ever recognized by a National Wrestling Alliance territory.

"It was our desire to have the Bahamas as a part of the Florida territory, and we thought Sweet Brown Sugar was the guy to get the job done," said Funk. "That's why we put the belt on him. On a business scale, it was good business going into the Bahamas. I want to give Eddie Graham credit, too. He was a great wrestler when he was wrestling, but as a wrestling promoter, he was one of the best in the country. Along with Vince McMahon and Jim Crockett, Eddie Graham was right there with them."

**The NWA Bahamas Heavyweight Championship belt**

Conventional wisdom dictates that Bahamian fans became accustomed to the NWA International Heavyweight Championship being defended by Dory Funk Jr. in main-event matches, and a championship that was neatly separated from any regions of the United States would be the most attractive prize that Bahamian fans could watch wrestlers compete for.

"It makes sense that they would want to create a title that Bahamian fans would care about after seeing the international belt defended in Nassau," said Kevin Sullivan. "The Florida belt and the Southern belt wouldn't have meant anything to them at that point."

Elsewhere on the July 3rd card, Hacksaw Butch Reed competed against Kendo Nagasaki (Kazuo Sakurada of Japan), who was managed by "King" James Dillon. Dillon would accompany Nagasaki to the ring after first doing battle with Barry Windham, and Brian Blair would wrestle Jimmy Garvin for the Florida championship.

By this time, Eddie Graham had no problem pushing Black wrestlers to the very top of his cards. In fact, at the time of his anointing as Bahamas champion, Sugar had already captured the NWA Southern Heavyweight Championship on three separate occasions, and his third run as champion had been ended by Jimmy Garvin only a few weeks prior to his acquisition of the Bahamas title.

"Black wrestlers only really got pushed at the top of the card in certain territories, like the way Bill Watts pushed the Junkyard Dog as the top star in Mid-South Wrestling," said Sullivan. "We figured you had to push a Black guy to the top of the card when you came to the Bahamas, and that's what we did with Sweet Brown Sugar."

"Skip Young fit the bill," added referee Bill Alfonso. "He was Black; the people wanted a Black champion. He had a hell of a body – he had that nice upper body, big chest, big arms – and he was *really* good in the ring. People identified with him pretty good, so it was a natural choice to give the belt to him. We were doing so well there, and we wanted to give the people their own champion and give them some good entertainment."

Although Sweet Brown Sugar spent a good portion of his career wrestling under a mask, he wrestled mask-free in the Bahamas. Some wrestling experts have argued that Sugar's best years in the wrestling business occurred when his face was obscured from the view of the fans.

After debuting in his native state of Texas, Sugar would go back and forth between Florida, Texas, and several other territories, but definitely achieved his greatest popularity while working for Eddie Graham.

"In 1982, 'Hacksaw' Butch Reed was the most popular Black wrestler in Florida, but Sweet Brown Sugar was a close second," added Barry Rose.

To underscore the trend that Graham and company thought pushing Black wrestlers in Nassau was the optimal way to conduct business there, a championship match for the Southern title was announced between Black star Butch Reed and Fijian wrestler King Kong Tonga even though there is no record indicating either was actually the Southern champion at the time.

With that being said, territorial wrestling title histories are notoriously incomplete and riddled with errors, and it is possible that reigning champion Jimmy Garvin briefly lost the championship to Butch Reed prior to that show before regaining it.

"It definitely helped to have Black wrestlers at the top of the card in the Bahamas without a doubt," opined Brian Blair. "Skip Young was amazingly over. I need to be clear, even with the crowd in the Bahamas being predominantly Black, they weren't prejudiced. They *always* cheered for the babyfaces. It just kind of helped when you had a good, hardworking, African American wrestler on your show in the Bahamas."

Like the other title belts in Florida, and also like several other championship belts worn by wrestlers competing around the entirety of North America, the Bahamas championship belt was created by Reggie Parks, a wrestler who was working for Championship Wrestling from Florida at the time.

"Making the Bahamas belt would have taken me at least a couple months because I was still on the road and wrestling quite a bit," said Parks. "I don't know if they would have waited until they had the belt ready before deciding to create a Bahamas championship. Making a new belt rarely held up a wrestling storyline unless the belt was created for a tournament, and even then, it didn't really matter. They could just announce the new championship and then introduce the new belt on TV when it was ready."

So great was the popularity of Sugar and Reed in the Bahamas that they were even made the collective faces of the new Bahama Island Wrestling Fan Club. The organization was not declared to have been officially aligned with Championship Wrestling from Florida, but the advertisements they ran in the local papers certainly suggested a fondness for CWF and its two popular Black performers.

For just one dollar, fans could join the organization and receive a "free" 8x10 photo of Butch Reed and Sweet Brown Sugar.

In an August 16th article of *The Nassau Guardian*, Charlie Major Jr. declared that Sweet Brown Sugar and Japanese wrestler Kendo Nagasaki would compete in the main event the August 28th Nassau Stadium show in a defense of Sugar's new Bahamas championship. This match was reaffirmed in the August 28th edition of *The Guardian*, but the advertised match would never happen. Sugar instead closed the show by wrestling Jimmy Garvin to a draw.

After returning to Florida with his title reign intact, Sweet Brown Sugar began defending his championship against a slew of challengers on shows throughout Florida. In September alone, he successfully defended the belt against Jerry Grey, James J. Dillon, Kendo Nagasaki, Jake Roberts, King Kong Tonga, Tommy Wright and Vic Rosettani.

Advertisement for the Bahama Island Wrestling Fan Club

"That was one of the best things about working in Florida," said Don Muraco, a thickly muscled Hawaiian wrestler who completed multiple lengthy swings through Florida during the 1970s and early 1980s. "In Florida, pretty much everybody was great, and it wasn't a WWF-type of place where you'd be working with the same person constantly. In Florida, you might work with a different guy every night. In a week, you could wrestle Dusty Rhodes, Buggsy McGraw, Jimmy Garvin or Steve Keirn all in the same trip around the state. We had a *lot* of talent there."

Given the intent of the Bahamas championship to be the main-event attraction in the islands, its regular defense by Sugar in Florida created a compelling case where it was an international championship identified with a specific country that was defended on the undercard of shows held in the United States. Moreover, given who and what the belt represented, it became symbolically tantamount to a classic "negro championship" with a unique twist, as it was ordinarily defended by a Black wrestler almost exclusively against non-Black competitors, regardless of the venue it was defended in.

On September 3rd, *The Guardian* reported on the events of the August 28th show, and announced the return match between Sweet Brown Sugar and Jimmy Garvin, except this time the match would be for Garvin's Southern championship even though the advertisement for the show stated otherwise.

**Sweet Brown Sugar – The 1st NWA Bahamas Heavyweight Champion
(Courtesy of Peter Lederberg)**

The article emphasized the unmatched popularity of wrestling as an attraction in Nassau, noting that cars were parked bumper-to-bumper up and down Fowler Street, and all along East Bay Street from the roundabout by Paradise Bridge all the way to the Nassau Yacht Club – essentially turning a full mile of Nassau's roads into an ad hoc parking lot.

"Bahamian people appreciate an exciting wrestling show," Major told the press. "We plan to keep our many fans entertained with shows throughout the rest of this year."

Major went on to make a somewhat surprising claim – that the majority of Bahamian wrestling fans were women – and also mentioned that future wrestling events hosted at Nassau Stadium would be moved to Friday nights because Championship Wrestling from Florida was booked for stateside events for the remaining Saturdays of that year.

In the middle of the same month, TK Promotions returned with another event at the Poinciana Sporting Arena, except the roster of wrestling talent would be supplied by the Malenko family rather than the Fabulous Moolah.

"My dad obviously liked the islands, because they were somewhat uncharted territory, especially with regard to coming down there and really working a promotion," said Joe Malenko, who wrestled on many of his father's shows. "My dad believed there was money to be made anywhere. My dad would walk through a flea market, a bowling alley, or the parking lot of a gas station, and he would say, 'You know, you could put a ring here!' And a lot of times, we actually did."

Boris Malenko would end up setting the stage for alternative wrestling companies to present shows in the Bahamas in more ways that he ever could have envisioned. After a falling out between himself and CWF promoter Eddie Graham separated him from the NWA office he had once served so faithfully, Malenko opened a wrestling school and set about training new wrestlers alongside his sons, Dean and Jody.

"The list of guys that trained under Malenko is legendary," said Rose. "There are probably hundreds of names who trained under him that were all top-flight workers. He was excellent at getting people to understand the psychological aspects of working in the ring. You can't take someone who isn't a great athlete and make them into a great athlete, but Malenko helped wrestlers to grasp the psychology of what the fans watching the matches were thinking, which can make *anybody* into a great wrestler."

In the June 14, 1982 edition of *The Tampa Tribune*, Malenko announced the launch of his new wrestling company – International World of Wrestling – accompanied by a new television deal with local Channel 28. The tail end of the article included a list of Malenko's chief trainees who were soon to debut in the IWW's wrestling ring. Included among them were Jim Savage, Black Stallion, Joe and Dean Malenko, and Tyree Pride.

"We were never worried about the Malenkos as opposition," stated Bill Alfonso. "They didn't have a lot of things you needed to be taken seriously, like strong TV. The office certainly wasn't thrilled about it; it was *our* territory. They ran several shows, but we didn't think they would last long. They were working with limited resources, and they didn't have the cash where they could fly in a bunch of big names. But that's how little indie promotions usually are."

By the time of the Malenkos' debut event at the Poinciana Sporting Arena September 17th, they had officially added the word "Association" to the end of their company name, and the show was formally conducted under the IWWA banner.

This show was headlined by The Gladiator taking on The Black Stallion. Former CWF regular Bubba Douglas was also on the card competing against Big Jim Burley, and "The Bahamian Freight Train" Andy Ifill made an appearance in a bout against Oscar LaDue. In a tag match, "The Wrecking Crew" faced off against Bob Cook and Vladic Smirnoff. For this show, TK Promotions charged $10 for general admission, with a $15-per-ticket charge for ringside seats that exceeded the price of the Nassau Stadium's ringside seating by a full 25 percent.

Not content only to hold events in Nassau, the Malenkos also brought the IWWA to Freeport, which led to one of Joe Malenko's most unforgettable hotel experiences during his tours of the islands.

"We were supposed to get out of there that evening, but we didn't get out quickly enough," said Malenko. "The airport literally shut down. We then all went into one of the hotel rooms where we did the show that night, which was in their ballroom area. We'd been changing in the hotel room, so we just all went back to the hotel and went to sleep in there. The security guy came and knocked on the door and told us we couldn't be sleeping in there, since there were 20 of us. So we left the room and wound up going to the casinos, and slept on top of the casino's tables until we could get a flight out of there in the morning."

Nine months into the year, 1982 had brought about the resurgence of pro wrestling in the Bahamas and the anointing of a beloved new hero. Little did Bahamian wrestling fans know that they would suddenly be separated from their champion, setting the stage for a newcomer to take his place.

## Eight: "Lucky I got out of there alive!"

As a special treat for Bahamian wrestling fans, September of 1982 marked the month when NWA Bahamas Heavyweight Champion Sweet Brown Sugar was given the opportunity to wrestle NWA World Heavyweight Champion Ric Flair in a match at Nassau Stadium.

The promotion for the show boldly declared the event to be the first ever instance of the NWA's world title being defended in the Bahamas, which was an outright lie. It may have been a full decade since the last defense of the world title in the Bahamas, but Gene Kiniski and Dory Funk Jr. had each defended the championship in Nassau within the range of most Bahamian wrestling fans' memories, with the latter defending it there on at least four separate occasions.

Considered by several experts and historians to be among the greatest wrestlers of all time, "Nature Boy" Ric Flair was one year into his first of many reigns he would have as the kingpin of the NWA. Luckily for him, Flair had somehow just managed to complete a volatile tour of the Caribbean with Carlos Colon's World Wrestling Council while still in possession of his championship belt.

During a bout with Jack Veneno in the Dominican Republic, Flair allegedly asked Veneno to deviate from the agreed-upon finish to their bout and defeat him out of fear that the crowd would riot violently if Veneno lost. Instead, Flair collected his belt from Veneno later in the evening without most areas of the wrestling world having any knowledge that an impromptu defeat of the reigning world champion had taken place.

In Nassau, Flair would have no such difficulties, as he retained his title against Sugar on September 24th in a match that they had essentially rehearsed two nights prior when wrestling one another at the Miami Beach Convention Center in front of 4,372 fans.

To those familiar with the practicalities of professional wrestling during the territorial era, it would have come as no surprise that Sugar did not win the world championship, nor would he ever have been a true contender to do so given the expectations of the day. The standard for long-term traveling NWA world champions in the early 1980s called for the title to be held by strong but moderately sized ring technicians who could carry less-talented performers through long, believable matches while maintaining the bout's entertainment value, elevating the credibility of their opponent in the eyes of local fans, and selling plenty of tickets.

Sugar may have been able to heighten the interest of fans in specific wrestling markets, but he was severely undersized compared with champions of that era, and he typically sprinted through rapid-fire matches that ended quickly. More significantly, as far as Black wrestlers in the early 1980s were concerned, there were still places within the

NWA's vast territorial system where they simply would not have been expected to attract fans as accepted world champions. In fact, there were places Black wrestlers were not booked for CWF events even in the state of Florida.

"I heard [Sugar] did a good job as champion," said Steve Keirn. "He was a good-looking young guy with a good body and great fire. Because of those things, he was probably appealing to the audience, not only in the Bahamas, but in places like Miami, too. As long as it wasn't in the interior part of the state. They were pretty backwards back in those days. They were more inclined to want to see White wrestlers."

To Keirn, the audiences in the central part of Florida had a completely different vibe than the cities along the coastal perimeter.

"The center of Florida was basically country people," continued Keirn. "You might as well have been in Georgia or Alabama. Every town and every city I've ever been to has a different audience. Some audiences were similar because of the area they lived in, and because they've watched certain types of wrestling for so many years. Some only wanted a certain type of wrestling or wrestler."

The October show at Nassau Stadium was headlined by Sugar defending his Bahamas title against Jake "The Snake" Roberts in the main event. The most prominent match on the undercard was a six-man tag team contest involving Butch Reed, Brian Blair and Ron Bass against Jimmy Garvin, Vic Rosettani and King Kong Tonga. Charlie Major encouraged Nassau's wrestling fans to arrive at the Stadium early, noting that tickets would be on sale starting at noon, along with t-shirts of both Sweet Brown Sugar and Butch Reed.

While working with Jake Roberts in Nassau on October 15th, Sugar factored into one of Brian Blair's favorite memories of wrestling in the Bahamas.

"I was out there standing next to Jimmy Garvin while watching Skip in his match with Jake Roberts," recalled Blair. "The fans were really into it. As usual, there were several fans watching from the tree outside of the stadium. Well, Skip got fired up and pounded his chest to get the crowd's approval, and some kid sitting in the tree just got so excited and put his hands up to cheer for Skip. As soon as he did that, he fell out of the tree and took several people with him."

Shockingly, and without warning, Sweet Brown Sugar abruptly left Championship Wrestling from Florida on October 26th following a match in Tampa for Jimmy Garvin's Southern championship. Proof of the unplanned nature of Sugar's walkout is evidenced by the fact that Florida newspapers continued to print advertisements of his participation in a Global Tag Team Championship tournament for three full days following his departure.

According to Blair, Skip Young was finished with the nonsense he had been coping with while working in Florida, and subpar payoffs from the Bahamas were a deciding factor in the instantaneous nature of the decision.

"Skip was kind of radical when it came to being against the promoters," said Blair. "He had talent and expected a bigger push. From what I've seen, if you're talented and humble and do what the office asks, eventually you'll rise to the top. Well, Skip was a little more vocal than a lot of guys when it came to voicing his displeasure with what was happening."

Part of what Sugar was displeased with, Blair explained, was how the CWF owners were enriching themselves with the money made in the Bahamas at the cost of the wrestlers – and particularly the main eventers.

"The people who owned the Florida territory played too many games," continued Blair. "The Bahamas was their cash cow. They would take the Bahamian money, bring it back to the office all in cash, and divide it between the shareholders. That's why our payoffs were always down. They were jacking Sugar around on his money; he was really peeved about it. Skip liked to ride with his Mexican wife, who he called 'Señorita.' He traveled with her instead of the wrestlers. Then he had a baby, so he had three mouths to feed on the road, including his own. He just got to the point where he couldn't take the games anymore and left."

# Bahamian Rhapsody

The claim that the Bahamas was a "cash cow" to the owners of Championship Wrestling from Florida is an interesting claim, and one that there is some support for. For a CWF show in Nassau in early 1983, the cost of tickets was $10 for general admission, and $12 for the ringside area. By comparison, the ticket prices for the Miami Convention Center during the same period were $4, $5 and $6, with $8 charged for ringside seats, although the Miami Convention Center was also a much larger venue.

Expanding this comparison outside of the Florida territory, fans of the American Wrestling Association hoping to catch the act of rising superstar Hulk Hogan were paying $7 for general admission and $10 for ringside seats. Fans of the popular Von Erich family in Texas were paying around $8 for their ringside tickets, and to catch the act of World Wrestling Federation champion Bob Backlund, wrestling fans in the comparatively wealthy northeastern region of the U.S. were spending $6 for general admission and an average of $10 for their ringside seats in many of the region's venues.

Without question, on a per-night, per-fan basis, tickets to watch wrestling in Nassau Stadium were among the most expensive in all of the professional wrestling world at the time.

Because Bahamian dollars are fixed to U.S. dollars, and are used interchangeably in the Bahamas, those dollars carried the exact same value with Bahamian banks. Stated plainly, wrestling fans in Nassau were charged double the average general admission price to see the same shows that were enjoyed by people in Miami, and 50 percent more than the fans who were paying to see the action from ringside.

Even in 1984, that pattern would still hold true; the average general admission price in Miami was $6, and in Nassau it was $12, with $10 and $15 being the respective ringside seat prices of each location.

As a final comparison point, from a financial standpoint, many Bahamians weren't faring as poorly as most of the wrestlers performing for them had apparently believed. The majority of the wrestlers spent the bulk of their time in the area right by Nassau Stadium and the adjacent Pond neighborhood, or crossed the bridge to party on Paradise Island. They seldom ventured into other areas of the island that had been developed with modern housing and accommodations, like the eastern end of New Providence Island, or the Cable Beach area.

"We were too dumb to even look at the ticket prices," said Blair. "We just went by what the owners told us. Even if there were only 1,500 paying people in Nassau Stadium, which would be a low number, that would be $15,000 at $10 per ticket. The highest gate ever reported to the wrestlers out of there was $12,000. The main-event payoff in Nassau was $400. The other guys on the card would make $250. They'd bring the cash back to Tampa, and every stockholder in the company would meet there together. All the stockholders would go up into Eddie's office and take their share at the expense of the boys who worked the shows."

With Sweet Brown Sugar now headed off to work hundreds of miles away in the Mid-Atlantic territory owned by Jim Crockett, Jimmy Garvin beat Terry Allen at the Miami Beach Convention Center in what was previously advertised to have been a defense of the Bahamas championship by Sugar against Garvin. With the victory, Garvin became the simultaneous holder of the Southern title *and* the Bahamas championship.

No matter what the reality had been of the events that had taken place over the course of two nights in late October, the story reported in Bahamian newspapers was that Jimmy Garvin had defeated Sweet Brown Sugar to become the NWA Bahamas Heavyweight Champion. With that, the belt that was originally intended to be carried by a popular Black babyface found its way around the waist of a despised White heel who could sufficiently enrage Bahamian fans until it was time to anoint a suitable new babyface as champion.

"Gorgeous" Jimmy Garvin had a pretty good idea of what would await him when he set foot inside of Nassau

Stadium with Sweet Brown Sugar's Bahamas championship belt around his waist.

"It didn't take much to make a Nassau Stadium crowd too angry, and they could get *really* angry," recalled Garvin. "I just think old school wrestling fans could be really aggressive, as opposed to soccer fans or tennis fans. A tennis fan isn't going to jump onto the court and hit someone with a racquet, but at a wrestling match, there's no telling how many people might take a swing at you. That's the sort of heat you could create with an audience, and in the Nassau area, that heat could go *way* up high."

By late 1982, Garvin was a well-established star in Florida, and had already won every meaningful championship in the company. Despite his main-event pedigree in The Sunshine State, it was clear from the outset that Garvin, as a White heel wrestler, could only ever be the Bahamas champion on a short-term basis.

"First of all, you couldn't be that big of a heel in the Bahamas," said long-time CWF referee Bruce Owens. "The fans reacted big to everything the heels did, and overdoing it would send them over the edge. A White guy in the Bahamas as a heel could only ever be a transitional champion, because you wanted a Black guy in there who could win and make the people happy."

One month after Sugar's departure, the most logical choice to inherit the Bahamas championship, "Hacksaw" Butch Reed, wrestled his final match for the company on November 30th before leaving to work in Atlanta and St. Louis. Just like that, the Florida territory lost its two most popular Black babyface wrestlers in one fell swoop. To fill the void left behind by the two departing stars, Charlie Cook was quickly ushered back into the company, and Rufus Jones was rushed into Florida from St. Louis as well.

"The reason they kept two Black guys together as a team is because Black guys would draw fans in some key areas," said Larry Hamilton. "And if they thought they had a Black guy with an attitude problem who they couldn't control, they would bring in another Black guy who they thought could control the guy with the attitude problem. Something similar happened when I was with guys like Mark Regan and Pez Whatley. They were considered the hotheads, and I was the one they counted on to calm Mark and Pez down."

In Nassau, Charlie Major Jr. reported to the fans the official but fabricated story of how Garvin acquired the Bahamas title. In the November 19th edition of *The Guardian*, under the headline "Windham seeks revenge for Brown Sugar," Major explained to fans how Barry Windham would rectify the situation in the ring and avenge the loss of the Bahamas title by Sweet Brown Sugar to Jimmy Garvin.

"It was the first time Sugar put his title on the line, and he was unsuccessful," Major told the press.

Continuing on, Major turned his attention to the enhanced police presence that had been visible at Nassau

Stadium at recent events, having received direct support from the Commissioner of Police.

"Some of the fans get totally involved in the matches, and they want to get near the ring," Major told the press. "The police will be there, so it will be no problem for the fighters."

**Jimmy Garvin: The 2nd NWA Bahamas Heavyweight Champion**
**(Courtesy of Peter Lederberg)**

No matter what Major told the press, the fans who arrived at Nassau Stadium that night were there for the sole purpose of heaping misery upon Garvin, and when he cheated his way to victory over Barry Windham, the hatred of the fans boiled over.

"I had to fight my way out of there. It was terrible," said Garvin. "For our safety, they had crowd-control barricades, and they had police with dogs. Well, the police didn't like me either, and you *know* whose side the dogs are on."

The barricades at Nassau Stadium ordinarily offered about 10 feet of protective space for the wrestlers to move within, but when the crowds surged toward, the space narrowed to the point where the wrestlers – and the heels in particular – could become trapped.

"To make matters worse, as you went down to get to the dressing room, the bleacher seats started to come into play," continued Garvin. "You're still walking in a straight line, but the seating is going up. You have people kicking at you and throwing Heineken bottles at you. The fight wasn't over until you got through the dressing room door. It was horrifying."

After escaping from the mob and dodging the deluge of debris being rained down upon him, Garvin finally made it to the dressing room door.

"The guys in the dressing room had been peeking through the doors, but they didn't want to open it because the people would be throwing stuff like Heineken bottles," added Garvin. "Right when I got there, the guys swung the door open, I threw myself through it, and as the Heineken bottles were hitting my back, they slammed the door shut again."

Upon being informed that the Bahamian fans had been informed in the press that he had beaten Sweet Brown Sugar for the belt and that Windham was supposed to avenge the fallen ex-Bahamas champion, Garvin said, "So *that's* why I got my ass kicked! Lord have mercy! I was lucky I got out of there alive with that kind of buildup! I got beat to death!"

Shortly after returning from his match in Nassau against Barry Windham with the Bahamas belt still securely fastened around his waist, Garvin quickly dropped the Bahamas championship in Tampa on December 7th to its next Black babyface owner, "The Freight Train" Rufus R. Jones. Given what happened following Garvin's prior match, someone apparently thought better of inviting him back into Nassau Stadium as the defending champion once again.

Rufus Jones was a mainstay of the wrestling territories in the Midwest who also spent some time in Georgia and the Carolinas. He was known to excite the crowds in his prime, but by late 1982, Rufus was nearly 50 years old, and he was not even close to being an athlete on the level of Sweet Brown Sugar.

"I was familiar with his work in the Carolinas where he'd made a lot of money working with Blackjack Mulligan," said Buggsy McGraw. "By no means was Rufus a great worker, but he was a downhome, Black, southern wrestler with a sizable fan following of both Blacks and Whites. He built this following by being highly charismatic and entertaining in the ring."

In the January 18, 1983 edition of *The Nassau Guardian*, Charlie Major Jr. introduced Jones to the Bahamian fans as their new Bahamas champion ahead of CWF's first Nassau show of the new year, which was set for Saturday, January 29th.

Apparently Major had been repeatedly badgered by questions from concerned friends and fans, because he vocalized that popular stars Butch Reed and Sweet Brown Sugar were expected back for the next show, which would have been a boldfaced lie unless someone from the CWF office actually informed Major that this was a possibility. Sugar would not return to Florida until October of 1984, and Reed had left for Georgia and would never be back to wrestle in the Bahamas... at least not inside of a CWF ring.

In the aftermath of that show, a letter to the editor from Mr. J. Albury was printed in *The Guardian,* praising the Royal Bahamas Police Force for the role they played in curtailing disruptive behavior at Nassau Stadium's first wrestling show of 1983.

"On arriving at the stadium, there were several hundred people standing outside," wrote Albury. "I thought the stadium was already full and those outside couldn't get any seats, only to find out they were the people who would not normally pay, but jump the walls and make a nuisance of themselves."

The announcement of the forthcoming Nassau Stadium show also caused Kevin Smith and Charlie Thompson to move their first wrestling show of 1983 from January 29th to February 12th in order to avoid a scheduling conflict with the CWF event. The final lineup of matches, which was once again filled with wrestlers from Boris Malenko's IWWA company, was also vastly different from the originally scheduled card.

The original main event of IWWA International Heavyweight Champion Jim Savage defending his belt against Black Stallion was replaced by Cyclone Negro defending his Pan American Heavyweight Championship against "El Tigre" Luis Astea. The co-main event would feature midget wrestlers Little Coco and Billy the Kid, who were actually given priority photo placements in the February 9th edition of *The Nassau Guardian* due to the novelty of having midget wrestlers performing in Nassau once again.

On the undercard, Jim Savage teamed with Dr. Red Roberts in a tag team match against Black Stallion and Tyree Pride. In light of the significance Pride would later hold to Bahamian wrestling fans, the fact that his name was erroneously mangled into "Tarry Reid" is retrospectively comical.

"The Bahamian Freight Train" Andy Ifill also competed on the undercard, and Kevin Smith promised that both Ifill and former Bahamas Wrestling Alliance Heavyweight Champion Edward Penn would be factored into future events at the Poinciana Sports and Entertainment Arena.

The man who would become famous as "The Haitian Sensation" Tyree Pride was born in 1949 under the name Samuel Peter in Micoud, St. Lucia. Pride eventually immigrated to the United States, moved to Opa-locka, Florida, became naturalized in 1981, and found his way into Boris Malenko's wrestling school.

Shortly after concluding his training with the Malenkos and being factored into their plans for the IWWA, Pride made a financially influenced decision about the most optimal way to brand himself as a wrestler.

"When I looked at Florida, I didn't see a lot of St. Lucians here," said Pride. "I decided it was better to call myself 'The Haitian Sensation' because I knew there were a lot of Haitians in Florida, and I could do way better with that name."

While Tyree Pride may not have been a legitimate Haitian, his command of Creole brought tremendous credibility to his performance, which was quite convincing even with full-blooded Haitians.

"In St. Lucia, the language we spoke was *very* close to Haitian Creole," explained Pride. "I could do interviews in Creole, Spanish, and I could even speak to people from Aruba in Papiamento. I had it all down."

When Malenko's company first promoted its show in Nassau under the IWWA name, Pride claims it was he who helped the Malenkos get into the Poinciana Sports Arena.

"Charlie Thompson was the guy I made the connection with," said Pride. "I set the event up with him and Kevin Smith."

Also wrestling on the card that night was Rusty Brooks.

"The Thompson-Smith shows were pretty much independent shows, and had the look and feel of an independent show," said Brooks. "They told us once we got to Nassau we were going to go to the radio station and do some promoting. After we got into the hotel, Kevin Smith came and picked us up in a Gremlin with a huge speaker strapped to the roof, which looked kind of like the car in the *Blues Brothers* movie with Jim Belushi. We spent the afternoon riding around the city screaming 'Wrestling tonight!' over the speaker."

Similar to the complaints of wrestlers who performed at Nassau Stadium, Brooks described the lack of police presence and involvement at the Poinciana Arena as contributing to some wild episodes.

"During one match, I had a tag team partner named Dr. Red Roberts," Brooks stated. "He was wrestling, and I was supposed to run in and interfere in the match. I was standing by the dressing room door waiting to run in, and all of a sudden, a fan climbed into the ring and hit Red in the head with a chair! He just *threw* the chair at him. I ran to the ring and grabbed the guy by the jacket, pulled his jacket over his head, and started dragging him toward the back to the arena."

It was at that moment when Brooks said he noticed the Bahamian policeman standing next to him, casually watching the proceedings while garbed in his ceremonial white uniform.

"I looked at the policeman and asked him, 'Didn't you see that?'" continued Brooks. "He laughed in my face and said, 'Fuck you, man!' In anger, I did something really stupid: I grabbed *the policeman* and threw him down. Then I ran to the dressing room door, but it was locked! By now, the people were all throwing things at Red and I, and we ran under the bleachers to the other locker room door that the babyfaces entered through. Thankfully, we were able to get through that door, and they shut the door right away as soon as we got inside."

Boris Malenko walked over to ask Brooks what was going on as soon as he and Roberts entered what they thought was the safe haven of the locker room, and that was precisely the point when the power went out in the arena.

"It was *scary*," remembered Brooks. "They eventually got the power back on, and then Kevin Smith came in. I was screaming at everything that moved around me. Kevin walked up to me and said, 'What happened, man? What happened?' I was incensed, so I grabbed him and pushed him against the wall and said, 'I'm gonna *show* you what happened, *man!*'"

Before things could escalate any further, Malenko restrained Brooks and pulled him away from Thompson.

"Malenko said, 'Stop, kid! You're gonna get us killed!'" said Brooks. "We were on the first flight out of there in the morning. I never worked for Thompson and Smith again."

Joe Malenko remarked that sort of behavior from community police officers was typical at wrestling events.

"A lot of the cops of small towns – but *especially* outside of the U.S. – if they're going to protect anybody, it's going to be their local friends," said Malenko. "Now do they want you killed on their watch? Probably not. But are they willing to turn a blind eye to *some* things? Yeah. Absolutely."

According to Brooks, Charlie Thompson also seemed to think he could get away with murder when it came time to pay the wrestlers.

"I recall when we were all lined up outside the hotel room Thompson was using as an office, waiting to get paid," said Brooks. "He tried to short me on the money, and I asked him what was going on. He started listing off the things I took out of the hotel refrigerator as deductions from my pay."

The situation devolved into a shouting match, but Brooks claims to have left with everything Thompson owed him.

"Joe and Dean Malenko were standing right outside the door when Charlie and I were arguing," said Brooks. "Joe asked if I got what I was promised. When I told him I had, Joe said, 'Can you come in and represent us to make sure we get what we were promised, too?' I said, 'No, brother. You're on your own.'"

Upon hearing that story retold, Joe Malenko simply laughed and stated, "I'd have a harder time believing Rusty left anything at all inside of the refrigerator!"

In a profile piece written about him by *The Fort Lauderdale News*, Dr. Red Roberts – whose real name is Dr. Michael Brannon – told a story about a similar incident he dealt with during one of the Poinciana shows of the early 1980s.

Roberts tells the story of pinning Tyree Pride just 20 seconds into his Poinciana Arena match held on February 12th after first insulting Pride and the Bahamian fans. Wooden folding chairs were flung from the crowd into the ring. The next thing Roberts knew, he was waking up at Princess Margaret Hospital and was told he had gone too far. In the same article, Roberts also mentioned being stabbed.

Malenko couldn't remember those riotous incidents specifically, but agrees they could conceivably have happened.

"They were fired-up crowds, for sure," agreed Malenko. "That was also a good thing, though. One of the greatest matches I ever had was in Nassau against a guy named Jim Savage. We worked a match and that whole place just started rocking. My dad just looked at me when I got back to the dressing room and said, 'Holy shit!' It was a moment in time. It was one of those matches where everything clicked and the whole crowd got behind it, and it got so loud that you couldn't even hear yourself think."

While it's true that Malenko was part of his own pull-apart brawl at the Poinciana Inn, he recalled it taking place a long way from the wrestling ring.

"We were at the hotel in Nassau, and I had only one towel in my room, so I went to the front desk and told the guy I needed another towel," said Malenko. "I was being very nice about it, and he was being very ornery about it. Eventually, I just dove over the counter to get a towel from him. I don't recall any fists being thrown over it, but everyone came running out and all hell broke loose. So later on in my life, whenever I would ask for a towel, everyone would be sure to give me one. It became this stupid joke that followed me around for 15 years, that I was the guy who always needed a towel."

It should be noted that even in his first appearances in the Bahamas, Tyree Pride was able to foster a connection with Bahamian wrestling fans that would have them immediately running to his aid. This foreshadowed events that would play out time and time again in Nassau wrestling rings. However, before that would happen, the islands of the Bahamas were going to get swept up by "The American Dream."

## Nine: The American Dream

Over at Nassau Stadium, the next scheduled outing for Bahamas champ Rufus Jones did not put his title at risk, as he teamed with Charlie Cook to battle Kevin Sullivan and Kangaroo #1. In the main event, Angelo Mosca took on crowd favorite Barry Windham, while Roy Welch and "Bad" Leroy Brown faced off in singles contests, as did Terry Allen and Jake "The Snake" Roberts.

Neither Jones nor the Bahamas title made an appearance at all on April 1$^{st}$ at Nassau Stadium, but the accompanying article in *The Nassau Tribune* suggests that he was not missed. Dusty Rhodes main-evented the show against Kevin Sullivan, and the reporter covering the event described Nassau Stadium as being sold out with the venue "jammed to overflowing." On the undercard, Terry Allen and Scott McGhee defeated one of the Fabulous Kangaroos and James J. Dillon.

**Terry Allen holds one of the Fabulous Kangaroos in a headlock while James J. Dillon and Bill Alfonso look on (Bertie Johnson/Nassau Tribune)**

For an Englishman like McGhee, trips to the Bahamas created a unique challenge when it came time to re-enter the United States.

**Rufus Jones as the NWA Bahamas Heavyweight Champion
(Courtesy of Peter Lederberg)**

"I was coming back to Florida from wrestling in Japan and trying to get back into the United States," began McGhee. "The immigration guy saw all these Bahamas stamps. On my passport, it's stamped all over with 'Bahamas, Bahamas, Bahamas.' They thought I was some kind of drug smuggler

123

because they ripped my suitcase apart. The only thing that saved me was I had one of the Japanese posters with me that had all of the wrestlers on it, and I was on the poster. When they saw it, they all started laughing. I was thinking, 'You can laugh all you want as long as you let me in the country!'"

During Florida tours, Rufus Jones had spontaneously ceased all defenses of the Bahamas title at the typical Florida stops, with his final advertised defense of the championship coming on January 26th at the Hollywood Sportatorium against Jake Roberts. From there, Jones spent the final few months of his Florida tenure wrestling Leroy Brown and "The Professional" Len Denton before departing for Mid-Atlantic Championship Wrestling. When the Bahamas championship belt magically rematerialized at Nassau Stadium in April following Jones' exit, it adorned the waist of Angelo Mosca.

As a professional football player, "King Kong" Angelo Mosca was exceptional, having been recognized as one of the most decorated athletes in the history of the Canadian Football League. As of this writing, he shares the record for the most Grey Cup championship game appearances with nine, and he also won a total of five Grey Cup championships with two different teams.

Quite possibly, Mosca's most memorable involvement in mainstream culture happened in 2011 when he got into a fight with former British Columbia Lions quarterback Joe Kapp during a fundraiser involving Canadian Football League Alumni. Still seething over grievances from a Grey Cup championship game played five decades prior, the two septuagenarians came to blows on stage, and footage of the altercation later went viral on YouTube. The whole affair culminated in an appearance by Mosca on the *The Dr. Phil Show*, as he explained the root cause of the fight to America's favorite psychologist.

When it came to wrestling, Mosca capitalized on his fame as a football player in order to boost his marketability as a wrestling star much like Wahoo McDaniel, Dick the Bruiser, and other football veterans in similar situations had also done.

His background as a legitimate athlete, coupled with his reputation for having been a somewhat dirty player, made him a main-event performer in nearly every territory he wrestled in.

Despite Mosca's fame and reputation, many observers of Florida wrestling during the early 1980s regarded Mosca's wrestling performances as a consistent letdown.

"I don't think I *ever* saw Mosca have a good match in any territory," said Barry Rose. "His run in Championship Wrestling from Florida wasn't the longest, and I always got a feeling it was designed to assist with his son's debut."

Mosca's son, Angelo Mosca Jr., has been widely criticized by wrestling experts for being among the worst professional wrestlers of all time. A portion of that criticism is owed to the fact that Mosca Jr. was routinely elevated above seasoned veteran wrestlers and won championships at their expense, often while looking hopelessly lost during matches.

Equal criticism has been heaped upon Mosca Jr.'s interviews. In one infamous case, Mosca Jr. stammered his way through an interview on an episode of Mid-Atlantic Championship Wrestling before accidentally revealing the real name of famous masked wrestler "The Assassin" Jody Hamilton, who also happened to be the booker of the territory.

Regardless as to how the Bahamas championship belt came to be in Angelo Mosca's possession, he successfully defeated Blackjack Mulligan during his April defense of the championship, and then followed that victory with another successful title defense on May 21st at Nassau Stadium against Mulligan's son, the young Barry Windham.

Mosca's triumphs in the Bahamas clearly established him as a villain in need of unseating, and a suitable contender would soon arrive. On July 2nd, the announcement was made that Angelo Mosca's next Bahamas title defense would be against the former two-time NWA World Heavyweight Champion Dusty Rhodes. The article in *The Nassau Guardian* stated, "Rhodes promises to avenge the defeat of Blackjack Mulligan and Barry Windham, both of whom lost to Mosca in their attempts to gain the cherished Bahama Island title."

Charlie Major Jr. further dangled the carrot to Bahamian wrestling fans that a win by Rhodes would make future appearances by him in the Bahamas more likely.

"And if he does win, he should attract more of the big names in the wrestling circuit to challenge him for the title," Major gleefully told *The Guardian.*

In addition, the article recognized the Bahamas debut of "The Purple Haze" Mark Lewin as he faced off against Charlie Cook, and Major stipulated that dual victories by Rhodes and Lewin would result in a future match on Bahamian soil between the two. Major closed by posing the possibility of future midget wrestling at Nassau Stadium, which was not a facet of wrestling the CWF promotion was known for in that era.

The excitement for Rhodes' appearance in Nassau had crescendoed to such a degree that on July 8th, *The Nassau Guardian* went so far as to report the arrival time of Dusty

Rhodes' Bahamasair flight from Florida, and Major insisted that Bahamian wrestling fans should meet Rhodes at Nassau International Airport. From there, Dusty would be taken to meet with young fans at the Thelma Gibson and T.A. Thompson schools.

In wrestling territories during the 1980s, this level of promotional effort placed behind a babyface challenger was a strong indicator that a title change was likely, and this particular case was no exception. To the unsurpassed delight of probably every wrestling fan in Nassau Stadium, Dusty Rhodes successfully unseated Angelo Mosca to become the fifth NWA Bahamas Heavyweight Champion.

"Honestly, I don't even recall Mosca beating Rufus Jones for the Bahamas title," admitted Kevin Sullivan. "I'm pretty sure Dusty just gave the belt to Mosca for a few months so that it would be a bigger deal when he beat him for it."

Charlie Major Jr. and Championship Wrestling from Florida did their part to cash in on the title change. Whether the increase in price went directly to cover the cost of bringing in a major star like Dusty is a question we will never know the answer to. What we do know is Charlie Major Jr. advertised "championship prices" for Rhodes' arrival, which resulted in fans paying $12 for general admission and $15 for ringside seats to see one of the hottest professional wrestling attractions in the world capture the Bahamas title.

For the sake of comparison, the average price of general admission for the Miami Beach show two days prior, with Dusty Rhodes against Ox Baker in the main event, had been five dollars, with ringside seats going for eight. On a per-show basis, the price difference is stark, but to be completely fair, some Miami Beach fans would reliably support four shows each month while Bahamians typically only attended one.

Still, whatever gripes wrestlers may have had about Bahamian wrestling fans of that era, it can never be said they were skinflints who refused to shell out cash when wrestling came to Nassau. They gladly covered a sudden 20-percent increase in ticket prices to see their beloved hero win their nation's championship during Independence Day weekend.

Unfortunately for fans anxious to see more of Rhodes, his possession of the Bahamas championship did not result in more frequent trips by The Dream to the islands... at least not right away. There was a multi-month absence of wrestling by Rhodes and CWF from Nassau, which was certainly exacerbated by the reemergence of Sweet Brown Sugar on a Poinciana Arena card on October 22nd.

The popular Sugar, who was the first man to wear the Bahamas championship belt, and who had never been seen to lose the Bahamas championship by Nassau fans, faced "Pretty Boy" Larry Sharp on a card supported by a tag team match between the team of Charlie Cook and Tommy Gilbert, and the pairing of Scotty Williams and Super Texan. In addition,

Thompson and Smith also provided the midget wrestling action that Charlie Major Jr. was incapable of hosting in Nassau Stadium.

Almost immediately, Major countered by announcing the lineup for a show to take place on November 4th, with the main-event offering a Dusty Rhodes title defense against his former ally, "The Outlaw" Ron Bass. A few days later, a *Nassau Guardian* article discussed Major's latest wrestling program and offered up an opinion on what was apparently a hotly contested debate in the nation at the time: Whether or not professional wrestling was genuine combat, or if it was fake.

"No one knows for sure how much of it is real," the writer said, "yet most people enjoy it whether they believe it's real or not."

The unidentified writer then advanced the discussion by making three key appeals in support of the ongoing offerings of wrestling action by Bahamian promoters in the face of its potentially spurious nature.

First, he suggested the very presence of big-name wrestlers in the Bahamas was a treat for Bahamian fans who spend so much time glued to their television screens on Saturday mornings watching wrestling. Second, he argued on behalf of the valuable exposure a tourism-centered nation like the Bahamas received when famous Florida wrestlers spoke on television about how much they enjoyed the Bahamas and its people.

Last, but not least, the writer of the article admitted that the wait for wrestling to return to Nassau Stadium had been intolerable, but he assured readers the wait was well worth it given the return of "everyone's favorite – Dusty Rhodes – on the main card."

Potentially because they were informed that the reputation of professional wrestling as genuine combat was under a microscope of public scrutiny, Rhodes and Bass reportedly engaged in a 45-minute bloodbath in front of "a few thousand fans" in Nassau Stadium who stayed on their feet for the entire bout. The match reportedly made such an impression that *The Guardian* reported on December 4th how fans interviewed after Rhodes' disqualification victory over Bass went on to declare that wrestling unequivocally "is *not* fake."

As a result of the unsatisfying conclusion to this bloody affair, the December 3rd show at Nassau Stadium would be headlined by a return bout between Bass and Rhodes, and it would be a no-disqualification match. Bass declared before his fight with Rhodes that the title would change hands. There was no chance of this happening; Rhodes defeated Bass to delight his Bahamian fans and retained his championship gold.

As a round, White, bleach-blonde Texan, Rhodes may have seemed like an odd figure to attract such steadfast support from a mostly Black, island fanbase. Yet, this was consistent with the way Dusty was received by fans just about everywhere he performed, whether overseas, or in his home country.

"Dusty talked about the connection he had with the Black fans," said Howard Brody, former NWA president and the coauthor of Rhodes' autobiography. "Dusty had a philosophy that when he was booked on the card, *he* was the Black guy. He was so over with the Black fans, he didn't feel he needed to book any other Black wrestlers on the undercard in order for those fans to feel represented."

To demonstrate his point, Brody brought up a feud between Rhodes and Bearcat Wright, the very same Black wrestler who was commonly billed as being from Kingston, Jamaica, and who had wrestled in the Bahamas to little fanfare one decade prior. In an uncharacteristically clumsy slip of the tongue, Rhodes let a naughty word sneak out of his mouth during a live television interview segment in the midst of denigrating the Bearcat.

"Bearcat Wright was a Black heel, and during one of Dusty's promos for a show in Tampa, Dusty dropped the N-word in the heat of the moment in a promo that aired in Tampa," Brody explained. "The Black fans came out in huge numbers to see the match, except they backed *Dusty*. Even though he said that word, they still agreed with him. As a fan, you were stunned by how much love they had for someone like Dusty for them to be able to overlook something like that. It's a heavyset White guy with blonde, curly hair calling a Black guy the N-word, and they came out to support the White guy. It didn't make sense. *That's* how popular he was. For whatever reason, he had that connection with the Black fans, and he totally understood how much power he had."

Kevin Sullivan, who spent several years wrestling in Florida, concurred with that sentiment.

"You *had* to push a Black wrestler in the Bahamas," Sullivan said. "The *only* time you could get away with not pushing a Black wrestler in the Bahamas is when you had Dusty wrestling in the main event. He was as over as any Black guy who ever wrestled there, if not more so."

It's worth noting that during the reign of Dusty Rhodes as the Bahamas champion, the belt was never defended in the United States as it was during the reigns of Black babyface champions Sugar and Jones. Similarly surprising is the fact that Rhodes did not hold any other CWF championships during his run with the Bahamas belt. For all intents and purposes, it was a true main-event title run by a wrestling megastar that was intended for Bahamian eyes only.

In the grand scheme of things, the unadulterated possession of the NWA Bahamas Heavyweight Championship by Rhodes – a two-time NWA World Heavyweight Champion by that point, and one of the top-drawing attractions anywhere he wrestled – solidified it as the true main-event championship of the Bahama Islands. Yet a time was rapidly approaching when Bahamians would be graced by the presence of another pair of champions that they would be able to cheer for just as vocally.

## Ten: A Gold Mine

To kick off 1984, Charlie Major Jr. stormed out of the gate by announcing his first show of the year, along with plans to renovate Nassau Stadium and enhance its functionality. The first wrestling event of the new year was headlined by a slam-versus-pin match between Blackjack Mulligan and the 460-pound One Man Gang, in which Mulligan could win the match by successfully body slamming the mammoth Gang.

Also on the card would be Mulligan's son, Barry Windham, who was fully ensconced in his masked persona of "The Yellow Dog." He wrestled and defeated Cowboy Ron Bass.

While Major did say he expected at least 2,000 fans to attend the show headlined by Mulligan and the Gang, he used the bulk of his opportunity to have direct access to the press to criticize Nassau's local boxing scene, drawing attention to a dearth of both talent and fan interest as the reasons why boxing had not been the primary focus of his promotional efforts in recent months.

"The amateurs are not getting the support," Major told *Guardian* reporter Jerome Armbrister. "It's the people's attitude toward amateur boxing versus professional boxing. You get just as good action in amateur as in professional, and I hope, this year, Bahamians can support the amateur program. That's one thing that will be a savior for local boxing."

Major closed by suggesting Nassau Stadium could be used as a venue for rock concerts that year. Incredibly, the advertisement beneath the article persisted in promoting "championship prices" for the January 7th show even though no championships were on the line, and none of Championship Wrestling from Florida's active champions participated in the event.

Later in January, Dusty Rhodes made his return to Nassau Stadium on the 28th, along with the Bahama Island championship belt, to make a title defense against the new demonic version Kevin Sullivan. Major predicted that at least 3,500 fans would be in attendance to see the American Dream defend his belt against the Prince of Darkness, with at least 500 fans expected to be turned away.

"The word from Dusty is he will be out to stop Kevin Sullivan's visit to the Bahamas," Major told *The Guardian*. "He is one of the few to have a victory over Rhodes. Kevin Sullivan was absent from Florida, and now he has returned with a new bag of devil tricks. He expects to be the new Bahama Island champion."

Sullivan's new gimmick was simply the result of popular trends he had been looking to capitalize upon.

"MTV had just started, and the horror genre had been revived," said Sullivan. "New horror films were springing up, and because of that, all of the old horror films also became popular with a new audience. I was just following their lead and incorporating some of that material into my new gimmick."

The primary match on the undercard would pit "The Yellow Dog" Barry Windham and the newly arrived Billy Jack Haynes against Cowboy Ron Bass and Black Bart, who wrestled collectively as "The Long Riders." The article acknowledged how fans suspected the Yellow Dog to be Barry Windham, but it had not yet been proven. The debut of Hector Guerrero of the famous Guerrero family was also discussed, along with how he would be competing against Mike Davis for the Florida Junior Heavyweight Championship.

Major closed by hyping the eventual return of NWA World Heavyweight Champion Ric Flair, and perhaps as a result of outside pressure from fans hoping for the return of Black wrestling stars that were capable of main-eventing the shows, Major once again teased the return of Butch Reed, along with the possible debut of the Junkyard Dog.

It is impossible to know what the Championship Wrestling from Florida office might have been suggesting to Major about the acquisition of these two individuals from the uppermost tier of Black wrestling talent, but when Sylvester "Junkyard Dog" Ritter eventually did seek a new home after concluding the record-breaking run in Mid-South Wrestling that made him a superstar, he would first be making multiple trips to Mid-Atlantic Championship Wrestling before turning north to join the roster of the World Wrestling Federation.

Likewise, Butch Reed was also busy working high on the cards of Mid-South Wrestling, and appeared to be in no danger of sliding eastward to wrestle in Florida.

The Yellow Dog and Billy Jack Haynes were victorious in their respective bouts that evening in Nassau, with Haynes making a memorable impression on the female fans in attendance, who reportedly screamed their approval whenever Haynes flexed his bodybuilder-caliber physique.

On February 3rd, Jerome Armbrister wrote an article in *The Guardian* about the forthcoming lights-out dog-collar match between the Yellow Dog and Ron Bass, which took place on February 4th. Armbrister described the crowds at the recent back-to-back sellouts at Nassau Stadium, which each reportedly drew 3,500 paid fans, with a further 500 who were refused admission and hovered disappointedly outside of the Nassau Stadium entrance.

Armbrister also interviewed Bahamian fans for the article, which was a rarity in the coverage of wrestling up until that point.

"Yellow Dog" Barry Windham punches away at Ron Bass while Bill Alfonso watches closely (Derek Smith/Nassau Guardian)

Excited wrestling fan Aubrey Sherman, in explaining how she wanted Barry Windham to deal with Ron Bass, expressed her desires in a very Bahamian fashion when she said, "Yellow Dog is supposed to *mash him up*."

"I think Barry would use the clothesline," continued Sherman, switching to an analytical approach. "He will also use his elbow very effectively."

Another superfan, Mark Cunningham, was having a hard time picking a winner.

"It's hard to say, but Yellow Dog will pull it off for the Bahamian people," declared Cunningham. "Although, there is a chance Cowboy can use his size to beat the young guy."

Ultimately, Cunningham would be sent home happy after the Yellow Dog defeated Bass once again, which set the stage for yet another main-event match between the two only one week later on February 11th. This time, the pair would compete in a Texas Bull Rope match, which was touted as a specialty of the Cowboy, who had already defeated Dusty Rhodes in one such match.

"Bass regards himself as the king of the bull rope," Charlie Major told *The Guardian*. "He was very unhappy about the match last week. He is very confident that he will beat the Dog in the Texas Bull Rope match because the Dog has very little or no experience in that."

Major also announced the arrival of women's wrestlers to the show, with Leilani Kai and Judy Martin facing Despina Montagas and Penny Mitchell. Once again, the popularity of Billy Jack Haynes with Bahamian women was acknowledged in print. The man who "stole the hearts of Bahamian people… mostly the ladies" would square off against Black Bart, the partner of Ron Bass.

"Black Bart is very volatile and tough," said Major. "I'm expecting Billy Jack to be himself and give the fans the kind of action we had in his last two outings."

Furthermore, Major guaranteed another show on February 25th with Dusty Rhodes teased as the potential headliner, and an appearance by NWA World Heavyweight Champion "Nature Boy" Ric Flair in April. This would mark the fifth show in Nassau in only two months, which was a torrid pace considering the average during peak years had ordinarily been one show every four to six weeks.

Sadly, Rhodes did not return on February 25ᵗʰ, and Barry Windham wrestled in the main event against a newcomer to the Florida wrestling territory, "Hacksaw" Jim Duggan, while Billy Jack Haynes wrestled Ron Bass in the primary undercard match.

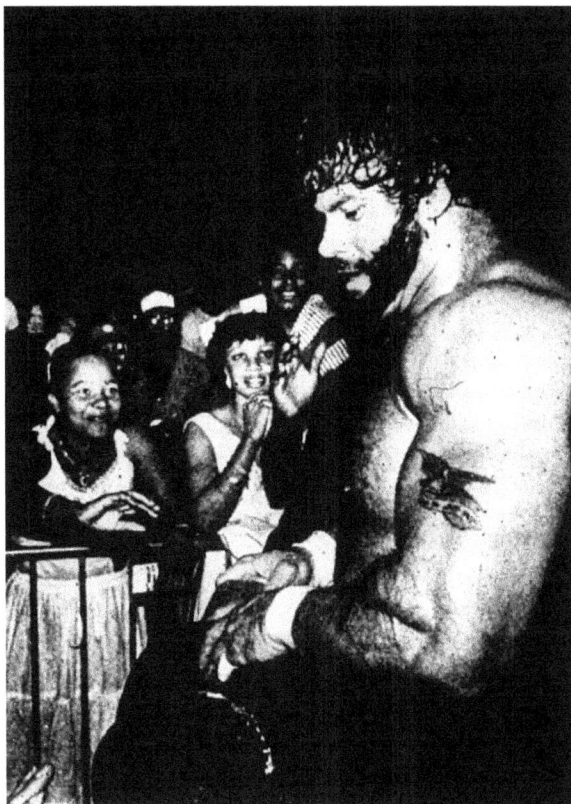

**Billy Jack Haynes walks to the Nassau Stadium ring while adoring fans look on (Derek Smith/Nassau Guardian)**

"Billy Jack will win," said wrestling fan Eugene Dawkins when he was interviewed by *The Nassau Guardian*. "He got the weight. He has a submission hold that can make any man respond. He can put a man's body to the mat. If he let

Bass get him in the air, it's all over because Bass have a good powerslam that no man can stop before the count of three. If (J.J.) Dillon don't interfere, it could be a good match."

Similarly confident in the prowess of her own favorite wrestler, Pamela Carey assumed Barry Windham would make short work of Jim Duggan because of his unstoppable clothesline.

"I think Barry would win because he can fight; he is good," Carey told Armbrister, *The Guardian*'s sports reporter. "He would use the clothesline. Why not? It worked on everyone else."

Finally, Eugene Dawkins, who was categorized as a wrestling expert by virtue of how he never missed any of Championship Wrestling from Florida's Saturday morning content, broke down the finer points of each match. After picking Barry Windham to beat Duggan due to the strength of his clothesline, Dawkins seemed to think the tag team contest between the team of Mike Rotunda and Mike Davis against One Man Gang and Kharma was an even matchup on the basis of the potency of Rotunda's airplane spin and the Gang's big body splash.

When it came to choosing a winner between Denny Brown and Hector Guerrero, Dawkins was similarly noncommittal.

"Denny Brown does the drop kicking," said Dawkins. "On the other side, Hector Guerrero has a vertical suplex, but if Denny Brown hits the atomic knee drop on him, no way he could get out of that. Plus, if Hector Guerrero put him to the mat and jump off the ring rope, it's all over. That takes all your energy."

Certainly, these were wrestling fans who took the outcomes of matches very seriously.

Making his first appearance in the Bahamas, "Hacksaw" Jim Duggan had just completed a highly successful stint with Mid-South Wrestling, which included a "Battle of the Hacksaws" against "Hacksaw" Butch Reed, one of the most popular wrestlers ever with Bahamian audiences.

It is quite possible that Charlie Major Jr. had been told about the imminent arrival of "Hacksaw" Jim Duggan from Mid-South the prior month, confused him with "Hacksaw" Butch Reed, and inadvertently raised the hopes of the Bahamian fans with his announcement one week prior only to dash them when a tall, rugged, physically imposing, but clearly White and unfamiliar wrestler was trotted out as the new Hacksaw in Reed's place.

On March 24th, Rhodes finally made his long-awaited return to Nassau Stadium to simultaneously defend his Bahamas title and to put an end to James J. Dillon's tenure there in a match with a stipulation attached to it: The loser had to leave the Bahamas for one year. Behind the scenes, Dillon was preparing to depart the Florida territory and move on to Jim Crockett's thriving wrestling promotion headquartered in Charlotte.

Very soon, the Crockett territory would begin to absorb sizable chunks of the most popular wrestling talent around the United States to counter the growth of the rapidly expanding World Wrestling Federation that was preparing to become a company with a national focus behind the surging popularity of its newest megastar, Hulk Hogan.

The effects of the nationalizing of professional wrestling would soon have a profound influence on the Florida territory, and would undoubtedly play a role in the way things would play out in the Bahamas as well.

In mid-April, Ric Flair returned to Nassau once again, making good on Charlie Major Jr.'s promise from a few months prior, which he was quick to remind the island's wrestling fans about.

"For one, it fulfills a promise that as long as the best talent is available, we'll get it here," Major told *The Guardian*. "It was something we were discussing for some time."

Getting Flair booked for Nassau during that trip may have been slightly more difficult than usual. The NWA World Heavyweight Champion competed six times over the course of five days in Florida between April 8th and April 12th, but then flew to St. Louis to wrestle former NWA champion Harley Race on the 13th. Yet, Flair lived up to his reputation for being willing to fly anywhere to defend his championship by climbing right back aboard a plane to fly to Nassau and meet Barry Windham in the main event of what was titled "Star Wars '84."

Keeping up the narrative Major had been feeding them, *The Nassau Guardian* reported this as the second time the NWA world title was being defended in Nassau, when in reality it was at least the 8th defense by a third different champion. Local wrestling fans expressed their thankfulness for Flair's presence and what it meant to the tiny nation.

"It shows the Bahamas is a top sporting place in the world," said Trevor, a local fan. "The tourists also come to wrestling, and Bahamians love wrestling, especially the women. Both [Flair and Windham] are very good, but I'll go with Barry Windham. Most Bahamians, even though they like Flair, will pull for Barry. But the fight could go either way."

Bahamian Rhapsody

As was his custom, Flair wrestled Windham to a one-hour draw in front of what *The Guardian* reported to be a "crowd of over 4,000" at Nassau Stadium. The retelling of the match itself described it to be a by-the-numbers Ric Flair match, in which Windham would batter Flair only for the champion to repeatedly cheat to gain the upper hand. Then, as the one-hour time limit drew near, Windham seized the upper hand and tried several pinning combinations only for Flair to narrowly escape from all of them as the clock ticked toward zero.

Major wasted no time in announcing that his next show would be April 27th, and would be headlined by a Dusty Rhodes title defense against "Mad Dog" Buzz Sayer, with Billy Jack Haynes, Ron Bass, Mike Davis, Billy Graham, Kevin Sullivan, Barry Windham, Mike Rotundo, Chavo Guerrero and Hector Guerrero also appearing on the card, along with defenses of the Florida championship and Southern championship.

When asked directly if he thought he might be overloading the card, Major replied by saying that Bahamian fans appreciate good wrestling, and he would continue to bring top wrestlers to the Bahamas. *The Guardian*'s article promoting the show underscored the unmatched popularity of "The American Dream" Dusty Rhodes with Bahamian wrestling fans, and talked about how "Superstar" Billy Graham was a favorite of old-time wrestling fans who had not been seen by the islanders in many years, likely as many as seven.

Following Rhodes' successful title defense against Sawyer, a match between he and Graham was hurriedly announced for May 12th. However, both the bout and the entire card were reportedly canceled on account of Rhodes having an opportunity to wrestle against the NWA's new world champion Kerry Von Erich in Lakeland, Florida. In the meantime, the advertisement for the show did throw a new wrinkle into the mix, as the match pitting Barry Windham and Mike Rotunda against Ron Bass and Black Bart was advertised as being contested for "The Bahama Island Tag Team Title."

During this stretch of Championship Wrestling from Florida shows in the Bahamas, the NWA United States Tag Team Championship had not been defended in the island nation. Seemingly, there was a desire to have championship tag team matches take place in the Bahamas, but there also appeared to be some reluctance to defend championships bearing the name of the United States on a Bahamian show.

At the time that the Bahama Island tag team title defense of Windham and Rotunda was first announced, "The Long Riders" Bass and Bart were the reigning U.S. tag team champions.

Two weeks later, when the Bahamas Island tag titles were officially defended for the first time in Nassau, the reporting by *The Guardian* drew a further distinction between the U.S. tag title and the Bahamas tag title. The article stated that Windham and Rotunda would be defending their Bahamas Island tag team championship against the U.S. tag team champions, Ron Bass and Black Bart, but only the Bahama Island titles would be on the line during that match. This match would be on the undercard of the "Battle of the Full Nelsons" between "Superstar" Billy Graham and Billy Jack Haynes.

"We had heat with the Bahamas back then," said Kevin Sullivan. "Now, when I say 'heat' in this case, I'm talking about the United States having heat with the Bahamas. Our government was in the middle of trying to bust their prime minister, Pindling."

Beginning in late 1983, Bahamas Prime Minister Lynden Pindling had been under investigation after allegations were made by the U.S. Justice Department that he and two of his cabinet members accepted monthly bribes to the tune of $100,000 per month from Norman's Cay resident Carlos Lehder, a member of Colombia's Medellín Cartel. Lehder reportedly used his home on the tiny island as a staging area for shipments of cocaine to the United States.

"Pindling and his crew make the Bay Street Boys look like schoolboys," former Bahamas parliamentarian Edmund Moxey told *The Miami Herald* in January of 1984.

Later in the year, admitted drug smuggler Edward Hindelang, who was snared in the U.S. investigation into the Bahamas known as "Operation Grouper," testified about bribes that were supposedly paid to Pindling through an intermediary to effectuate the release of captured drug boats by Bahamian police.

With the U.S. government working hard to investigate and incriminate the Prime Minister of the Bahamas, the Florida wrestling promotion did not wish to find out whether or not the mere mention of the name of its premier tag team championship might instigate a riot at Nassau Stadium.

"I recall that they had championship belts down there that we used when we came out," said Rotunda. "But we didn't bring them back and forth. They were able to stay down there in the Bahamas. We also did Freeport shows, so we would have had them in Nassau and Freeport, but they would have stayed down there when we flew back to Florida."

The Bahamas tag title accomplished the goal of allowing the name of the Bahamas to be used in a tag team championship match, and also enabled the ongoing promotion of the babyfaces as champions even if they lost the U.S. titles back in Florida, especially because Windham and Rotunda were both so popular with the Bahamian people.

"Barry Windham was *really* popular there in Nassau," said Sullivan. "He was seriously a big cowboy. We would go out scuba diving, and we'd be half in the bag, drunk. Barry would be down there kicking away at snakes, only to have us come up and find out they were some of the deadliest snakes in the world. That's just how Barry was back then. He was fearless."

"Sometimes we would stay overnight there, and we'd go to a club, and the Bahamians *definitely* knew who we were," said Rotunda. "They were always excited to see us, and they treated us well since we were babyfaces. I don't even know if the heels went out at all when they stayed down there. Barry and I were free to do our own thing, and we went out to the clubs afterward. The fans were always respectful when we'd see them around town. The heels didn't have it nearly as easy."

Jimmy Garvin confirmed that heel wrestlers in the Bahamas were wise to sequester themselves if they wished to return home safely.

"I think I was hiding most of the time that I was there," laughed Garvin. "I would land there, go to the hotel, and I would hang out at the bar that served food inside the hotel. That was the one place I was safe. In that day and age, the heels would have been very scared to go out when we had that much heat."

Rotunda was also sympathetic to what the heels endured on a nightly basis inside of Bahamian wrestling venues.

"When they came out, rocks and debris would fill the ring because the fans would throw stuff at the heels even from over the walls," said Rotunda. "It was pretty freaky. Luckily, I was a babyface at the time, so we didn't get as much thrown at us, but I felt sorry for the heels for sure."

From Bart's perspective, the debris being thrown in his direction wasn't even the most dangerous of the physical threats he faced when wrestling Windham and Rotunda in Nassau Stadium.

"I remember Mike Rotunda stretching my ass in the ring every night," said Bart. "Barry Windham was a worker, but Mike Rotundo is a *real* shooter. Then there were the rocks the people would throw at us. Kids were selling them at the door for 25 cents each, and there was no guidance system on them. They might have been trying to hit us, but the babyfaces got hit plenty of times."

To be fair, Bart admits he went too far on his interviews about Bahamian fans in his efforts to get heat, which he immediately regretted.

"I was cutting a promo about the Bahamas, and I called the fans a bunch of 'blue-gum monkeys,'" lamented Bart. "I didn't mean anything by it, and I regret it, but I was trying to get heat. I didn't mean it as a racial slur. I knew that was a mistake. I want you to let the people down there know that I love them, and I appreciate them coming out and watching the wrestling every time we were there. It was the best time of my life. That whole territory – including the Bahamas – was my first big break. Nassau was a gold mine. If we could do it again, it would *still* be a gold mine."

Rotunda agreed with the sentiment that the Bahamas was a financially beneficial place to work whenever he was working at the top of the cards.

"The reason we kept going back there is because the houses were so good; *especially* in Nassau," said Rotunda. "It was a nice payday for us back then. It wasn't like the regular spots we'd hit in Florida every week. It was like we'd go to Nassau every six weeks and get a nice little payoff of $800 to $900. It would boost your personal profit margin a great deal. Back in the early '80s, that was a *very* nice payoff for one night.

146

Mike Davis set me up doing these radio remote things where I would tell people how to rent TVs and rent beds. I would do that with him in the morning, and then we'd get on the plane and go to Nassau, so that whole day was a nice day for picking up extra money."

From Black Bart's perspective, every trip he took to the Bahamas felt like a vacation as long as he could overlook the rocks being hurled in his direction at the Stadium every time he emerged from the dressing room.

"That was one of the best times of my life," said Bart. "We were on top. Everything was selling out. When I went to the Bahamas with Bass and J.J. Dillon, Joe Higuy from The Bridge Inn would pick us up at the airport, and the basketball players from his team would take us to the hotel room. One time when we were at The Bridge Inn, I drank 21 triple Seagram's 7 and 7's. The bartender stopped putting any liquor in it because he figured I'd had enough. I told Joe about it, and he fired the guy. I didn't mean to get that guy fired, and I hope he knows that. I appreciate him for trying to take care of me."

Rotunda also had fond memories of their meals at The Bridge Inn.

"Going to Joe Higuy's restaurant with Kevin Sullivan, that was the first time I ever had conch chowder," recalled Rotunda. "They had big bowls of conch chowder for us in the afternoon, and then we'd work at night. For some reason, I also remember seeing a lot of cars down there being driven around with a bunch of wax on them and thinking, 'What the hell is that?' Barry said, 'I don't know. I guess everyone must wax their cars on the weekends,'" because of all the cars we saw being driven around with the wax still on them. I guess they'd let it sit, and then take it off and shine it up on Sunday. That always stuck in my mind."

In just two years, the Bahamas had gone from a nation that had never received formal acknowledgement by the National Wrestling Alliance to a country with two separate NWA championships bearing its name. Moreover, they were represented by three of the most exciting professional wrestlers active anywhere in the wrestling world. However, the Bahamas would soon be stripped of all its active wrestling champions, seemingly in one fell swoop.

## Eleven: The Shakedown

On June 14th of 1984, wrestling fans in Nassau finally got to witness a title match between "Superstar" Billy Graham and Bahama Island champion Dusty Rhodes. This was the exact same pair that had main-evented New York's Madison Square Garden three times during the 1970s. Back then, Graham was in the midst of his unprecedented run as a semi-long-term heel world champion for the World Wide Wrestling Federation, and Dusty was loaned to Vince McMahon Sr. by promoter Eddie Graham to pose an acceptable challenge to the Superstar.

In appearance, the two grapplers were polar opposites from one another. Billy Graham was the physical archetype that would define professional wrestling during much of the 1980s and 1990s. He had the massive, impeccably tanned physique of a bodybuilder who was also unmistakably on steroids.

By comparison, Dusty Rhodes was adorned with a prodigious agglomeration of adipose tissue, which belied the fact that Rhodes hid the strength and cardiovascular potential of an authentic multi-sport collegiate athlete beneath those layers of body fat. Further, Rhodes was more than the equal to Billy Graham in both overall size and charisma, and he was also the more well-rounded wrestler between the ropes once the bell rang to signal the start of the action.

Billy Graham, whose real name was Eldridge Coleman, was an outstanding athlete in his youth, and he even played professional football in the Canadian Football League. After an Achilles injury forced him to give up his football aspirations, Graham transitioned to wrestling. By that stage of his life, he had already won the West Coast version of the Mr. Teenage America bodybuilding competition, and by the time he began wrestling, he had been an occasional workout partner to the most famous bodybuilder of all time, Arnold Schwarzenegger.

As 1975 dawned, Graham had already won his first world wrestling championship – the International Wrestling

Association World Heavyweight Championship, recognized by
the International Wrestling Enterprise of Japan – and Coleman
followed that accomplishment by winning the "Best Arms"
distinction at the 1975 Mr. America bodybuilding competition.

Then in April of 1977, Graham accomplished his
greatest career achievement by winning the WWWF
championship. It was during that championship run that he
and Rhodes sold out Madison Square Garden three
consecutive times, with the final two matches in their series
consisting of a Last Man Standing match and a Texas Bull
Rope match.

When he made trips to wrestle in Florida, Graham was
recognized as the "cousin" of both Eddie Graham and Mike
Graham, although the relationship was in storyline only.
Further, the Superstar had adjusted his presentation noticeably
since his time as a world champion in New York, and he was
reintroduced to Floridians as a bald-headed, mustached karate

fighter who wore baggy pants and a black belt that ostensibly communicated his prowess in martial arts.

Although the Superstar's interview technique and delivery were still among the best in the professional wrestling industry, any Bahamian wrestling fans hoping to see the bleach-blonde, clean-shaven, tie-dyed juggernaut who had captivated the Northeastern United States just a few years prior was sorely disappointed.

"This was not the same Billy Graham who wrestled for Vince McMahon in New York and held the WWWF title," said Barry Rose. "This was karate-fighter Billy Graham, and the presentation simply wasn't the same, and it wasn't as popular with the fans as it would otherwise have been."

Rhodes retained his title against Graham, but in doing so, he had also defended his Bahama Island championship for the final time. One month after the match between Rhodes and Graham, Vince McMahon Jr. fired his most unmistakable shot to date in the escalation of a national wrestling war when he acquired a controlling interest in Georgia Championship Wrestling, and access to the promotion's national cable programming slot on WTBS along with it.

Known as "Black Saturday," the move by McMahon granted the WWF a momentary monopoly on the nationally viewable pro wrestling action available on cable television.

In August, Rhodes would follow others by making a permanent move to Jim Crockett's Mid-Atlantic territory, which was now the undeniable stronghold of the National Wrestling Alliance, and which was about to begin a rapid consolidation of whatever top-tier wrestling talent was not tied to WWF contracts.

Meanwhile, no clear explanation for Rhodes' departure would be announced in the Bahamas for several months, probably because no one had a clear picture yet of precisely what was happening, nor how it would affect Rhodes' schedule. The Dream's popularity made him a frequent traveler, and it may not have been plainly apparent that he would be unavailable to wrestle in the Bahamas for several years.

In between Dusty Rhodes' final defense of the Bahamas title and the initiation of a national wrestling war, Charlie Major Sr. passed away on the morning of June 30th. The death of the Bahamian sports legend occurred only nine days after a declaration by St. Bonaventure University that it would be constructing a new running track and naming it after its record-setting track-and-field star.

Following the death of Charlie Major Sr., the frequency with which both wrestlers and bookers of CWF shows would make accusations about being swindled out of money they were owed at Nassau Stadium would increase dramatically.

"They would skim off the top. It's like a natural thing for local wrestling promoters to do," accused referee Bill Alfonso. "There was just a little larceny. It's common in independent shows and smaller shows. People deal with cash. They'll say $5 for the wrestlers; $5 for me. They'd say the house would be a $40,000 gate, but he'd only report $28,000. You can't argue with the guy, because you still have to get off the island. It obviously wasn't *super* bad, because we kept going back. Charlie Major Jr. was the only promoter that I knew there for the whole time I was with Championship Wrestling from Florida, and *everybody* still made money on those shows."

Nearly one month later, on July 27th, Barry Windham and Mike Rotunda also made the final defense of their Bahama Island tag team championship belts before they both followed Rhodes to Jim Crockett Promotions. Just like that, the Florida territory had lost three of its top wrestlers, and from the perspective of a Bahamian wrestling fan, both of the Bahama Island championships had seemingly been vacated overnight.

The promotion of the August 17th Nassau Stadium show reflects the bewilderment that endured behind the scenes in Championship Wrestling from Florida during that time. Both the advertisement for the show and *The Nassau Guardian* article written to promote it mention the Bahama Island title being on the line in the main event, but the main event was never identified.

Then again, with so much turmoil surrounding the departures of key CWF talent, the announcement of a championship match could just have easily been the result of confusion or outdated information.

The matches that night involved the tag team of the Break Dancers taking on Kevin Sullivan and Billy Graham, and another tag-team contest pairing the Hollywood Blondes against Scott McGhee and the One Man Gang. In singles competition, Dory Funk Jr. wrestled against the newly arrived "Pistol" Pez Whatley, and Billy Jack Haynes took on the Saint.

The most likely candidate to replace Rhodes as a future Bahamas titleholder would have been the new Black babyface wrestler Pez Whatley, but Haynes was so popular in the Bahamas that he also would have been a decent candidate to carry the belt. However, Haynes was also in the midst of making his exit from the Florida territory, and neither his absence nor the losses of any of the Bahamian favorites would escape public notice.

On the night of the September 29th show at the Stadium, an incident took place which resulted in an outrageous use of a real-life event being falsely applied to explain the absences of some of the Bahamian fans' most popular grapplers. During the show itself, Ric Flair defended his NWA World Heavyweight Championship against Pez Whatley, while Kevin Sullivan tussled with Scott McGhee, and the One Man Gang challenged Jim Neidhart. Behind the scenes, Sullivan, Flair and the One Man Gang were reportedly accosted by Bahamian police officers in the heel dressing room.

"I remember that perfectly," said Sullivan. "The policeman had an 8-ball of cocaine, and he was trying to get it in our hands. He was also trying to take apart Flair's world title belt. It was a shakedown. I felt like they were trying to get a payoff, or to extort money either from us or from Charlie Major."

News of the incident was leaked to *The Nassau Tribune* by a source which Sullivan believes might have been his local friend, Bahamian businessman and Bridge Inn owner Joe Higuy, and the details appeared in an October edition of the newspaper. Within the article, the confidential informant is identified only as "the number-one friend of all the visiting wrestlers," and the article cites reports that detailed how the wrestlers were placed against the wall and searched for drugs by uniformed Bahamian police officers.

"These guys don't even bother with the stuff," the informant told *The Tribune*. "But when they were searched for drugs, they couldn't believe it. Most of them have already vowed that it was their last time out in Nassau."

The informant went on to explain that about a dozen wrestlers had dealt with harassment of that nature from the local police. Conveniently, the list of wrestlers who Bahamian fans were advised that they should never expect to see again stemming from this harassment included several popular wrestlers who had either already left the Florida territory for greener pastures, or who would soon be departing.

The list of outbound wrestlers included Dusty Rhodes, Blackjack Mulligan, Barry Windham, Scott McGhee, Billy Jack Haynes, Mike Davis and Kevin Sullivan. A "popular referee" connected with Championship Wrestling from Florida was also added to the list of those who were not interested in returning to the Bahamas.

Major responded by submitting a statement to *The Nassau Guardian*, stating, "There was a situation at the last show held Saturday, September 29, where the policemen wanted to check out some of the wrestlers. This was done and the lawmen were satisfied that everything was in order."

*The Guardian* referenced a prior declaration from Major that his company would never host wrestlers who had been involved with drugs or had problems with the law, which were factors that would ordinarily result in a work permit being immediately revoked or invalidated.

While elements of the reporting certainly appear to have been based on factual events, Bahamian wrestling fans had been skillfully instructed to reroute any blame for the absences of their favorite wrestlers that they wanted to level at Championship Wrestling from Florida or Charlie Major Jr. over toward the Royal Bahamas Police Force for their alleged harassment of the wrestlers.

Considering the frequency of tales involving babyface wrestlers being treated favorably by Bahamian police officers, along with the stories of heel wrestlers being treated with a commensurate degree of disdain, it is almost unfathomable to think fan favorites like Rhodes, Windham, Haynes or McGhee would have been subjected to anything constituting harassment for drug possession or drug use on the part of the police.

As this was playing out in the press, the *actual* use of illegal drugs had truly spiked in the Bahamas with devastating consequences. The very next day after the dressing room shakedown had taken place, Knight-Ridder Newspapers published a syndicated report by Carl Hiaasen and Jim McGee detailing how the Bahamas had a become a critical hub for South American drug smugglers in their efforts to bring cocaine into the United States.

While the report focused most of its attention on familiar accusations of corruption and bribery involving Bahamian officials who were criticized for being paid to look the other way, the report also focused on the effects of drug use being felt by Bahamian residents, including the emergence of new problems: drug addiction and drug-related suicides.

Nassau's lone drug rehabilitation clinic was having to turn people away as a result of being filled to capacity, and drug-influenced suicides were occurring at a previously unimaginable rate of one per month. Elsewhere, Bimini Island commissioner Wilton Stubbs estimated that 80 percent of his island's unemployed teenagers were freebasing cocaine.

To his credit, wrestler Scott McGhee had been booked as a speaker in Bahamian churches to encourage children not to use drugs.

"Gordon Solie contacted me out of the blue and asked me, 'Scott, can you give the youngsters over there some advice on keeping away from drugs?'" explained McGhee. "They were very receptive. The parents would say 'Thank you so much for what you said to our kids.' This was in the early '80s, and some of the people had begun to have drug problems."

Of course, some of the wrestlers were legitimately hamstrung by drug problems of their own, just like many other professional athletes and performers of the 1980s.

Private investigator Kevin Rounsavall relayed the details of an interview with Billy Jack Haynes in which Haynes described himself as a drug smuggler who transported cocaine from the Bahamas to Florida on Eddie Graham's behalf. In all fairness, this story seems far-fetched, as no other wrestler has ever openly disclosed a link between Eddie Graham's wrestling operation and a drug smuggling ring. The Sunshine State was rife with cocaine during the 1980s, so there would have been no clear need for wrestlers to run the risk of getting busted while trying to sneak drugs into a U.S. state that was already teeming with intoxicating white powder.

"Everything was free to us back then, including drugs," said referee Bruce Owens. "In the dressing room of Miami Beach, they had this long bathroom. There was a metal shelf running along 10 sinks. The first time I walked in, there were three helmets from Miami Beach motorcycle cops, and the cops were hitting the coke. Back then, people in the wrestling business were considered big stars. We could walk in anywhere we wanted, and it was all free. When things are free, it makes bad habits hard to quit. You could go to the Bahamas and party with somebody on a yacht, and the next thing you know, someone has a bowl of coke out that's the size of a cereal bowl."

One month after the reported incident of harassment, CWF returned to Nassau with a main event of Dory Funk Jr. and Jesse Barr facing off against Pez Whatley and Larry Hamilton, with Scott McGhee against Jim Neidhart and Kruscher Kruschev versus "Superstar" Billy Graham rounding out the show.

Again, despite no championships being at stake during the program, despite both of the Bahama Island championships lying dormant, and despite the loss of many of Bahamians' preferred wrestlers, "championship prices" remained in effect. With general admission at $12 and ringside seats selling for $15, Nassau Stadium remained one of the most expensive venues to watch wrestling anywhere in the world.

This also marked the first Nassau appearance by Larry Hamilton, and he was blown away by the experience.

"When I first flew in it was just crazy at the airport," described Hamilton. "The Bahamians were all coming up to me; even security was coming up to me and talking to me. When I did the interview for the Bahamas, I said, 'I'm an island boy! I love the islands, I love the water, and I can't wait to get to Nassau!' I didn't know there were Hamiltons in the Bahamas that were attorneys there. So, I think the Bahamian fans assumed I was related to the Hamiltons. Then when I got there and did the press conference, I had to tell the people that I wasn't related to the Bahamian Hamiltons. But they still loved me anyway."

November brought the return of a popular face when former Bahamas champion Sweet Brown Sugar rejoined Championship Wrestling from Florida, which was a news story that warranted its own article in the November 9th edition of *The Nassau Guardian.*

**Pez Whatley and Sweet Brown Sugar at Nassau Stadium (Nassau Guardian)**

In the write-up, Sugar's sudden unexplained departure from Florida in 1982 was acknowledged, but it was also explained that he had been granted something equivalent to free-agent status, as if Sugar had not been working for NWA-sanctioned territories for the bulk of the prior two years.

In reality, Sugar spent most of that period wrestling in Mid-Atlantic Championship Wrestling, Georgia Championship

Wrestling, Southwest Championship Wrestling, and World Class Championship Wrestling, all of which were still territories under the governance of the National Wrestling Alliance.

"This match gives Sugar an opportunity to travel, and it is also good from a financial standpoint," Charlie Major Jr. told *The Guardian.*

Sugar was booked to wrestle against The Saint on the November 16th card, while Southern champion Pez Whatley was also featured on the show competing against Jesse Barr in the main event, with Larry Hamilton wrestling Krusher Kruschev on the undercard. For the first time, there were three popular, Black babyface wrestlers simultaneously featured on a CWF event at Nassau Stadium, and two of them were proven main-event commodities.

As 1984 cruised to a close, Sugar and Whatley participated in two more Nassau Stadium events which were built around their presence, on December 1st and 29th respectively. In the midst of these proceedings, an order was placed to create a brand-new Bahama Islands title belt which closely resembled the NWA National Championship belt used in Georgia.

"Mike Graham had called me up, and he said they wanted me just for TV, and also for the Bahamas," claimed Hamilton. "He said he wanted to put the Bahamas belt on me, but I was going away to work for the Fullers, and then over to Japan. By the time I was ready to come back, the belt was on somebody else."

The answer to the question of who the new Bahamas champion would be became one of the most challenging riddles to solve during 1985. By the time the year was over, it would see a death, a departure, and a mild defection, but in the end, an enduring champion would indeed be crowned.

## Twelve: Pistol and Pride

B y 1984, the Malenkos had concluded the promotion of
their IWWA shows in the Bahamas, but Tyree Pride
took steps to continue running wrestling shows in the
Bahamas on his own terms. Throughout the process, Pride was
flanked by "The Jamaican Jammer," Bobby Wales, who he got
started in the professional wrestling business.

"My friend, Carlos Cardigan, introduced me to Tyree,"
remembered Wales. "We bought some steel, and Tyree welded
it together to create a ring. That's where we started training,
right there in Tyree's backyard."

Burt Baum, a Miami resident and lifelong wrestling fan
who grew up watching matches in Laurel Gardens, New Jersey,
responded to an advertisement Pride placed in a Miami
newspaper looking for a partner to help him promote
wrestling. This is according to Burt's son, Howard, who was
only 18 years old at the time, but who had already been a
ringside photographer for Championship Wrestling from
Florida for two years.

Howard described the arrangement as a classic
"money-mark" scenario, in which a wrestling fan who acquires
financial resources decides to indulge a fantasy of getting
involved in the pro wrestling business.

"When my dad answered Tyree's ad, I had no idea how
egregious it was to be involved in an outlaw wrestling
promotion," said Baum. "I wasn't privy to the politics. I
thought I could be involved in a little wrestling promotion on
the side with my dad and Tyree, and still shoot photos for
CWF like no one was going to say anything to me."

Baum's father formed and bankrolled the World
Wrestling Alliance with Pride and Wales handling much of the
promotion. Baum then assisted his father with the task of
locating wrestlers to compete for the newly formed WWA.

"We got to travel up to Tampa and watch a few local
wrestling shows, but a lot of it involved watching tapes,"
explained Baum. "We watched Malenko's tapes, because he

just got done doing his local promotion, and I was involved with picking out guys who I thought were good and who we could use on our shows."

After the first set of WWA tapings, Baum said he walked into the next CWF show in Miami assuming he would be photographing the matches at ringside as per usual. He was wrong.

"Lo and behold, the night after our first taping, Bill Alfonso came up to me and said, 'Oh man... Duke Tanaka wants to see *you!*'" laughed Baum. "Then Chris Dundee told me I was done with shooting at ringside and with selling my photos by the entrances."

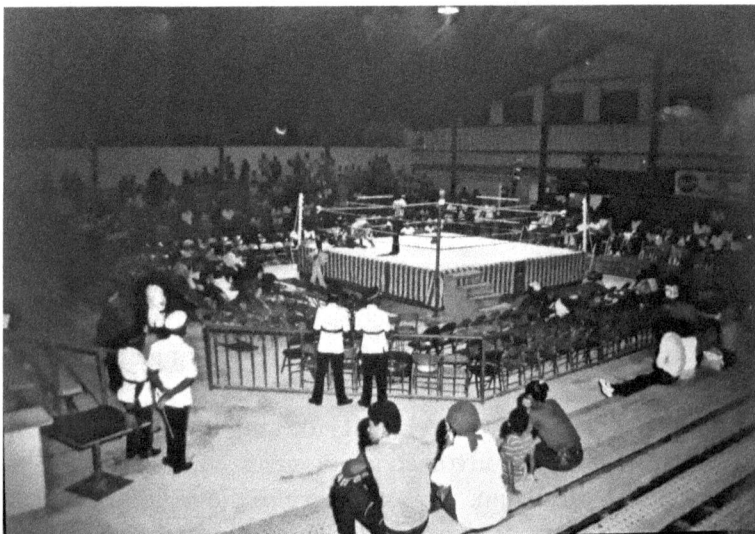

**Inside of the Poinciana Sports Arena (Courtesy of Howard Baum)**

In Nassau, the Baums' WWA acquired the slot previously occupied by the Malenkos' IWWA at the Poinciana Arena, and Howard recalled accompanying his father to those events to take photos on a few occasions.

"The business end of things was handled entirely by Tyree," explained Baum. "He was the intermediary between us and Charlie Thompson. "The hotel room at the Poinciana Inn was hot, horrible and bare-bones. If I'd been on my honeymoon, it would have been terrible, but I was only 18, so it was an adventure to me. The café adjacent to the arena had the best fried chicken and conch chowder that I've ever had. One of my fondest memories of the event was of sitting around with the wrestlers eating food out of that cafe."

In order to enhance the talent level of the wrestlers showcased at their events, Pride and the Baums turned to old territorial favorite Cyclone Negro, who also served as the WWA's Brass Knuckles Champion.

"The brass knuckles belt was Cyclone's personal belt," said Baum. "He was one of those brass knuckles champions who never lost his belt. Other than that, we also had a world champion and world tag-team champions."

Compared with crowds in the United States, Baum described the Bahamian crowds at the Poinciana Arena as being decidedly more raucous.

"Americans might have been getting smarter to the inner workings of the wrestling business, but they seemed not to have gotten the memo over in Nassau," said Baum. "The crowd was cheering for everything, including the women and the midgets. We had the brass knuckles matches with Cyclone Negro and Scott Williams to satisfy bloodlust, and then Tyree and Dr. Red Roberts were wrestling in our main events."

Also wrestling in WWA's main events as Pride's tag-team partner was Tiger Conway Jr., a second-generation wrestler from Texas who had worked regularly in the territory during the mid 1970s.

"About a month after I worked with Tiger over in the Bahamas, he got a call to wrestle for Florida in the NWA," said Pride. "Since I knew him, he took me to the dressing room and introduced me to everybody. Right away, Chief Wahoo McDaniel came up to me and said 'I heard people talk about you. Everywhere you go you draw because of your wrestling style.' I said, 'Chief… I'll tell you what… All you have to do is put me on TV on Wednesday and Saturday. You're going to see a difference when you come to the Miami Beach Convention Center."

By this point, the WWA had *already* folded as a wrestling promotion, which is a failure that Baum attributes to the inexperience of Pride and Wales.

**Tyree Pride and Tiger Conway Jr. (Courtesy of Howard Baum)**

"Tyree was hard-working, but he didn't have the sophistication at the time to be a great promoter, and Bobby Wales was more of a dreamer," said Baum. "Bobby seemed like he was simply hanging around Tyree, but Tyree really drove everything with his force of will. A lot of people didn't like Tyree for various reasons, but he was the hardest-working person I've ever been around in the wrestling business."

To emphasize the self-sufficiency of Pride, Baum recalled when he watched "The Haitian Sensation" go above and beyond the call of duty for the sake of ensuring that all fixtures were in their proper place prior to a wrestling event.

"There was a light on the ceiling of our building for one of our TV tapings in Miami, and Tyree just shimmied 80 feet up a pole to fix the light on his own," said Baum. "He could have gotten himself killed before our show even started. He and Bobby may not have been great promoters, but Tyree was an *extremely* hard worker."

Still, it would be nearly eight months before Pride would be featured prominently on any CWF events. Eddie Graham was still in charge of Championship Wrestling from Florida, and he was no fan of wrestlers with a connection to the Malenkos. However, a seismic shift in the landscape of wrestling in the Florida territory was about to take place.

The new year began promisingly enough, but disaster was looming on the horizon. The first show of 1985 was headlined by a loser-leaves-town tag team match. Sweet Brown Sugar and Dutch Mantel faced Jim Neidhart and Krusher Kruschev on January 12th with the stipulation in place that the losing team had to leave the Bahamas for one full year.

In hindsight, it is obvious that this match was designed for the babyfaces to defeat the heels, because any finish to a Nassau Stadium match resulting in Sweet Brown Sugar being banned from the Bahamas would almost certainly have instigated a riot.

At least this time, Championship Wrestling from Florida had the luxury of explaining the departures of wrestlers through in-ring events. The Russian Kruschev, who was really Minnesotan Barry Darsow, was leaving Florida to join Jim Crockett's expanding territory in the Mid-Atlantic. Meanwhile, Neidhart would be traveling to the World Wrestling Federation where his brother-in-law Bret Hart had been competing since November.

Also featured on the show were Brian Blair and Jesse Barr, which was a match Charlie Major Jr. stressed as being of great significance.

"Barr, the Florida champion, is a very fierce competitor and was recently embarrassed by Blair who entered the ring during a match (during a match between Barr and another opponent) in a chicken costume and ended up pinning Jesse Barr," Major was quoted in the press. "So it is expected that this match could be the best of the card for the night."

"That's one of my favorite moments of my career that was ever caught on tape," laughed Blair. "I hit the ropes wearing that chicken suit, but I couldn't see clearly out of the holes in the mask when I went to give Jesse the flying forearm. I came off the ropes and absolutely blasted Jesse with my forearm right in the face, in full view of the camera."

As per usual in Nassau, all of the key babyfaces won their matches that night. The next event, on January 25th, featured the Nassau debut of Michael "P.S." Hayes of the Fabulous Freebirds. The charismatic Hayes had become one of wrestling's most well-known stars over the course of the multi-year feud in Texas between his Fabulous Freebird stable – consisting of Hayes, Terry "Bam Bam" Gordy and Buddy "Jack" Roberts – and the Von Erich family.

To ensure a warm reception for Hayes in Nassau Stadium, Charlie Major Jr. played up the warm relationship between the incoming Freebird and Sweet Brown Sugar.

The first of the two main-event matches involved Sugar and Whatley against the "Pretty Young Things," Norvell Austin and Koko Ware – a rare meeting between two Black tag teams. The main event was a return bout between Florida champion Brian Blair and Jesse Barr, with Barr pledging to get revenge for his defeat earlier in the month.

Behind the scenes, disappointment over his Nassau payoffs from January had left Blair upset with the CWF management team.

"That first night, I was main-eventing with Jesse coming off of the angle we worked with the chicken suit," explained Blair. "I could see Nassau Stadium was packed. I went and asked Lester what the house was, and he told me it was only $12,000. It told him that was bullshit. Our payoff wasn't great, but it wound up being okay. Jesse and I still decided to complain about it later on."

Blair then explained to Welch how a Blair-Barr rematch would attract even more fans to Nassau Stadium.

"I was right," said Blair. "That second night, there were even more fans in the Stadium. It was obvious. I went up to Lester to ask him what the house was, knowing full well it should be more than the last time. Lester kept telling me he hadn't counted it yet, and he'd tell me later. We met up at the Bridge Inn later that night. Lester told me some story about how he set his briefcase down with all of the money in it, and it supposedly got stolen. After all that, Jesse and I wound up getting an even smaller payoff for an even bigger house. I didn't believe Lester's story for a second."

**Brian Blair kicks Jesse Barr (Andrew Seymour/Nassau Guardian)**

Even before that return bout could happen, tragedy struck. On January 25th, 1985, Eddie Graham committed suicide by shooting himself in the head with a handgun... *twice.* *The Orlando Sentinel* reported that Graham, who was 55 years old, was found dead in his bed by his wife Lucille early in the afternoon after she returned home from visiting relatives.

Although no single cause has been cited for Graham's suicide, reasons that are commonly listed include financial debts, marital problems, and pessimism toward the long-term outlook of his wrestling company, which was now facing competitive threats on multiple fronts.

Vince McMahon Jr. had broken several decades' worth of formal and informal agreements with respect to territorial boundaries in the aftermath of Black Saturday, and he was actively running events in the defined territories of other promoters, including Eddie Graham's. The WWF had run shows in Miami and Jacksonville at the tail end of 1984, providing Graham with the first sophisticated, well-funded competitive threat that he had ever dealt with since he'd arrived in Florida 25 years prior.

The wrestling business leaves its performers with little time to mourn, and the company pressed on. For its February 23rd show at Nassau Stadium, CWF advertised a one-night tournament to crown a new Bahamas champion and fill the vacancy caused by Dusty Rhodes' departure for Mid-Atlantic Championship Wrestling during the previous year. The Saint, Pez Whatley, Jesse Barr, Dutch Mantel, Buddy Roberts, Rick

Rude, Bill Irwin and Brian Blair all competed for the brand-new championship belt.

In the end, Pez Whatley won the championship, but never defended it in Nassau. Within one month of winning the tournament, Whatley left the Florida territory to work for the Crocketts in Charlotte, along with the revived version of Georgia Championship Wrestling known as "Championship Wrestling from Georgia."

"Pez was a super nice guy, but something happened with him and he just decided to leave," recalled Bill Alfonso.

The original plan may have been to put the Bahamas championship belt back around the waist of Sweet Brown Sugar, but Sugar left the CWF in the middle of February to work for World Class Championship Wrestling in his home state of Texas. Aside from working for a few dates in Florida in July of 1985, Sugar never again wrestled consistently for CWF.

The remainder of 1985 would be absolutely devastating for Championship Wrestling from Florida. Before it was over with, the company would also lose Brian Blair, Hercules Hernandez, Jesse Barr and Buggsy McGraw, leaving them further depleted of both established and newly built stars.

In the meantime, Tyree Pride worked his first match for CWF at the Miami Beach Convention Hall during the summer of 1985, teaming with Cowboy Lang in a losing effort against Rip Rogers and Little Tokyo. Then, he made his first appearance on a CWF television show which aired on October 5th. For many wrestling fans in Florida, this was the first time they were made aware of The Haitian Sensation's existence.

Wearing short, green tights, Pride employed a variety of aerial maneuvers that were impressive – if a bit sloppy – to successfully dispose of his masked opponent known as "The Marauder." After finishing off his opponent with a flying cross chop, which Gordon Solie generously referred to as a "body ram," Pride approached the announcing desk and graciously answered the questions of "Mr. Solie" before looking into the camera and delivering an interview in Haitian Creole which Pride stated was intended exclusively for "my people."

One week later, Tyree Pride faced "Ravishing" Rick Rude in a main-event match at the Miami Beach Convention Center, and the venue reportedly did better business than it had done in years. Tom Archdeacon of *The Miami News* wrote about the event in the October 16ᵗʰ edition of the paper. In an article titled "The Pride of Little Haiti," Archdeacon detailed how buses filled with Haitians from Little Haiti arrived one after another, all filled with Haitian immigrants who could scarcely wait to cheer their hero to victory.

Archdeacon interviewed Miami Beach promoter Chris Dundee, who attributed the entirety of the event's success to the undersized Tyree Pride.

"He's the one drawing the money in here," Dundee told Archdeacon. "Look at the crowd in here – 80 percent Haitian – and it's all because of him."

Archdeacon went on to identify Pride as the first real hero the Haitian immigrants had representing them in any local Florida sports.

**Tyree Pride being interviewed by Gordon Solie**

"When we got down there, Kendall Windham and all the boys came up to me and said, 'Tyree, thank you for the house!'" remembered Pride. "They knew I was the one who brought all those people in there at the Convention Center."

When Rick Rude began indulging in his standard rule-breaking tactics, several Haitian fans broke through the barricade to point out the infractions to the referee. Each time, police officers corralled the fans and moved them back behind the barricade.

After Pride won the match, a near riot ensued as fans surged toward the ring to get closer to him. As the police hustled Pride back to the dressing room, a young Haitian woman with an infant in her arms rushed forward and begged Pride, "Bless my child!" He took the child, kissed it, and handed it back to the exuberant woman.

Tom Archdeacon was asked what these events mean to him now, decades later, with the knowledge that Tyree Pride was not actually of Haitian descent.

"I'm not sure how the Haitian fans would have reacted to the truth," Archdeacon said. "I'm sure the celebration would feel a little hollow and there would be a sense of betrayal with some. But I also think many would still celebrate the moment and the concept of a conquering Haitian hero. No one else was championing their cause, their ethnicity, or their people, and he was doing so in glorious fashion. They had to still love and appreciate that. He was the one sporting guy who made them proud to be Haitian."

On the next edition of CWF television, Pride replicated his performance from the previous episode, with the only addition being the challenge he issued to the winner of that weekend's forthcoming match in Nassau between "Pistol" Pez Whatley and "Playboy" Buddy Rose for the NWA Bahamas Heavyweight Championship, with Pride wrestling earlier in the night against Bob Roop.

The Whatley-Rose match was officiated by Bruce Owens, who believed he was sent there to handle the match because no one else from the officiating team wanted any part of it.

"Buddy Rose went over on Pez Whatley with a screwjob finish where he had his feet on the ropes," described Owens. "The fans *tore up* the stadium. I had to count the pinfall where I was, but the people could see that I clearly saw Buddy's feet on the ropes. In the dressing room, we had to contemplate giving the belt back to Pez, because the police turned on us, and they were allowing the people to remove the doors from the locker room. It was *so* ugly. We were stuck in there for an hour. We were lucky that the Queen of England was on the island for some reason. The Queen's security came in with machine guns and got us out of there safely."

As far-fetched as that story sounds, it overlaps perfectly with the lone visit Queen Elizabeth II made to Nassau during the decade of the 1980s, from October 11th to October 18th of 1985.

Barricaded in the dressing room, Owens says that he and Rose indulged in some cocaine before dangerously wandering out onto Fuller Street at 3:00 a.m. and then walking down Bay Street and then south toward the Pilot House.

"We beat on Kevin Sullivan's door until he let us in," said Owens. "When Kevin saw me, he said, 'Jesus Christ, Bruce! Your eyes look like a barn house!'"

In essence, Whatley was loaned back to the Florida territory for one night for the sole purpose of having him visually drop a championship he had never defended before, and in a company he no longer regularly worked for, just to make the fans murderously incensed at Buddy Rose – the man who cheated him out of it.

"You weren't going to draw a crowd in the Bahamas with a White guy as your Bahamas champion, unless he was wrestling a Black guy," Owens stated. "Otherwise, you would have been wasting your championship to have it on a White guy on a long-term basis. Your audience in the Bahamas is going to be either Bahamian or Haitian, which is a Black audience either way. If you sent a White guy in as a heel, it was just so you could take the championship off of him."

That's precisely what happened. One week later, in front of a packed Nassau Stadium, Tyree Pride overcame the onslaught of Buddy Rose and won the Bahamas title with a high crossbody block delivered from the top turnbuckle. Referee Bill Alfonso counted the pinfall, awarded the championship belt to Pride, and then beat a hasty retreat out of the ring as fans poured in and began to dance in celebration. Hector Guerrero also entered the ring to congratulate Pride, but clearly thought better of lingering in the ring as fans continued to pour in.

"Hector Guerrero got out of the ring as fast as he could!" remembered Pride. "Bill Alfonso just disappeared!"

After what transpired the previous weekend in Nassau following the inflammatory finish to the match between Whatley and Rose, Alfonso said he was not going to make any assumptions about the temperament of the crowd on that evening.

"That was a tough crowd who took the shit seriously," said Alfonso. "Tyree was one of their heroes. The people *loved* him. There was a spot during the match where Tyree gave Buddy a sunset flip, pulled his pants down, and showed his ass to the crowd. They went nuts for it!"

**Tyree Pride – NWA Bahamas Heavyweight Champion**
**(Courtesy of Peter Lederberg)**

So began the reign of what many fans consider to be the signature NWA Bahamas Heavyweight Champion. It would be reign that was equally memorable for Tyree Pride, his followers in the Bahamas, and also for any of the heels who attempted to steal his championship in front of his swarms of adoring fans.

## Thirteen: Rocks, Bottles, and Conch Shells

The first Nassau show of 1986 resulted in one of the most controversial incidents to ever take place in Nassau Stadium. That night, Tyree Pride was scheduled to defend his Bahamas championship against "The Taskmaster" Kevin Sullivan inside of a steel cage. Sullivan was fully immersed in his demonic gimmick by now, which was especially inflammatory when presented to the devoutly Christian Bahamian audience.

"When Kevin had an interview and you saw it on television, you had to come see Tyree beat the hell out of Kevin Sullivan," said Pride. "He had more gimmicks than anyone else I'd ever seen."

Those gimmicks included such activities as snake charming, and Pride was legitimately afraid of snakes.

"Before one of his interviews, Kevin asked me, 'Hey, Tyree… can I throw this snake on you?'" remembered Pride. "I'm sure someone told him I didn't like snakes, and that's why he asked me that. There was no way in hell I would let him do that to me!"

As Sullivan and Pride stood there and discussed their upcoming match in Nassau Stadium, Charlie Major Jr. began explaining to the two participants of the cage match exactly how he wanted everything to unfold.

"Keep in mind, this isn't a place where babyfaces typically lost," explained Sullivan. "Charlie looked at us and said, 'Here's what I want you to do for the finish. I want the referee to get knocked down. I want you to get blood on Tyree. Then I want Purple Haze to come down to the ring and you should hang Tyree from the cage.'"

Sullivan said he could not believe what he was hearing. He was well aware of the assortment of horrors that had befallen other wrestlers who had incensed the crowd at Nassau Stadium even with mild heel hijinks.

"The chicken-wire fence that protected us from the stuff the crowd threw at us didn't quite go all the way to the door," said Sullivan. "There was a time when one of the Bahamians in the crowd had a cinder block and threw it at King Tonga, and it hit him in the head. He had to walk it off like it didn't hurt. Another time, Jake "The Snake" Roberts had heat with some of the guys in the dressing room, and they wanted to get back at him. The boys let a bunch of fans into the heel dressing room, and they wrapped a rug around Jake and beat him with sticks the same way you'd beat a rat."

With these incidents dancing through his mind, Sullivan said he turned to Major.

"I asked him 'You want me to hang a Black guy... *out there*?! There would be no protection for me!'" said Sullivan. "Then Charlie Major said, 'Don't worry, Kevin; I'll be there to make sure you get back okay.' I didn't really believe him."

Sullivan remembered seeing very odd behavior from some of the Bahamian and Haitian fans at ringside as he walked out to the ring that evening.

"This woman was standing at ringside doing this weird voodoo ritual thing with a chicken," said Sullivan. "Once I got near her, the chicken shit all over her face."

Toward the middle of the match, Sullivan took control of the action and opened up a cut on Pride's forehead.

"The blood was shooting out of my head and hitting people in the third row," recalled Pride. "Everybody wanted to kill Kevin Sullivan right then, from that alone."

Then, as planned, Mark "Purple Haze" Lewin made his way down to the ring with a rope in his hands, opened the cage door, and climbed inside of the ring. Lewin and Sullivan then strung Pride up on the cage by his neck. The Nassau Stadium crowd went absolutely nuclear.

"People were throwing rocks, bottles, conch shells and whatever they could get their hands on at the bad wrestlers," Pride said. "It was a *disaster.*"

As Sullivan started trying to make his way to the cage door, he noticed the fans surging through the barricade to get to him. True to his word, Charlie Major Jr. was down on the arena floor outside of the cage to meet Sullivan.

"I opened the door, and the fans started to come after me," said Sullivan. "That's the most threatened I'd ever felt in my entire career. I immediately grabbed Charlie Major, held him up, and used him as a human shield all the way back to the locker room. I was completely unscathed; *Charlie* needed 47 stitches."

"That's the gospel truth!" laughed Pride. "It happened exactly the way Kevin said. He put Charlie Major in front of him and used him as a shield!"

After the hanging incident, Pride remembered Sullivan and Lewin being arrested by the Bahamas Police and charged with assault.

"I had to go over to the police station the next day and talk to them," said Pride. "They dropped the charges and let everybody go. The Bahamian people took everything so seriously. Nobody ever drew more money in the Bahamas than me and Kevin Sullivan."

Despite the incredible response the match had received from the crowd, Pride was not happy with the amount of money that made its way into his pocket.

"Charlie Major Jr. was a guy who would try to beat you with your money every week," Pride lamented. "You would go over there, and he would play like he had a million. When it was time to pay the guys, he would look around and make the guys wait a long time before they could get paid. It was very hard to get money out of his hands. He was so tight with everything."

However, Pride withheld no credit from Charlie Major Jr. when asked to appraise the quality of the food served at the Nassau Stadium restaurant

"If you woke up in the morning with a hangover the day after a show, Charlie Major had *the best* boiled fish with lemon and Johnny cake as a hangover remedy," laughed Pride. "That was the best Bahamian boiled fish I ever had!"

Two months later, Pride faced off against Jerry Grey during a CWF television episode in which Pride, clad in yellow, dominated Grey for nearly the entire match. Then, as the bout drew to a close, Pride ascended the turnbuckles and attempted to leap onto Grey, only for Grey to dip out of the way.

Instead of landing on Grey, Pride crashed face first into the mat, and Grey covered him. Even though Pride raised one of his shoulders off the mat, the referee still counted to three, and Jerry Grey became the new Bahamas Heavyweight Champion in what was a very rare, televised title change for the Florida territory.

"Jerry Grey was very young when he started in the business," said CWF referee Bruce Owens. "He was only 18 or 19 years old. He got over very well as a pretty-boy, blonde heel. That was one of those times they took the belt off Tyree to make money. Tyree always wanted to be the champion, but the chase is required to make a championship mean something."

For Grey, it was his first and only opportunity to reign as a champion in CWF.

"The fans were very rowdy to me, especially with me being a White Bahamas champion, which was very rare," Grey stated. "It was Wahoo McDaniel's decision to have me win the belt on television, because it would be seen by so many people. Wahoo wanted to spike business in Nassau, and that's *exactly* what happened."

Bob Roop explained that *he* booked the title change, in part, to reward Jerry Grey for his hard work on the undercard.

**NWA Bahamas Champion Jerry Grey**

"Jerry was a hell of a good talent," said Roop. "I just didn't have any way to put him in the main events. He had been a guy who had put other people over in the lower card, and it's hard to take a guy like that and elevate him into another role quickly, at least not without butchering somebody else. I figured I could give him a bit of a financial reward for his hard work if I put him in the Bahamas with Tyree."

The rematch between Grey and Pride was scheduled for March 15th in Nassau, and it was intended to be an undercard match supporting the main event featuring a defense of the NWA World Heavyweight Championship by "The Nature Boy" Ric Flair against Wahoo McDaniel.

"Ric Flair actually saw the crowd in Nassau that night and told me that Tyree and I would be going on last," Grey said. "He knew the crowd was there to see Tyree try to win the belt back from me."

Grey lost the title right back to Pride that night, but several Haitians in the crowd felt Grey should pay a more severe price for having temporarily dethroned their hero.

"Sir Oliver Humperdink was my manager for that match, and we had to run back to the dressing room like football players, tackling people and knocking them over," laughed Grey. "Once we got inside the dressing room, it took all the heels in there just to hold the big, wooden door closed from all the people who were trying to get inside. We had to wait in there for hours until everything was over and the people were long gone. Keep in mind, this all happened *after* I dropped the belt back to Tyree, so I can't imagine what would have happened if I'd actually gone over on him!"

From a financial standpoint, Roop recalled the match between Pride and Grey not drawing any less than other main event matches CWF held in Nassau.

Bruce Owens remembered these rapid-fire title changes as serving the additional purpose of reminding Pride who was in charge.

"Tyree got to a point where he was being pretty vocal about his pay, and in reality, all the office had to do was put it on a heel, let the heel get the heat for it, and then let the next babyface beat him for it," Owens stated. "The Bahamas belt was tailor-made for an island person, but it couldn't *always* be the island person taking the belt. The people wouldn't buy that scenario forever."

Once his threat to Pride's title reign was turned away, Grey found Bahamians to be far more friendly to him.

"I wrestled in the Bahamas about 30 times over the course of my career," said Grey. "The people always told me I was their champion afterwards, and I enjoyed all of my time there."

Just a few weeks after regaining his championship, Pride was further rewarded with a shot at Ric Flair's NWA World Heavyweight Championship at the Miami Beach Convention Center. As the traveling world champion, Flair's job was to come into a territory and make that territory's local babyfaces look like world beaters. With Flair and Pride booked to work together in Miami Beach, Roop knew he was sure to pack the building.

"You should have seen the look on Flair's face when he saw Tyree, who was at least four or five inches shorter than he was," laughed Roop. "Flair thought I was ribbing him – or playing a joke on him – when I put him in the ring with Tyree. Instead of acknowledging Flair's surprise, I just told Flair what I wanted to happen in the match just like it was any other match."

In front of a building packed with Haitian immigrants who had relocated to Miami, Flair made Pride look incredible before narrowly escaping with his world title reign intact.

"Next to beating Rose for the Bahamas title, the best night of my life was when I wrestled Ric Flair in Miami Beach," Pride said. "To go from where I'd been to wrestling the NWA champion in front of all the Haitian fans was a very proud moment for me."

Unfortunately, it seems as if some members of CWF's management once again thought Pride was getting too big for his britches. At least that was the impression Bruce Owens received.

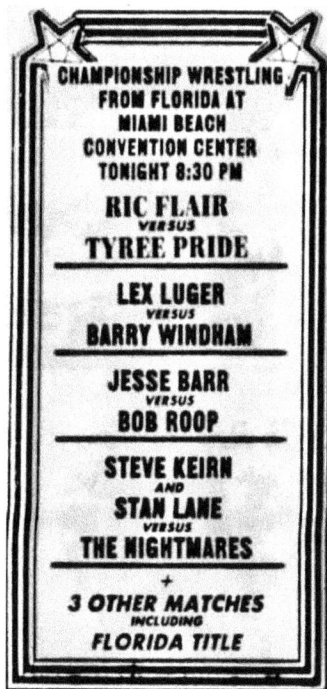

CHAMPIONSHIP WRESTLING
FROM FLORIDA AT
MIAMI BEACH
CONVENTION CENTER
TONIGHT 8:30 PM

**RIC FLAIR**
VERSUS
**TYREE PRIDE**

**LEX LUGER**
VERSUS
**BARRY WINDHAM**

**JESSE BARR**
VERSUS
**BOB ROOP**

**STEVE KEIRN**
AND
**STAN LANE**
VERSUS
**THE NIGHTMARES**
+
**3 OTHER MATCHES**
INCLUDING
**FLORIDA TITLE**

"Tyree could pack the house, but he started wanting too much," Owens stated. "I think that's the time they wanted to temper him down a little bit, and that's why they took the belt off of him for a while. I know there was a point where he was griping about money, and they said, 'Look, you're being paid well, and if you go anywhere else, you're not going to make this much.'"

Booker Bob Roop remembered things a little bit differently.

**Ron Bass taunts Tyree Pride with the Bahamas championship belt (Courtesy of Peter Lederberg)**

"It's true that Tyree was insufferable at times," Roop admitted. "He had a Napoleon complex for sure. Me putting him against Ric Flair for the world title may have given him that attitude. At the same time, I don't remember ever getting to the point where I felt like I needed to punish him."

Still, Roop *did* book Pride to lose the Bahamas title again – and in Nassau of all places – to the "Outlaw" Ron Bass on May 31st. As a precaution, Roop booked the ending of the match to occur quickly and legally.

"In the Bahamas, I wasn't going to do a hot finish to screw Tyree out of the title," Roop laughed. "I'm sure we did something where Tyree missed a big move, Bass covered him for the pin, and we got him out of the ring quickly. Anything else would have been too dangerous. If I'd screwed him out of the title in some way, we'd *still* be trapped there. Screwing Tyree meant being trapped in the heel dressing room all night waiting for the rioters to leave."

"To me, Ronnie Bass was one of the nicest guys you'll ever want to meet, but if Bass wanted you to do something and you didn't want to do it, he would stick on your butt until you did it," said Black Bart, Bass' longtime friend and Long Riders tag team partner. "And then if you didn't do what Ronnie wanted you to, he would make sure you did it whether you wanted to or not."

Roop also told a story about Bass that exemplified his tendency to do exactly what he wanted in the ring. Before telling the story, Roop underscored what a good and believable ring worker Bass was, and how likable he was on most occasions.

"Ron was one of my main heels at the time," began Roop. "There were some political things going on in the office back then. Luger was the Florida champion, but Gordon Solie hated him. Luger had an arrogant attitude in real life, which helped his believability. He had a million-dollar body, but he had a kindergarten mind for wrestling. He didn't treat Gordon with the reverence that Gordon felt he was due."

Roop explained how he and Solie got in the habit of collaboratively going over their ideas for the CWF television program since Gordon had 40 years of familiarity with the Florida territory that he could draw upon for ideas.

"I talked about getting the Florida belt off Luger to create some heat, and Gordon thought we should put it on Ron Bass," explained Roop. "There were other guys I could've done it with, but I thought Bass would be fine in that role, so that was the plan we made. If I remember correctly, we were going to do the title change on TV, but I don't think Ron knew about it."

A few days later, Ron had a match at a fairground show against a young wrestler named "The Falcon," who was Steve Brinson. The decisions Bass made in that match soured Roop on the idea of making him the Florida champion.

"My idea was to put the Falcon over because it was a fairground show, and losing at the fairground show wouldn't hurt Ron," said Roop. "Ron was directing the match because the Falcon was green, and also because he was the heel, and heels usually led the matches. Ron was supposed to give the Falcon a comeback, and then the Falcon would beat him. Ron was supposed to beat the crap out of him for 10 minutes, give him a comeback, and then the Falcon was supposed to catch him in a small package out of a slam attempt."

According to Roop, instead of doing as he was asked, Bass went out and pounded on the Falcon the entire time. Then, the Falcon gave Bass the small package and pinned him out of the blue, but the crowd failed to react for the finish to the match because there had been no intrigue preceding the ending, which is what inserting a comeback for the Falcon into the match was designed to accomplish.

"When he came back to the dressing room, I said, 'Hey Ron, didn't you forget something?'" said Roop. "Ron had a smirk on his face, so he knew what I meant. Then he said, 'Like the comeback?' Then he got an even bigger smirk, snapped his fingers and said, 'Oh yeah...'"

As a result of that episode, Roop said he decided not to give Bass the Florida championship. This decision irritated Solie, who was hoping to see Luger lose to Bass on television. Roop explained how Solie campaigned feverishly to have Bass fired from his booking role after that.

"Except for that one personal experience, I had nothing but the best feelings for Ron Bass," stated Roop. "He could be disrespectful, though. That move he pulled was basically his way of slapping the booker in the face."

At the following show in Nassau on June 13th, Pride was not booked to appear, which Roop chalks up to Pride simply not being available as it would have made "no sense" to book a show in Nassau without him. Instead of defending his newly won championship against Pride, Bass instead defended against "The Total Package" Lex Luger, who was still in the very early stages of a career that would see him become a multi-time world heavyweight champion.

"Luger was as green as grass at the time," explained Roop. "Again, he looked like a million dollars, but he was a terrible worker. He rode in the car with me every day for six months, and I was schooling him the entire way. I actually went out to the ring with him at times in a managerial capacity because I didn't want him getting lost and looking around like he didn't know what to do."

One of the most disgusting documented episodes to ever take place at Nassau Stadium involved Luger and Roop. As the two were leaving the ringside area after a match, Roop remembered a moment when Luger stopped for too long to flex and interact with the fans, which is something wrestlers – and especially heels – were always advised not to do in Nassau.

"As Luger is standing there, some lady in the audience took a sippy cup full of piss and threw it right in Luger's face," said Roop. "Some of it even got in his mouth. He sprinted back to the locker room to try to wash it out of his mouth, but the water to the fountains had been shut off. He actually had to go over to the toilet and scoop toilet water into his mouth to try to get the urine out."

"I was there to see that as well," added Ricky Santana. "Luger wound up having to run around the back of the building and all the way back to his hotel room at the Pilot House just to take a shower."

Santana also helpfully pointed out how the Bahamian crowd was relatively mild when compared with some of the other Caribbean islands where Santana spent many of the most productive years of his wrestling career.

"In the Bahamas they *would* throw things," said Santana. "The island mentality was very blood-and-guts and rock-and-bottle. You kind of got accustomed to it. In Puerto Rico and some other places they would *burn* things. I saw them literally burn Bronco's truck because he made a derogatory statement about the Black fans and going to the town where you could only see their teeth in the audience if they smiled."

The reporting of the outcome of the match between Bass and Luger has caused historical confusion for those chronicling the histories of wrestling championships. On the episode of United States Class Wrestling which promoted the July 5th matches in Nassau Stadium, Ron Bass appeared twice. On both occasions, he was referred to as the Bahamas Heavyweight Champion, and even appeared with the title belt during his match against Chris Champion.

It was suggested in the United States for years that Lex Luger won the Bahamas title from Ron Bass at the June 13th show, but the presence of the Bahamas belt around the waist of Bass in early July, coupled with CWF declaring Bass to still be the Bahamas champion during that same time, casts doubt on this claim.

The primary source of the confusion seems to stem from the nature of the tag team match booked for July 5th in Nassau, which was declared to be an "Australian Rules" match. Pride and Bass were the captains of their respective teams, and the championship of Bass would go to Pride if either Bass or his partner Ed Gantner was defeated. Luger scored the pinfall that night, and captain Tyree Pride was awarded the title and became a three-time Bahamas champion as a result.

To be fair, *The Nassau Guardian* later added to the confusion by reporting in its July 26th edition that Pride defeated Lex Luger for the Bahamas title. This was also interpreted by some people that Luger simply handed the Bahamas championship to Pride because he wasn't interested in it.

"That's a lie," said Pride. "Lex Luger *never* touched the Bahamas championship."

Bruce Owens also denies that an event that could be perceived as disrespectful to the Bahamas title would ever having taken place anywhere, let alone in Nassau.

"Our championships were always treated with respect," Owens said. "We would never just have a wrestler hand it to another wrestler, or act like they didn't want to keep a championship once they had it. It's just not something we would have allowed to happen."

The outcome of the July 5th match set up a logical rematch, in which Pride had to prove that he was capable of defeating Bass one-on-one without the assistance of a teammate. Ever the conquering island hero, Pride successfully defeated Bass in the July 26th main event to retain his championship and prove his worthiness to wear it.

With a Caribbean-spawned hero dominating oversized Americans in the ring each month in front of a packed Nassau Stadium, Bahamian wrestling fans were on the receiving end of an additional treat when Charlie Major Jr. addressed the vacancy of the Bahama Island Tag Team Championship during an interview.

"The title has been inactive for some two years now, and will be recommissioned in the very near future," said Major. "To say if it will be on the next two cards would be wrong, but we are working on it."

Only the team of Barry Windham and Mike Rotunda had ever held the NWA Bahama Island Tag Team Championship, and Major's suggestion that new champions would be crowned could rightly have been interpreted by Bahamian fans that the state of professional wrestling was perfectly healthy in their corner of the world. Little did they suspect that they were actually witnessing a Championship Wrestling from Florida company that was in the midst of its death throes.

## Fourteen: "I'm a Conchy Joe!"

Pride's reclamation of the Bahamas title was short-lived, and despite his popularity in the islands, he was soon in the process of being phased out of Championship Wrestling from Florida's plans. Just as quickly as Pride had regained and defended the Bahamas championship, he lost it to 25-year-old Chris Champion in Orlando on August 3rd. Like Pride, Champion was a student of the Malenkos, and he was a brand-new addition to the CWF promotion. He would also successfully defend the championship against Pride on August 30th in Nassau.

**Chris Champion conducts an interview holding the Bahamas title belt**
**(Courtesy of Peter Lederberg)**

The failure of Pride to recapture the Bahamas championship might have appeared to be a telltale sign that he would soon be eliminated from the company's future plans completely, but that initially seemed not to be the case. Pride was quickly paired with his friend, Jamaican wrestler Bobby Wales, to form "The Caribbean Connection." Meanwhile, Champion would lose his Bahamas title to masked wrestler "The Falcon" Steve Brinson on September 28th in Orlando, the same city where he'd collected it. This title change occurred almost simultaneously to Pride and Wales being cut altogether from the CWF roster.

**The masked Falcon during his reign as Bahamas champion
(Courtesy of Peter Lederberg)**

It was also approximately around this time that Kevin Sullivan assumed the role of head booker for Championship Wrestling from Florida. After acquiring the CWF booking duties, Sullivan evaluated the landscape of the company and decided things would function more smoothly if there were fewer championship belts. He also decided a heel-against-heel program pitting himself against Bad News Allen should be the conduit through which the process of belt elimination should take place.

"I went back to the late '50s and early '60s with the idea of taking the two best heels and putting them in a program together," Sullivan said. "I thought Bad News was the right guy to book in that position because he was the real deal and had his judo background. He was dead-ass serious."

Allen Coage won a bronze medal in judo for host nation Canada in the 1976 Montreal Olympics just one year after winning gold at the Pan American Games in Mexico City. Coage was then trained to wrestle in Japan by pro wrestling legend Antonio Inoki before returning to North America as a full-time wrestler.

After several years of working for Stampede Wrestling in Calgary, Bad News Allen came to Championship Wrestling from Florida very late in 1986, and Sullivan booked him as an absolute killer.

To begin the process of setting CWF's two top heels on a collision course with one another, Sullivan booked Allen to take the Bahamas championship from the Falcon on December 7th in Orlando. In the process, the Afro-Canadian Allen became the lone Black wrestler to carry the Bahamas title as a heel. A little more than a month later, Sullivan would win the Southern title from the departing Lex Luger who was on his way to the Mid-Atlantic.

From there, Sullivan and Allen would clash in several matches that the Taskmaster remembers quite vividly.

"We did a cage match in Daytona Beach, which hadn't been drawing well for us," described Sullivan. "I bet Mike Graham $500 that we would outdraw the Lakeland show, which usually did significantly better. Bad News was such a great talent, and the heel-against-heel thing was a novelty. In the end, I wound up with Mike's money."

As the two heels feuded, Sullivan booked Allen to simultaneously hold *all* of the CWF singles championships simultaneously – the Florida title, Southern title and Bahamas title.

"I viewed it as hitting the reset button for the company," said Sullivan. "Bad News was leaving anyway. He had already decided he was heading off to wrestle in Japan."

During his January 10th Bahamas title defense against Lex Luger, Allen used several of the tactics he would become world famous for when he began wrestling for the World Wrestling Federation one year later.

"Bad News Allen drew the wrath of the fans from the outset, as he began pounding on the favored Lex Luger as Luger made his initial attempt to enter the ring," *The Nassau Guardian* reported.

**WRESTLING**

NASSAU STADIUM — FOWLER STREET

NWA

GRUDGE MATCH

BAD NEWS ALLEN vs. KEVIN SULLIVAN

SCOTT HALL vs. KAREEM MUHAMMED

ON SATURDAY, FEBRUARY 7th, 1987 AT 8:30 P.M.

$5,000 CHALLENGE MATCH

KENDALL WINDHAM vs. ED "THE BULL" GANTNER

OPENING MATCH

RON SIMMONS vs. JERRY GREY

TICKETS AVAILABLE AT THE NASSAU STADIUM TELEPHONE: 23882
RINGSIDE $15.00 GENERAL ADMISSION $12.00 CHILDREN $5.00

At the conclusion of the match, Bad News performed what would become his trademark stunt of walking out on the match and getting himself counted out when things began to go unfavorably for him. As *The Guardian* stated, "The fans were left dissatisfied as, in the heat of the battle, Allen walked away from the ring."

With Allen's departure from CWF imminent, and with the judo master still holding all three title belts, Sullivan claims that he took that opportunity to book himself to win the Bahamas championship from Allen in Nassau on February 7th, even though the match was not advertised as being for that particular championship.

"It was a heel-versus-heel match, but that's really one of the first times I was ever cheered at all in Nassau," remembered Sullivan. "I'd say the crowd was about 50-50 in favor of each of us. I think they'd usually want to cheer for the Black guy, but I did local interviews suggesting to the people that Bad News was a Haitian and I was more of a Bahamian. I hung out in the Bahamas a lot, so a lot of the locals were familiar with me."

The subject of the presence of Haitians in the Bahamas was a very touchy subject in the Bahamas during the 1980s. In an issue of *The Orlando Sentinel* from December 1st, 1985, Bahamian official H.C. Walkine was quoted as saying the Bahamas was not interested in accepting the return of Haitians who had attempted to immigrate to the Bahamas without authorization, even though the Haitians in question had all lived in the Bahamas for periods of two to nine years.

"If they are illegal immigrants, we don't want them to land in the Bahamas at all," affirmed Walkine. "We have no intention of accepting people that are here illegally. We have enough of them as it is."

The article revealed that approximately 40,000 Haitians living in the Bahamas illegally had been ordered to return to Haiti during the previous week.

Around the time of Sullivan's match against Allen, *The South Florida Sun Sentinel* published a feature article about Bahamas national security minister Loftus Roker. In the report, Roker discussed the recent $12 million purchase of three new cutters that were added to the Bahamian government's naval fleet, with a stated goal of halting would-be Haitian immigrants at sea before they could reach the islands of the Bahamas and immigrate illegally.

After expressing admiration for the desires of the Haitians to be free, Roker concluded by saying, "I have an obligation to the Bahamian people not to reduce our standard of living and turn the Bahamas into a Haitian slum."

"In the Bahamas, especially back then, calling your opponent a Haitian would definitely have been a very viable way to get heat on them," commented Omar Amir. "Bahamians have looked at Haitians in a certain negative light for a long time. Many Haitians migrated and tried to live the best life they possibly could by starting over in places like the Bahamas. I think a lot of Bahamians descend from Haitians, and they just don't acknowledge it or talk about it. It's a touchy subject even to this day."

Sullivan was not shy about his love for the Bahamas and Bahamians, at least when directly approached on the streets of New Providence Island. He lived with his friend Joe Higuy in a 13-room house on Love Beach for nearly a year, and he had also been known to hang out in the Over-the-Hill region of Nassau, where tourists were discouraged from traveling.

Despite his adoption of the Bahamas as a second home, Sullivan still maintained his heel persona in professional settings, and taunted the Bahamian public in print. For example, in the April 4, 1987 issue of *The Nassau Guardian*, when promoting his match with Jimmy Valiant, Sullivan was quoted as declaring himself to be a Bahamian from Spanish Wells.

"It was true; I *did* spend a lot of time on Spanish Wells," insisted Sullivan. "When Bahamians talked to me on the street back when I was wrestling Tyree Pride, I would say, 'I'm a Conchy Joe! How can you cheer for this *St. Lucian* guy over a Conchy Joe?!'"

Sullivan's use of the term "Conchy Joe" demonstrates that he certainly picked up enough Bahamian slang to learn the term commonly applied to native Bahamians who were either predominantly or exclusively of European descent.

Spanish Wells businessman Anthony "Buddha" Pinder very fondly remembered Sullivan's time on his relatively remote fishing island off the northern tip of Eleuthera.

"Frankly, I'm surprised Kevin can remember *anything* about that time due to all the partying he was doing back then," said Pinder.

The public statement of affiliation with Spanish Wells made by Sullivan could also be construed as a heel swipe against the majority of Bahamians who were Black. In the 1980s, Spanish Wells was still classified as a sundown town in which non-Whites were not permitted to be present after sunset.

"Not only did I hang out in Spanish Wells, I also went right next to it over on Current Island," claimed Sullivan. "The best lobster fishing trip I ever had was off Current Island. In Nassau, I worked out with all the Bahamian guys at Peter Young's gym. They were a little hesitant to come over and talk to me at first, but I could squat over 800 pounds at the time, so eventually they came up to me to strike up conversations, and I got to be friends with all those guys."

Aside from claiming to have taken the Bahamas championship from Allen, Sullivan also claims to have never lost it, which would make him the final man to ever hold the NWA Bahamas Heavyweight Championship during the CWF era. Regardless, the accepted story in the U.S. had been that the Bahamas championship had been absorbed into the Southern championship, which Sullivan *also* captured from Brown on February 25th and then never lost. Either way, Sullivan has a claim to being the final NWA Bahamas Heavyweight Champion, and he isn't shy about making it.

"I'm *still* the undefeated Bahamian champion," Sullivan boasted. "No one ever took that belt away from me in the ring."

Only a few more shows held beneath the banner of Championship Wrestling from Florida were held in the

Bahamas following Sullivan's acquisition of the Bahamas championship, which was reflective of the steady decline of the CWF territory in the midst of repeated talent raids by the World Wrestling Federation.

It was also representative of the intra-NWA talent grabs by Jim Crockett Promotions. The Charlotte-based headquarters of the wildly popular Mid-Atlantic territory had now expanded to such an extent that it had effectively consolidated the wrestling territories of America's southern states.

When the financial reins on the Florida territory were tightened, Nassau and Freeport were among the first locations placed on the chopping block. The Bahamas was a locale with a growing reputation for being a spot where presenting wrestling shows was more trouble than it was worth, and also a place that was only regarded as monetarily viable if events were held there every four to six weeks, as opposed to Florida cities that CWF had traditionally visited every week.

By then, Tyree Pride was already spearheading wrestling tours of the Bahamas on his own with a ragtag group composed predominantly of rookie wrestlers, several of whom he'd helped to get started in the business, including a young Mike Droese.

"I was wrestling as an amateur in high school," said Droese. "At the end of the year we did this fundraiser where the wrestlers from Championship Wrestling in Florida came and appeared at our school gym at Killian High School to help our wrestling team. A bunch of those guys were there, including Lex Luger, Tyree Pride and Barry Windham. I was too much of a chicken shit to ask anybody about how to become a pro wrestler even though I was interested. My dad took it upon himself to go in the locker and start bugging wrestlers, and Tyree told him where there was a school close by."

The wrestling school that Droese was steered into was owned and operated by Pride's friend and frequent tag team partner, Bobby Wales. It was a tiny school located in a warehouse in nearby Opa-locka, where Droese found Wales to be a very accommodating teacher.

"Bobby is probably one of the greatest teachers I can imagine, and he had a *lot* of patience," said Droese. "I was the poster child for ADHD where I really tended to hyper-focus on certain things when I really wanted them. I was in great shape since I'd just come off wrestling season, so combine that with how focused I was on every little thing he taught me."

Droese explained how he would occasionally get too rambunctious and overzealous during his training, and Wales would need to force him to relax.

"Bobby would always slow me down," said Droese. "Usually I was focused enough to where Bobby would teach me something and I would usually get it in one or two tries. I got through the basics so quickly that I was able to have my first match in just six months."

Over the course of those six months, Droese also acquired his first pro wrestling ring name based on the attire he wore to Wales' training sessions.

"When I was in practice with Bobby, I had on this green shirt I got from high school for wrestling and playing football," said Droese. "We were the Killian Cougars – 'KC.' I had this big 'KC' on the front of my shirt, so Bobby just started calling me 'Mean Mike Casey.'"

Droese had barely concluded his six-month crash course in wrestling training before Pride and Wales hauled him along with them on a multi-island tour of the Bahamas. Some of the nights featured appearances by veteran talent with name recognition like Buggsy McGraw and Ox Baker.

Simply as a consequence of Pride's booking choices, Droese managed to annoy one specific veteran on his very first night of the tour.

"The first night we wrestled in Freeport, and I had to wrestle Chick Donovan," laughed Droese. "Since I was Tyree's boy, Chick had to put me over. Tyree was still keeping the heels and the babyfaces in separate locker rooms, and the referee was running back and forth bringing over the finishes to our matches. I heard that Chick Donovan apparently did not like being told he had to put me over. I can understand why. Chick had been in the business for years, and I was this new kid who didn't even have five matches under his belt."

Despite Donovan's consternation over having to lose to a rookie wrestler at a low-level independent event in Freeport, Droese confirmed that Donovan managed to maintain his professionalism once they both met in the ring that night.

"I went out there, and we didn't even have a finish planned," said Droese. "We locked up, and Chick said, 'Just listen to me.' He put me everywhere I needed to be and made me look like a million bucks, and I had *no idea* what was going on. That dude walked me around the ring so effortlessly. When you hear it said about a wrestler that he can work with a broomstick and have a great match, that's what Chick Donovan did with me that night."

Droese conceded that the standards of the show probably weren't at the level of what Bahamian fans were accustomed to seeing even though those attitudes weren't reflected in their reactions to the matches they were viewing.

**The Poinciana Inn (Courtesy of The Nassau Tribune)**

"The fans were always really great," said Droese. "They were pretty excited about watching wrestling down there. I just think they really enjoyed the shows we were putting on and got into it. Then again, I was so inexperienced that I was so hyper-focused on what was happening in the ring, and I didn't even see or hear the fans much when I was in the ring because I was half lost. The sad thing is I was actually one of the most experienced guys Tyree had down there, even with only six months of training and so few real matches under my belt!"

In some respects, this ramshackle Bahamian tour served as an extension of Droese's training, and helped him to learn from some experienced veterans.

"Buggsy McGraw was actually the one who taught me how to throw a punch properly during that tour," said Droese.

"He taught me to throw my punches from up high to down low so that the people in the nosebleed seats could see what you were doing."

"Yeah, that sounds like something I would have told somebody to do," admitted McGraw.

Regrettably, Droese didn't have the funds to venture too far from the Poinciana Inn when he wrestled in Nassau.

"We weren't really given any money, so we couldn't go very far," said Droese. "I think Tyree got a deal on the hotel we were in. We drew people into the restaurant by hanging out down there, so they kind of took care of us. I was just happy to be there. I was only an 18-year-old kid, and I couldn't believe I was on tour in the Bahamas. Of course, we weren't making shit for money. Any money that was made probably went to Tyree, but I don't think there was much money being made anyway."

Upon successfully returning from his first tour of the islands, Droese would be rebranded by Pride as the long-lost nephew of legendary wrestler Harley Race: "The Surfer Boy Harry Race." Within seven years, Droese would eventually settle on a gimmick as a garbage man before enjoying a multi-year stint wrestling for the WWF as Duke "The Dumpster" Droese.

In defiance of the demise of Championship Wrestling from Florida, the Bahamas would remain a sought-after territorial acquisition by North American wrestling promoters, and a scramble was about to ensue to see if anyone could capitalize on the death of the territorial giant and claim the Bahamas for themselves.

## Fifteen: Reclaiming Paradise

Despite the implosion of Championship Wrestling from Florida, it would have been reasonable for casual wrestling fans in Nassau to presume that nothing cataclysmic had occurred once a familiar triumvirate emerged in 1988 to fill the gap and bring wrestling back to Florida, and by proxy to the Bahamas as well.

Mike Graham, Gordon Solie and Steve Keirn decided rekindling wrestling in Florida was worth a genuine attempt if Jim Crockett Promotions and the newly centralized National Wrestling Alliance were going to abandon it.

**Steve Keirn with a member of the Royal Bahamas Police**

"I'd been in Tennessee, and I was ready to come home to Florida," explained Keirn. "I was wrestling for Championship Wrestling from Florida along with my partner from 'The Fabulous Ones' Stan Lane right until the end. That's when they came into the locker room and told us that all future events had been canceled. Months later, it was myself, Gordon and Mike who all kicked around the idea of keeping the territory running, keeping the television slot, and trying to run the territory on our own with no backing."

The trio named the new company "Florida Championship Wrestling," and they quickly signed a deal with Channel 3 – WEDU – to produce television broadcasts featuring Solie's familiar voice calling the action, along with a new color commentator, "Diamond" Dallas Page. They then set about introducing fans of the Florida wrestling territory to a new cast of characters.

"We started using characters nobody had ever seen before," Keirn recalled. "We were short on veteran wrestlers; I basically had to start training almost all of the guys who initially worked for us in FCW. That included Dusty Rhodes' son, Dustin. Mike Graham still had ownership of the CWF building at 106 North Albany, and we literally had guys who were working for us that were sleeping in the building every night as they were trying to save money and learn how to wrestle."

Despite Keirn's desire to include the Bahamas as a part of a reconstituted Florida territory, other promoters were already hard at work attempting to capitalize on the absence of an official National Wrestling Alliance claim on the Bahamas. It was in March of 1988 that Larry Hamilton brought his Continental Wrestling Association to the Bahamas to run its first show there.

"Charlie Thompson was really good to me, and he would always come to the matches at Nassau Stadium," said Hamilton. "I would talk to him, and he told me he wanted me to stay over at his place, which was the Poinciana Inn. Then he told me he also had an arena, and I asked him if we could run matches there. He told me that's exactly what he wanted to offer me, because Eddie Graham and Florida wrestling were dead. He also said he had a kid named 'Bahama Rock' John Hunt that he wanted me to run matches with."

While John Hunt had appeared on the undercard of Tyree Pride's 1987 Bahamas tour under the distended name of "Home Boy Bahama Rock Curly Hunt," Hamilton acquiesced and featured Hunt as a star attraction at his wrestling events at the Poinciana Sports Arena.

The two clashed at their first show at the Poinciana Sports Arena on March 26th of 1988, with Hamilton's Southern Heavyweight Championship on the line. The occasion was marred by one of the most memorable cases of fan interference in Bahamian wrestling history. While Hunt held Hamilton in a sleeper hold and the Southern champion began to fade, his bodyguard "The Black Assassin" climbed into the ring and clobbered Hunt with a piece of wood.

Seeing one of their own in trouble, several Bahamians in attendance folded up their chairs and either charged the ring with the chairs in hand, or lobbed them into the ring in the direction of Hamilton and the Black Assassin as the police struggled to regain control of the Sports Arena.

Building from the heat generated by that incident, a follow-up event was swiftly scheduled for Friday, May 6th at the Poinciana Sports Arena.

"Well this fight on Friday night, I think this is going to be one of the biggest matches ever in the Bahamas," Hunt told the press. "The last time it was a good fight, but a lot of people got involved in it. This is the revenge, so this time we want everybody who didn't get a chance to see it the first time to come out this time and see it for the final time."

Hunt also included a plea to Bahamian fans not to get involved in his match with Hamilton, while also urging the police to do their best to keep the frenzy to a minimum.

"With enough policemen there, I think you can keep it under control," remarked Hunt. "Tyree Pride, the Haitian Sensation, will be there to back me up and watch me when I'm in the ring. For my fans, I want them to come and support me and try to keep under control. Just come and support me."

The article included an additional appeal to fans in the form of a threat that Bahama Rock might lose his "wrestling license" if Bahamian fans attempted to intervene in the contest. Pride's student Tyrone Pryor was also added to the undercard of what unmistakably included the largest foreign contingent of Black wrestlers in the history of a Bahamian wrestling event, along with considerable star power.

# ★WRESTLING★

## T. K. PRODUCTIONS
### Presents

# "A NIGHT OF CHAMPIONS"

### on Friday, 6th May, 1988 at 8:00 p.m.
### at THE POINCIANA ARENA, Bernard Road

"The Revenge of The Bahama Rock Thunderbolt Explosion No. 2"

**LARRY HAMILTON**
Vs.
**'The Bahama Rock' JOHN HUNT**
For The U.S. Coastal Heavyweight Championship Belt

**Dirty DUTCH MANTELL Vs. The Sensational TYREE PRIDE 'The Haitian Sensation'**
For The Continental Heavyweight Championship Belt

**THE PRETTY YOUNG THINGS Vs. WAHOO McDANIEL and THE CHIEF**
Tag Team Match For The U.S. Coastal Tag Team Belt

**THE MASKED SUPER STAR Vs. Jumping JERRY BAZEL**
For The Florida Heavyweight Championship Belt

**ROCKY JOHNSON Vs. THE BLACK ASSASSIN**

**THE JAMAICAN DREAM Vs. B. O. DACIOUS**

**TYRONE PRYOR Vs. BLACK BEAUTY**

Ringside: $20:00    General Admission: $15:00    Children: $5:00

Tickets obtainable at: **All Pro Sports Shop, Just Rite Bakery, Andros Inn and Poinciana Hotel**

In addition to the defense of what was now known as the U.S. Coastal Heavyweight Championship between Hamilton and Hunt, the participants on the remainder of the show included some reasonable star power, with "Dirty" Dutch Mantel, Wahoo McDaniel, Tyree Pride, and Rocky Johnson all featured.

Hamilton said that he had big plans to develop Hunt as a wrestling representative in his native islands.

"I went in with the U.S. Coastal title against Bahama Rock," said Hamilton. "I was eventually going to put my Bahamas championship belt on him, but he fell in love or something and disappeared, and Charlie Thompson and I couldn't get in touch with him after that."

Meanwhile, Charlie Major Jr. was pleased to welcome the reimagined version of the wrestling organization that Bahamian fans were most familiar with back to Nassau Stadium. Major's statement to the press of the Bahamas involved an explanation that he had decided to shift his personal allegiance from the National Wrestling Alliance over to the new Florida Championship Wrestling organization due to internal squabbles amongst the NWA's top brass.

The first FCW event held in Nassau would feature several familiar faces, as frequent tag team partners Steve Keirn and Mike Graham would defend their FCW tag team championship against The Mighty Yankees in the main event, while Scott McGhee would make an appearance on the show's undercard.

McGhee was admittedly no longer the same worker he had been in previous years.

"I had a really bad car accident up in Calgary and didn't go to the hospital," said McGhee. "I got a friend to sew my head up. That was a big mistake. I had a subdural hematoma with two blood clots on the left side of my brain, and it caused me to have a massive stroke."

Although he eventually returned and agreed to wrestle for FCW, McGhee conceded that he probably shouldn't have been anywhere near the ring.

"Even though I could wrestle still, my dexterity wasn't quite the same," said McGhee. "I said, 'Please, whatever you do, don't put me in a tag match.' That was because I had big trouble just going through the ropes. In the Bahamas, it was double tough, because the ropes were closer together."

Even though he was limited in the ring, McGhee could not detect any differences in the reactions of Bahamian wrestling fans to his ring activity compared with their responses earlier in the decade.

"The Bahamians always took their wrestling very seriously, which was a good thing," claimed McGhee. "This was especially true considering we weren't able to use the ropes, and the ring was so hard that we didn't want to take many bumps. Working a match there was like starting a fire; you had the wood, the gasoline, and the match. Well, the crowd was already like wood soaked in gasoline. We were so over with the crowd just by being there, and they were volatile. All you had to do was drop the match on the wood, and the place would erupt. It didn't take much to get them worked up. We always had to keep that in mind."

Health issues aside, McGhee also claimed to have had a wonderful time in Nassau outside of the ring as well.

"Denny Brown and I would wrestle matches against the Skyriders, and then Denny and I went over to Paradise Island and had a good old time," laughed McGhee. "We would head over there to the pool or beach and try to get into as much mischief as possible. I don't know why a wrestler would say they didn't like working there; I *loved* it. Then again, I was a babyface, and there weren't too many things that scared me back then anyway. Everywhere I went on the island, people came up to me and shook my hand."

Despite McGhee's report that Bahamian fans enjoyed their first taste of FCW action, they were apparently unimpressed enough to make their feelings known to Charlie Major.

Bahamian households with disposable income had already been the recipients of satellite-derived television signals from across the U.S. for a decade. Any Bahamian with a satellite dish was familiar with the fact that many of the wrestlers who had once entertained them with great regularity – including Dusty Rhodes, Lex Luger, Rick Rude, Barry Windham, Mike Rotunda, Brian Blair, Kevin Sullivan, Ron Bass, Hercules Hernandez and Bad News Allen – were busy wrestling for either Jim Crockett Promotions or the WWF.

Moreover, even those without such access were able to purchase pirated copies of wrestling pay-per-view events at local video stores. Wrestling's secrets were becoming increasingly more difficult to conceal from Bahamian fans.

In the summer of 1988, Bahamian sports fans in general were also highly preoccupied with something else at that moment. The Los Angeles Lakers had just successfully completed their quest to repeat as NBA world champions. This resulted in Bahamian Mychal "Sweet Bells" Thompson winning his second-consecutive NBA championship, and cementing an entire generation of Bahamians as members of Lakers Nation.

Thompson, who had also been the first overall pick of the 1978 NBA draft, had been the first Bahamian to win an NBA title, and became the most successful Bahamian to compete in a major American sports league since baseball star Ed Armbrister. Thompson was rewarded for his efforts with a second consecutive parade through Nassau held in his honor.

Major issued what amounted to an apology ahead of the June 25th return of FCW to the Stadium, along with a slightly more honest explanation of what had happened to the National Wrestling Alliance. Specifically, Major suggested that the National Wrestling Alliance had once been located in South Florida, but had recently moved to Charlotte.

Either Major didn't have a full understanding of what had actually happened, or he thought the truth might be too difficult for casual Bahamian wrestling fans to understand. While the National Wrestling Alliance had once been a multi-territory organization, NWA president Jim Crockett, Jr. – whose family had owned and operated the Mid-Atlantic wrestling territory headquartered in Charlotte for decades – had essentially absorbed and consolidated the NWA territories to form a single, nationally-focused wrestling company.

Championship Wrestling from Florida had been one of many casualties of these expansionary efforts that were either directly absorbing and depleting wrestling territories, or causing them to swiftly fade into obsolescence and insolvency.

Major promised that the quality of FCW shows would improve with time, "and that some of the new talent will mushroom into some of the big names of the sport of professional wrestling." Continuing on, Major promised that more famous names would soon arrive, but added that in the meantime he believed that he and FCW had "... an obligation to the public to provide them with continued action."

The words of Major served to be reasonably prophetic in relation to the June 25th show, as "Scotty the Body," who would blossom into the American wrestling superstar known as Raven within a decade, would make his first appearance in the Bahamas on that very show.

**Lou Perez is helped out of Nassau Stadium by Mickie Jay
and Bret Sawyer (Nassau Guardian)**

Shortly thereafter, in early July, Major announced the expansion of wrestling action into previously unreached Bahamian islands, beginning with Abaco. The first organized wrestling event not held in Nassau or Grand Bahama would take place at Abaco's Ocean View Park in Dundas Town on July 15th.

"History is being made next week," said Major, before divulging his concerns about the access of the wrestlers to suitable dressing rooms on Abaco, as well as raising the question of sufficient security. "I always felt that people in the Family Islands were a bit more disciplined. I will get my chance to prove that on the 15th. This is no one-shot deal. I am optimistic that it will be a complete success, and perhaps we can make this an ongoing thing. I believe that Abaco is a sports-minded community, and they have a tremendous wrestling following."

Wrestlers appearing on this history-making event included Keirn, Graham, future WWF women's star Luna Vachon, and the returning Tyree Pride. The next night in Nassau, Pride would be in the main event competing for FCW's version of the World Junior Heavyweight Championship owned by Denny Brown, which was a bout deemed worthy of lengthy recounting by *The Nassau Guardian*:

> "At the start of the match, Tyree took complete control in getting Brown on the canvas, but on the two count Brown would somehow overpower him and get out of a near pin. This near pinning continued for a few minutes into the match, but was suddenly stopped as Brown took advantage of an opportunity and took Tyree by surprise. Near pinning once again ensued, but this time it was Tyree who was being pinned.
>
> At this point, the crowd started clapping and shouting, 'Get up, Tyree!' Tyree finally did get up and was once again in control of the fight.
>
> Then suddenly, out of nowhere came Denny Brown. He charged into the ring and knocked the referee out. He then began to pound the strength out of Tyree. At this point the only thing that the screaming spectators could do was to watch.

It seemed as though Brown had gotten enough as he quickly disappeared out of sight.

Tyree was then announced the winner of that last and perhaps most exciting match."

Judging from that description, it is clear that Pride won the match as a result of a disqualification and was not awarded the championship. A return bout was announced for August 13th, with Brown once again defending against the Haitian Sensation, except this time the victor would be determined inside of a steel cage.

"Tyree Pride was obviously getting the better of the match and it was felt that he might have wrestled the title from Brown that night," Major told the press. "But much to the surprise of everyone, coming from the dressing room was Jim Backlund who came to the aid of Denny Brown."

The second main-event encounter between Brown and Pride would also be the second steel-cage bout in the history of the Bahamas, preceded only by Pride's memorable steel-cage clash with Kevin Sullivan.

Pride successfully captured the FCW World Junior Heavyweight Championship from Brown during their cage match, and when he returned to Nassau in September to defend his newly won belt, it marked the renewal of his rivalry with "The Prince of Darkness" Kevin Sullivan.

The rest of the card revealed how other experienced wrestlers had emerged to help fill out the FCW roster, including veterans Dick Slater, Danny Spivey, Brett Sawyer and Bill Irwin, who wrestled as "Super Destroyer." Also added to the roster were two members of the Laurinaitis family – Johnny Ace and The Terminator – the younger brothers of wrestling megastar Joe Laurinaitis, who performed under face paint as Road Warrior Animal.

As the top draw in Nassau, Pride continued to defend his World Junior Heavyweight Championship at the Stadium even though challengers like Dick Slater, who he wrestled twice in back-to-back October encounters that left him bloody, were far too large to be realistically classified as junior heavyweights.

The Nasty Boys tag team also joined FCW in October. Major acknowledged that the two former American Wrestling Association stars and future holders of championship gold in both the World Wrestling Federation and World Championship Wrestling "were a big hit with fans."

"We knew Steve Keirn from when he showed up in Tennessee when we were wrestling there," explained Nasty Boy Brian Knobbs. "Jerry Sags and I had just gotten fired from the AWA. After that, we showed up at Steve's door in Tampa and said, 'Hey, Steve! Remember when you told us we could come down any time? Well, we're down here for a job!'"

Rather than sleeping at the Sportatorium with several other members of the other FCW roster, the antihero team with the 1980s punk gimmick found other accommodations.

"First we stayed at the Tampa Bay Motor Lodge, which was a dump, and then Mike Graham gave us his Suburban to live out of," said Knobbs. "Mike finally asked us to help him with something, but we stayed out partying until 8:00 a.m. and weren't there to help Mike with whatever it was he needed. The next day, he left a message for us to drop the truck off and leave the keys, so then we didn't have a car to drive either!"

The Nasty Boys were quickly joined on the cards by young Dustin Rhodes, along with the giant construction-hat-wearing wrestler "U.S. Steel," who was Dusty Rhodes' brother-in-law Fred Ottman. AWA veteran Scott Hall also joined the lineup in time for the company's year-ending Nassau card on December 30th.

Shortly after this FCW event, Hamilton returned to Nassau with his rebranded Coastal Championship Wrestling, and utilized a classic wrestling trope to gather attention from the Nassau media. A scuffle between women's wrestlers Bambi and Black Venus broke out when Venus became annoyed that TK Productions representative Adrian Thompson was devoting too much time to interviewing Bambi.

*Nassau Guardian* reporter Andrew Coakley was present on the scene and reported the words that were exchanged in the lounge of the Poinciana Inn:

"'Hey, what the hell are you doing?' shouted Black Venus as she came across the room, making her way towards Thompson. 'You're going to talk all the time to her? And what about me? You're going to ignore me and not talk to me? Is that what this is all about? She is nothing! Do you understand me?'

What ensued was the slapping of Thompson by Venus, followed by a brawl and a hair-pulling session. CCW commissioner Ben Masters, Rocky Johnson and Larry Hamilton broke up the fight, which led to the following exchange:

'Who do you think you are, shoving me?' demanded Johnson. 'You want to get it on now, huh?'

'Gentlemen, please!' said Masters, trying to restore order. 'Please. Saturday night at the Poinciana Arena! This is not the place nor the time!'

'Why not try and do it now?!' responded Johnson.

'Saturday night at the Poinciana Arena, not here,' remarked Masters.

'Hey, man, you'll get your chance, all right?' Hamilton said, pointing at Johnson. He held up his belt in front of Johnson. 'This is what you want?' he asked. 'You'll never see the day you wear this.'"

Also present at the press conference was "Pistol" Pez Whatley, who hadn't appeared in the Bahamas since being screwed out of the Championship Wrestling from Florida version of the Bahamas championship in his match against Buddy Rose. Whatley was set to face Doug Furnas to crown the inaugural holder of CCW's brand new version of the Bahamas championship at the forthcoming event.

"Well, everybody knows that the Pistol man is the real Bahamas champion," boasted Whatley at the press conference. "I don't even know why we're having this match, because when I left here, I was the champion. Doug Furnas, I know that he's one heck of a wrestler and one heck of a strong man, but I've been the baddest one walking and talking on this island for a long time, and I will continue to do so!"

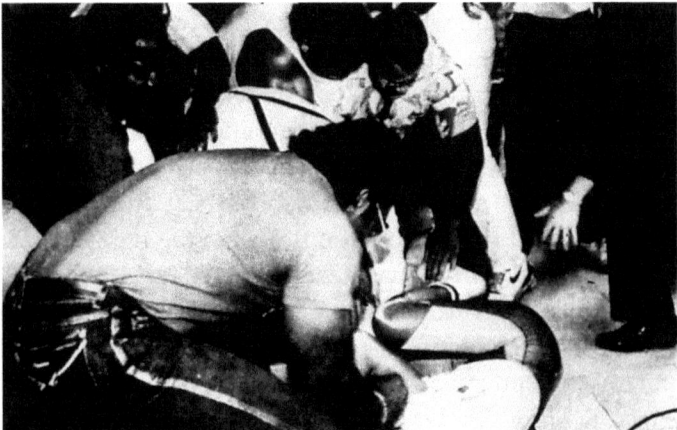

Aftermath of a scuffle between Black Venus and Bambi at the Poinciana Inn (Derek Smith/Nassau Guardian)

**"Pistol" Pez Whatley**
**CCW Bahamas Heavyweight Champion**

Whatley would go on to capture the Bahamas championship that evening, making him the first wrestler to hold multiple versions of Bahamian gold. To represent his organization's Bahamas championship belt, Hamilton used a Caribbean championship belt that had been given to him by a third party; expert championship beltmaker Dave Millican evaluated it and determined it to be an original Caribbean tag team championship belt made by Reggie Parks for the World Wrestling Council during the late 1980s.

"I also recall putting the Bahamas championship on Dutch Mantel during that period," said Hamilton.

In early 1989, the World Junior Heavyweight Championship of Tyree Pride was phased out in favor of the FCW Caribbean Junior Heavyweight Championship. A closer inspection of the championship belt reveals the initials "CCW" at the top of the main plate. The CCW initials appear to indicate that the belt was originally intended to be used in Hamilton's Coastal Championship Wrestling organization before Pride began making appearances for FCW.

"That was Tyree's personal championship belt," said Keirn. "It looked good, so we let him use it."

A momentous shakeup in the early months of 1989 for both the Bahamas and the entirety of the region serviced by Florida Championship Wrestling was caused by the return of Dusty Rhodes.

The American Dream had been fired from World Championship Wrestling not too long after the organization had formed. Jim Crockett Promotions had been purchased by billionaire media mogul Ted Turner after profligate spending had landed JCP in dire financial straits. In WCW, Rhodes had pushed the creative envelope by bleeding on camera while being spiked in the eye by the Road Warriors, Hawk and Animal, and this unapproved bloodletting contributed directly to his dismissal.

Coincidental with Rhodes' arrival, FCW changed its name to "The Professional Wrestling Federation" to accentuate its intention of appealing to fans beyond the physical boundaries of Florida.

"Dusty was definitely a guy who was going to put people in seats," said Keirn. "In Florida, he was the hottest thing here, and the hottest thing that was ever around here."

When the PWF brought wrestling to the Bahamas with a familiar and popular face like Rhodes on the card for the first time in five years, Keirn recalls the fans responding with joy.

"The Bahamian fans were great people, and they had a blast at our shows," stated Keirn. "It was almost a celebration for them. It was one of the only forms of live entertainment that would come there from outside the country on a regular basis that they had an interest in. We were on television in Florida twice a week, on Saturday and Sunday. I'm not sure what the Bahamians' programming was, but it was one thing they could relate to."

Not content to simply place advertisements in Nassau's newspapers and hope for the best, Keirn sent out a street team to raise awareness for Rhodes' return.

"I put Dusty on the back of a truck and had him riding through the streets of Nassau playing the drums and telling people to come to Nassau Stadium," said Keirn.

Knobbs and Sags of The Nasty Boys was right next to Dusty throughout the ride.

"Dusty was calling it 'Flamingo Madness,'" laughed Knobbs. "Sags and I were there next to Dusty, and he was cutting up the whole time and had us laughing. He said, 'Would you believe the American Dream is riding down the street in the back of a truck on a 100-degree day in the middle of Nassau, Bahamas?!'"

Now possessing an ownership stake in the PWF, Dusty returned to headlining shows at Nassau Stadium for the first time in more than five years, and the crowds were raucous for the return of the former NWA Bahamas Heavyweight Champion. Rhodes wrestled the renamed "Big Steel Man" Fred Ottman in the main events of PWF's shows in front of sellout crowds, and defended his brand new PWF Heavyweight

Championship in the process. The Nasty Boys also received thunderous applause from the Bahamian fans, especially for their matches against Johnny Ace and the Terminator.

"Wrestling the Terminator and Johnny Ace was a highlight for us, because no one had ever gotten that type of pop over there except for guys like Tyree Pride and Dusty Rhodes," recalled Knobbs. "And here we were just three years into the business, and we were getting that kind of pop as babyfaces in the Bahamas of all places! They were fantastic matches and we enjoyed wrestling over there. People were literally climbing the trees to watch the matches, that's how crazy it was."

From Knobbs' perspective, wrestling in Nassau was a highlight of his entire career even though he was flat broke at the time and struggled to find food.

"It was a great experience and a good time for a couple of guys in their 20s with no money," laughed Knobbs. "The funny thing was that we didn't get paid until after the shows, and we were only making 50 bucks for the trip. So, before the matches, we were hitting up Johnny Ace since he was the only one with a credit card. We'd complain, 'Johnny, we have no money yet! Buy us a cheeseburger or some fries or something!'"

To Bill Alfonso, who was a referee in both CWF and the PWF, there was little difference between the reception the two companies received from Nassau fans at the Stadium.

"The crowd was still raucous when I was over there with the PWF, but it was always raucous if you had stars that the people knew," said Alfonso. "If we went over with Dusty and Steve Keirn and Mike Graham, it felt like another Florida wrestling show. It was very similar. Dusty demanded professionalism and had no tolerance for bullshit, so it was a grade-A show all the time. He was one of my favorite people in wrestling. He was my boss as the booker, and I learned so much from him. I learned how to produce and be a booker and a finish guy, which helped me a lot when I was in Extreme Championship Wrestling a few years later."

Bahamian Rhapsody

With Nassau Stadium packed and Dusty Rhodes in the main events, the wrestling programs of 1989 had Bahamians feeling like it was 1984 all over again. That's precisely when Bahamian fans received a grim and sobering reminder of how crestfallen the ending to 1984 had left them.

## Sixteen: Blame the Nasty Boys

Despite the pleasant reception received by Dusty
Rhodes and the rest of the PWF roster from the vocal
wrestling fans of the Bahamas, any triumphs were
short-lived. After only a few short months of appearing for the
PWF, both Rhodes and his brother-in-law Fred Ottman left
Florida behind in order to sign with Vince McMahon's World
Wrestling Federation.

Instead of wearing his customary ring gear on WWF
programming, Rhodes was attired in a memorable but atypical
polka-dotted outfit, while the gargantuan Ottman was renamed
"Tugboat," and supplied with a sailor hat and candy-striped
tank top.

"Dusty left to play the polka-dot guy in the WWF
without any warning, and people were bailing on us left and
right," described Keirn. "Dusty bailed at a *really* bad time
because he left us with a Learjet expense among other bills he'd
run up. Our company's truck also got repossessed. Everything
was in my name because I was listed as the president of the
company."

Coincidentally, Rhodes also departed with the PWF
heavyweight championship belt, which would be handed to
Lex Luger in WCW years later – complete with a temporary
metal plate grafted on top of it to hide the "Professional
Wrestling Federation" name – as an emergency belt
replacement after Ric Flair had been fired by WCW, and left
for the WWF while bringing the original WCW championship
belt along with him.

Despite the dire straits Rhodes left Keirn and the
PWF's other original owners in, Keirn harbored no resentment
toward the departing wrestling icon who left him in such a
terrible bind.

"Even to the day he passed away, Dusty and I were
friends," said Keirn. "He was my big brother. Big brothers can
bully you and belittle you, but if someone says something
about you, your big brother has your back. Did I like Dusty all

the time? Hell no! Sometimes I hated him. When Dusty bailed, he was probably hurting for money. I never even brought it up to him."

**Brady Boone preparing to land across the knees of Steve Keirn (The Nassau Tribune)**

In the wake of the departures of Rhodes and Ottman, the PWF continued to make appearances in the Bahamas throughout 1989, and expanded its reach onto additional islands that had previously been untouched by professional wrestling. In addition to Nassau Stadium, the Freeport YMCA, and Abaco's Ocean View Park, Steve Keirn and Charlie Major brought PWF action to the Palmetto Point Park in Eleuthera.

"A lot of wrestling fans will be there. The wrestlers are really enthused and looking forward to their first trip to Eleuthera," stated Major to *The Nassau Guardian*, before adding that he was presently looking at hosting wrestling events on other islands, "namely Andros and Exuma."

The primary matches on the Eleuthera card would be Steve Keirn defending what was once again the most prestigious championship remaining in his company – the Florida Heavyweight Championship – against Kendall Windham. Undersized Tyree Pride also defended his personal championship – which was supposedly a *junior* heavyweight championship – against Nick Busick, a stocky, explosively strong ex-powerlifter who weighed 260 pounds.

Principal ownership of the PWF was then acquired by Wayne Coulter according to an August 18th, 1989 article of *The Tampa Tribune*. The same article describes a chaotic scene in Nassau where Coulter got roughed up by the audience. Bill Alfonso described that as just an average night at Nassau Stadium.

"I felt like I was in danger there more times than I can guess," laughed Alfonso. "Any time there was a match where a popular babyface got screwed, the crowd would start throwing rocks and brushes and shoes, so I'd have to have eyes in the back of my head to keep from getting hit with a rock or a Beck's bottle or a Heineken bottle."

Whenever trouble brewed, Alfonso always had a pre-planned strategy for escape.

"I'd have to slide out of the ring, do whatever I had to do to protect my head, and then try to make it back inside," said Alfonso. "All the heat is being drawn by the bad guys; they weren't trying to hit me. So I could simply slide out of the ring while the bad guy is taking all the heat."

Keirn said Wayne Coulter was ultimately ineffective in his PWF managerial position because he was incapable of relating to the wrestlers.

"Coulter wanted to have a leadership role, but if you were not part of the wrestling business, it was hard for you to break from a zero level to a level of control because you had no respect for your talent," explained Keirn. "We were trying to polish Wayne up to see what he could do, but when you walk into the dressing room and try to tell wrestlers what to do, the guys in there need to respect you."

Given the personal nature of wrestling, Keirn said it's almost impossible for non-wrestlers to effectively communicate to wrestlers why they should be willing to accept the desired match outcomes proposed by the bookers.

"The only way they're really going to respect you is if you've done it, and if you've done it all your life," said Keirn. "Wayne was never going to be able to explain to a wrestler why they should lose a match when he's never been asked to lose a match before in his life."

With Rhodes no longer headlining shows, Keirn would lean heavily on Tyree Pride to be an attraction at Bahamian wrestling events.

"I would use Tyree Pride because he was a Haitian," Keirn stated. "There are a lot of Haitians living on the island, and he would speak in Haitian Creole to them when he did his interviews."

Upon being informed that Pride was actually St. Lucian by birth, Keirn jokingly said, "It's a good thing he never mentioned that to me because I never would've booked him again! Seriously, though, Tyree did a great job. I liked Tyree. He had a bit of an ego, but a lot of guys have egos in our industry."

"Tyree Pride really was the Haitian Sensation down there," added Knobbs. "He had *tons* of fans."

Unavoidably, in the middle of one of the PWF shows headlined by Pride at Nassau Stadium, a riot broke out during Pride's bout against Kendall Windham, which came as a surprise of no one familiar with the reactions of Bahamian fans to Pride's matches in Nassau.

"The police in the Bahamas have clubs as weapons, and that doesn't stand up well to a folding chair when it's being used as a weapon," laughed Keirn. "I remember watching them try to hold the audience back. They were waving their clubs around to keep order, but they also looked like they were getting scared and getting ready to run all at the same time. Kendall Windham was out there trying to fight the audience, and I had to run out there in the middle of it."

Keirn described folding chairs flying into the fray like frisbees.

"I had to grab Kendall Windham and say, 'The only place to be during a riot is under the ring. Get under the ring! Get under the ring!'" described Keirn. "We all went bailing under the ring until the audience calmed down. That's actually the safest place to be during a riot. The fans in the Bahamas were usually like a keg of dynamite ready to have a fuse lit."

**Luna Vachon crashes down on top of Candy King**

Special arrangements were critical in order for the PWF to make trips to the Bahamas profitable, or even to keep from losing money on them, and Keirn said he was required to rely on favors and subsidies to make the arrangement work.

"Running shows in the Bahamas started off as an easy thing because we had a deal with Bahamasair back then," explained Keirn. "They would fly us there and back for free as long as we put an advertisement on our TV show for them. Colin Lightbourn, the owner of the Pilot House and the Poop Deck, comped all of our rooms and our food, so we didn't have to pay any of the basic expenses. We also had a Bahamian business partner, which allowed us to go through customs without any hitches. Running a show in the Bahamas can be a pretty big money-loser for a promoter who doesn't understand the whole system and doesn't know how to benefit from it."

In the meantime, other organizations tried their hand at promoting events in Nassau. Blackjack Mulligan held an event at the Poinciana Arena during the fall of 1989, with Buggsy McGraw being among the wrestlers invited to perform on the card.

"There was hardly anyone in attendance; the place was practically empty," said McGraw. "The show went on, and when it was all over with, Blackjack issued me the payoff with all of these hundred-dollar bills. I asked him how he could afford to do this when no one showed up, and he told me not to worry about it."

Also present at the show was Jerry Grey.

"There were *literally* four people in the crowd," Grey said. "Blackjack told us all that Charlie Major had sabotaged the show and somehow stopped people from showing up."

The answer to the question of how Blackjack Mulligan had been able to afford to issue such generous payoffs for a poorly attended show was answered in the early months of 1990. While waiting at the airport to board his Bahamasair flight for an event in Nassau, Keirn was ushered away to tend to an urgent matter involving Brickhouse Brown. The wrestler had been caught trying to get a gun through the security checkpoint in his luggage.

"The security team was holding him up against a wall," said Keirn. "He was blaming the whole thing on his wife, claiming that she had put the gun in his bag to intentionally set him up because she hated him and wanted him to get arrested."

In the process of attending to Brown, Keirn also lost track of Blackjack Mulligan and Kendall Windham, who had been with him at the airport prior to the distraction.

"I get on the plane, and there's no Blackjack and no Kendall even though they'd just been with me in the airport," continued Keirn. "So we had *three* guys advertised for the show who didn't show up."

Mulligan and Windham had already been arrested for their involvement in a massive counterfeiting ring by undercover officers on December 22nd of 1989. Apparently afraid that the pair might attempt to flee the country to avoid sentencing, the authorities collected them and detained them at the airport.

Aside from this mishap, the PWF continued to run shows in the Bahamas undeterred during the early stages of 1990. The organization made its first trip to Spanish Wells of all places – an island with a population of only around 1,000 people at the time.

Local businessman Anthony "Buddha" Pinder, who had become a legitimate acquaintance of Kevin Sullivan during the latter's scuba diving adventures in the greater Eleuthera area, helped to facilitate the arrangement that brought wrestling to what was, at least at the time, one of the least-visited locales in the Bahama Islands.

"Spanish Wells was unbelievable," described Keirn. "I went there because I was told It was the lobster capital of the world. I assumed it was also the cocaine capital of the world because everybody had these big gold necklaces on. The thing was, at night, they wouldn't allow any Black people on the island. Everybody Black had to leave! Spanish Wells was full of blonde people, and it seemed like all of them were lobster fishermen. They had plenty of money and nothing to do, which is exactly what a wrestling promoter like me wanted to hear."

According to Keirn, everything in the Bahamas seemed to be progressing at a sustainable level right up until the Nasty Boys trashed portions of the Pilot House with fire extinguishers, thereby destroying the goodwill the wrestlers had built up with Colin Lightbourn over the years.

**The author of this book with businessman Anthony "Buddha" Pinder on Spanish Wells**

"The Nasty Boys didn't do major damage, but it was more than enough to get us kicked out of there," Keirn admitted.

Brian Knobbs of The Nasty Boys tells the story a little bit differently.

"We didn't *trash* the hotel. The real deal was that there was a lot of sex, drugs and rock and roll going on, as they say," began Knobbs. "Mickie Jay was staying with Ron Slinker, and they had some illegal substances on them at the time, which were plentiful to get over there. We banged on the door, and they opened it. Sags had a fire extinguisher and just doused the room."

Whatever drugs Jay and Slinker had been partaking in that evening were now on the floor, having been absorbed into the foam from the fire extinguisher that had coated the hotel room.

"The whole thing was intended to be a joke on Mickie Jay, but it *did* get us kicked out of there," continued Knobbs. "Keirn always blamed us, but that's typical. The Nasty Boys get blamed for *everything*. We were always either in the vicinity, or we were directly involved. Don't get me wrong; we did a *lot* of things, but there was also a lot of stuff we didn't do and got blamed for it anyway!"

While Keirn missed visiting the Bahamas with regularity, there were elements of those trips he certainly didn't miss.

"I still have nightmares about sitting in those fiberglass chairs at Immigration," stated Keirn. "Every time we landed, we got hauled away to sit in a room until Charlie Major showed up with our work permits. Sometimes we were sitting there for three hours before he showed up. Then he'd walk in, talk to the folks at Immigration for a couple minutes, and then he'd say, 'Okay, let's go.' It made us wonder why he couldn't have called to tell them we were okay, or what took him so long. It seemed like sometimes he didn't even remember that we were coming in."

Keirn said he also missed intentionally driving a hard bargain during his negotiations with vendors at Nassau's famous Straw Market.

"The salespeople would invite me over to look at a shirt," said Keirn. "I'd look at the shirt and say, 'It's better in the Bahamas, huh? Okay... how about I give you *a dollar* for it?' They'd say, 'Mr. Keirn! That's not fair! You're rich!' and I'd say, 'What does that have to do with it? Make me an offer!' I always got a kick out of starting negotiations there with a dollar no matter what the item was."

With PWF wrestlers running afoul of Colin Lightbourn and instigating the dissolution of an agreement at the Pilot House that had allowed the wrestlers to receive favorable accommodations in Nassau for quite some time, Keirn abruptly halted the running PWF events in the Bahamas.

Now without a nearby wrestling organization to regularly bring to the Bahamas, Major searched elsewhere, and soon partnered with Fred Jung of the Canadian International Wrestling Federation. The pair quickly booked an event called "Wrestling Riot in The Bahamas" on May 19th at the Poinciana Arena, and not at Major's Nassau Stadium for some reason.

"We are hoping that this show is very successful, and if it is, we plan to continue to have shows here," Jung told *The Guardian*, adding that this was the CIWF's first show outside of Canada in a bid to turn the company into an international success.

The main event featured a steel cage match between Don Muraco and Abbuda Dein, and was supported by a dog-collar match between the Junkyard Dog and "Cowboy" Bob Orton. Active PWF wrestlers like Tyree Pride, The Nasty Boys, Dick Slater and Scott McGhee filled out the bulk of the undercard.

**CIWF president Fred Jung and VP Allen Walker with Charlie Major Jr.**
**(Nassau Guardian)**

226

Major appeared to take a thinly veiled dig at PWF's perceived lack of reliability in his *Nassau Guardian* interview, stating that he had acquired signed contracts from all of the wrestlers booked at the event, and had personally spoken with the majority of them to verify their commitment to appearing at the show.

"They are all looking forward to putting on the best wrestling show the Bahamas has ever seen," promised Major.

Despite the hype for the CIWF event, Don Muraco elaborated that there was nothing particularly special about it.

"It was just a small independent show in Nassau," said Muraco. "I honestly don't know what I was doing that far east. That was just a quick show with a small crew. There wasn't a whole lot to it other than flying in, doing the show, and then flying back out in the morning. I'm sure it was nice to see Nassau and go to the beach. It's a lot different from Hawaii. The water in Hawaii is so mysterious and sudden. The Bahamian water is beautiful; the sand is grainy and fine. They also have different types of sharks there. I can't do much scuba diving, though. At my size it's tough to find a wetsuit that fits!"

The Canadian International Wrestling Federation never staged another event in the Bahamas, and for the second time in three years, the Bahama Islands would once again find themselves without a sustained source of live pro wrestling entertainment within a wrestling company's defined territory.

Despite this, others would set their sights on making the Bahamas a profitable location for wrestling events, including one of largest companies in the history of the wrestling industry.

## Seventeen: Grasping at Straws

The refusal of the Canadian International Wrestling Federation to return to Nassau didn't mean the wrestling world was altogether finished with the Bahamas. On September 29th, World Championship Wrestling visited Nassau Stadium, marking the first wrestling event in the Bahamas ever staged by a well-funded company with national television access and global ambitions.

Wrestling in Nassau Stadium probably imbued several of the wrestlers who worked that night with a sense of déjà vu. Most of the matches included former CWF wrestlers who thought they had left the occasionally threatening confines of the Stadium behind them when they began wrestling for a wrestling company bankrolled by a billionaire.

The event consisted of the tag team known as "Doom" – comprising Butch Reed and Ron Simmons – competing against the Rock 'n Roll Express, Lex Luger dueling with former NWA champion Harley Race, the Southern Boys wrestling against the Fabulous Freebirds team of Michael Hayes and Jimmy Garvin, Tommy Rich versus Blade Hunter, Candy Man paired with Bobby Eaton, and Tyree Pride – who was never under WCW contract and would have been an unimaginable participant for the company in almost any other setting – defending his personal Caribbean junior heavyweight championship belt against Kevin Sullivan.

"I was responsible for helping to put that show together, and I knew that Tyree and I would definitely help us draw there in case the fans didn't care about anything else," said Sullivan.

A bout scheduled between Mike Rotunda and Stan Lane had originally been on the card, but was canceled. Along with Bobby Eaton, Lane functioned as one half of the second version of "The Midnight Express" – a tag team guided by managerial legend Jim Cornette. Neither Eaton nor Cornette opted to make the trip to Nassau for the show.

228

"I never worked in the Bahamas, as the only time we were ever booked there was for WCW," offered Cornette. "And with relations between us and the company the way they were, and Stan having worked there before and shared stories of being pelted with rocks and piss and filthy conditions in the rings and locker rooms, Stan and I both no-showed on purpose. Bobby went and came back and told us we were right!"

In his autobiography, WCW's ring announcer at the time, Gary Michael Cappetta, described the event as uneventful, aside from him having to dodge "a few flying objects that burst through frayed strands of chicken wire." However, he ultimately chalked up the WCW management team's dissatisfaction with the event to its financial failure, which he attributed to the show's earnings being underreported by the Stadium's owner.

It was a criticism that was shared by others who had tried their hands at running shows at Nassau Stadium during its later years as a wrestling venue.

"Charlie was the classic case of promoters having deep pockets and short fingers," laughed Steve Keirn. "You could never get a good reading on how a show was doing. I'd even stand there with a counter and walk around to count the crowd myself. Then I'd go to the box office and check, and Charlie and I wouldn't even be close in terms of where the money should have been."

In the end, Keirn chalked up the refusal of wrestling companies to return to the Bahamas in later years to the difficulty in collecting what they were owed.

"How are you going to get off of the island if you have a dispute with a promoter with local connections?" asked Keirn. "You *still* have to leave. You really just had to get whatever you could from Charlie and be satisfied with it."

To be completely fair, Joe Malenko explained how everyone connected with an independent wrestling show is at tremendous financial risk no matter what country the shows are held in.

"I would say 80 percent of the independent shows I worked on were never worth it from a financial standpoint," said Malenko. "By the time you got to places and you had to deal with the ins and outs of being on the road, you walked away with practically nothing, or sometimes you were in the hole. More often than not, you would get stiffed. If you were working for an independent company anywhere, you were usually taking home the short end of the stick."

Far from merely attaching blame to other wrestling promoters, Malenko was able to draw from his experiences watching his own father pay wrestlers less than he had initially promised them.

"Even people who worked for my dad, he would sometimes have to tell them that he knew he promised them one thing, but he was a little short that night and would have to catch up with them later," said Malenko. "*Nobody* made great money. Even when you ran paid shows where everything was paid to you up front, you still had the expenses of getting there, staying there, and the time away. Most guys who were working on independent shows had other jobs, so they're taking time away from things that they're making money at to probably make a lot less by actually wrestling. On the flipside of that, if you take away the money piece, the chance to be in the ring and on the road with a group of guys has a pretty good value to it."

The following year, in June of 1991, International World Class Championship Wrestling made its own attempt at holding a show at Nassau Stadium. The event was billed as "Nassau Mania – Where Only The Strong Survive."

IWCCW was formed when the New-England-based International Championship Wrestling company – owned by the Savoldi family – purchased the rights to the famous name of World Class Championship Wrestling. The Dallas-based WCCW had been owned and operated for many years by the legendary Von Erich wrestling family, and had once grown a sizeable international following through the sale of its syndicated television programming.

Despite the relatively small size of their wrestling promotion, the Savoldis aired their programs in syndication throughout the U.S., and they followed the reach of their program all the way to Nassau for the June show, headlined by "Mr. USA" Tony Atlas defending the ICW World Heavyweight Championship against Tito Santana, and with an undercard buoyed by a match between Dory Funk Jr. and Abdullah the Butcher.

*The Nassau Guardian* reported in its June 5th edition that a spokesperson for D. Glen Promotions, the promoters for the event, identified both Abdullah and Funk as "bleeders." If this was an attempt to hype the match, it was a bit of a misrepresentation; Terry Funk was the Funk brother with the reputation for being a wild man and a bleeder, not the methodical technician Dory Funk Jr.

Atlas earned his "Mr. USA" alias by winning the "Mr. USA" bodybuilding competition on three separate occasions. He had also teamed with Rocky Johnson as part of "The Soul Patrol" to become the first African American tag team to win the WWF World Tag Team Championship in 1983.

In a somewhat surprising move for a heel wrestler, Atlas addressed the students of E.P. Roberts Primary School during a special assembly, stressing the importance of acquiring an education, and advising the very young children "money and drugs can be taken away from you, but your education, no one can take."

The appearance by Atlas as a role model at the E.P. Roberts assembly is surprising since he was working for IWCCW in a rule-breaking capacity, and his match the next night would be against Tito Santana, who wrestled almost exclusively as a fan-favorite throughout his career. Nonetheless, Atlas also spoke specifically of the challenges faced by Black youth, which is a message for which he was certainly a better conduit than Santana.

Charlie Major Jr. appeared alongside Atlas during the E.P. Roberts school assembly, and was identified as being the Nassau Stadium manager for the IWCCW show as opposed to

being the event's promoter. For this specific show, that
responsibility fell to Glen Lowe.

Rusty Brooks, who wrestled as "Cannonball" at the
IWCCW show, recalled staying at the Pilot House before the
show, and also eating at the Poop Deck.

"I wound up scuba diving with Dory Funk and one of
the other wrestlers," said Brooks. "We went to the dive shop
right next to the Poop Deck. Bill Apter from the wrestling
magazines was there next to the scuba shop doing interviews. I
think it was Kevin Sullivan I went to the Stadium with. The
show was already packed before we got there, and we did not
have an escort into the building."

Dory Funk Jr. recalled that particular scuba-diving trip
because of his surprising interaction with one of the ocean's
denizens.

"I remember that I ran up on an octopus," laughed
Funk. "I got quite a shock. I was looking at little fish, and all of

a sudden there was an octopus looking at me, and I never swam so fast in my life to get away from it. I swam all the way to the beach to get away!"

According to Brooks, Savoldi was unfamiliar with the Bahamian "island-time" practice of arriving late to the shows, and it made him nervous.

"Savoldi was panicking because he thought we were going to lose our asses, financially speaking," laughed Brooks. "I had to tell him not to worry, and that this was normal. Everything on the islands was about an hour behind time. It had to be intermission before the place got packed, and then you were left wondering where everyone suddenly came from."

Keirn was not at all concerned about the IWCCW event at Nassau Stadium would mean for his Professional Wrestling Federation.

"By the time June of 1991 came around, I was already making plans to leave the PWF behind," said Keirn. "I also had a Florida-based territory, and if someone was going to steal part of a Florida territory from me at that time, the Bahamas would be the part of the territory I'd want them to take."

Based on the results of the event, and IWCCW's handling of it, the show had not been optimized to ingratiate the company with Bahamian fans who were viewing the Savoldis' wrestling product for the first time. This is best exemplified by the main event, which was included in IWCCW's "The Best of Tito Santana" compilation, and which also includes footage of Santana being interviewed by Bill Apter out by the ocean.

The match was treated as a continuation of ongoing storylines within the promotion, to which the majority of Bahamian fans in attendance were not privy. Also, the conclusion of the contest involved the use of brass knuckles by Tony Atlas after interference by his manager.

To summarize, IWCCW held a wrestling event in a brand-new location where fans were accustomed to watching title-holding, Black babyfaces overcome White heels in matches that usually had clean finishes. However, even after the Black champion had regaled a local school's children with a stay-in-school message, fans impressed by that message and with no other knowledge of IWCCW's product came to the arena that night and watched the Black champion cheat incessantly before losing through an unsatisfying disqualification finish.

**Mike Graham executes a fireman's carry takedown on Starr Rider Blade at Nassau Stadium (Derek Smith/Nassau Guardian)**

The footage of the event also shows an uncharacteristically lukewarm crowd at Nassau Stadium, which is understandable given the factors involved with the presentation of the show. However, the most striking element to the show's footage is the use of a hilarious cutaway shot that shows a crowd consisting of an entirely White audience wearing long-sleeve shirts and sweatshirts. In all probability, it was footage extracted from an IWCCW event in Upstate New York, as it was clearly not taken within 1,000 miles of Nassau Stadium.

The Savoldis never ran another show in Nassau, and Steve Keirn and the PWF were also on their way out. Keirn held one final event at Nassau Stadium on June 29th of 1991, which wound up being the PWF's swansong.

"By 1991, I was grasping at straws," said Keirn. "When I wrestled Tyree Pride in Nassau, I was even pushing myself into being a heel to make the match happen. I knew I could make the crowd mad, but given what tended to happen in Nassau, did I really want to make the fans *that* mad?"

Keirn dropped the PWF Florida Heavyweight Championship to Pride at Nassau Stadium, and shut down his company shortly thereafter to accept a job with the World Wrestling Federation as "Skinner," a tobacco-spitting alligator wrestler from the Florida Everglades.

"Dusty pretty much put us in a financial hole that we could never climb out of," said Keirn. "I had to go work for the WWF as Skinner just to pay off those bills he left me with!"

With PWF officially closed, the Bahamas did not get much in the way of professional wrestling action for the next few years, with occasional visits like a pair of shows promoted by Wayne Coulter that featured Tommy Rich and the Junkyard Dog, both of whom were nearly a full decade past their respective primes.

Years later, World Championship Wrestling made its second trip to Nassau on May 7th, 1994, and they booked the first wrestling event ever to be held at the Queen Elizabeth Sports Centre, a logical venue for a company of their size.

The show was headlined by a WCW world championship match between Sting and Ravishing Rick Rude, and the undercard included a match for the United States title between Ricky Steamboat and "Stunning" Steve Austin, along with Dustin Rhodes and Arn Anderson facing the Nasty Boys, and Kevin Sullivan squaring off with Johnny B. Badd. Promotional materials for the event made the mistake of swapping the championships that were defended in the two most noteworthy bouts.

"We had a great house at that show, because it was rare for a major company like WCW to come to Nassau," said Knobbs. "I brought my wife Toni over there along with her parents, and I remember partying with Rick Rude and the boys over at Club Waterloo because we already knew everyone there from our days in Florida Championship Wrestling."

The very next month, wrestling megastar Hulk Hogan signed with World Championship Wrestling, which marked the adoption of an aggressive competitive stance by WCW against Hogan's former employers in the World Wrestling Federation. Any plans WCW may have had to return to Nassau were indefinitely put on hold, and the WCW event in Nassau in May of 1994 marked the final attempt by a major professional wrestling company with global ambitions to book a wrestling event at a Bahamian venue during the 20th century.

Southeastern promoter Hal Jeffery also tried his hand at promoting a wrestling event at Kendal Isaacs National Gymnasium on May 4th, 1996, and he brought Brian Blair, Steve Keirn, Jim Neidhart, Duke Droese, Rocky Johnson, and a few other wrestlers down to Nassau in an effort to see if any interest could be generated in wrestling.

"It was a one-time thing," said Jeffery, who was also helping Blair promote shows in India and Malaysia around the same time period. "The show didn't do very well, and we never went back there."

In retrospect, the only element from that show that stands out as momentous is that it marked the one and only time that Dwayne "The Rock" Johnson ever entered a wrestling ring in the Bahamas. The future movie megastar was in the nascent stages of his professional wrestling career, and he was also getting an opportunity to garner some in-ring experience just a short hop from his home in Miami while his famous father could carry the bulk of the action in a tag team match.

"Rocky told me he wanted me to give Dwayne my honest opinion about his wrestling, because he was really young, and Rocky thought his son had a bit of an attitude," recalled Blair. "Quite honestly, for it to be one of Dwayne's very first matches, it wasn't bad at all."

At this stage of its development, the Bahamas was already beginning to appeal to a new generation of tourists. The country had survived an early 1990s downturn in the tourism industry, and Sol Kerzner was already in the process of erecting a resort development on Paradise Island that would soon become one of the most enduring landmarks of the Bahamas – The Atlantis Paradise Island Resort.

Simultaneous to this, Nassau was starting to play host to a more diverse range of events that sparked worldwide interest; the 1995 World's Strongest Man competition took place in the Bahamas, with most of the events hosted and adjudicated either in Nassau or on Paradise Island, and within clear view of the water.

To his credit, Larry Hamilton was still making attempts to run shows in the Bahamas during the late 1990s, and he thought he had the perfect young wrestler on his roster to help him attract a rage-fueled crowd in Nassau.

"I wanted to put the Bahamas belt on a White guy and bring him into Nassau as the Bahamas champion," said Hamilton. "So I put the belt on Blare Rogers. Blare was so helpful when he came to work for me. When he wasn't booked, he would still come to the TV tapings in Jacksonville to commentate. He said, 'Larry, I really want to be a part of this. I don't want to be left out.'"

After getting three shows booked in Nassau during the summer months, Hamilton explained to his partner "Soulman" Alex G that he wanted to bring a White champion to Nassau as the Bahamas champion, and that Rogers would be a good pick because Hamilton's first choice was unavailable.

"I really wanted to go in with Kevin Sullivan, but there was no way I could get him away from WCW," continued Hamilton. "I actually called Kevin and told him I had this kid named Blare Rogers who was a super nice guy who was young, talented, had good size and could think in the ring. Kevin told me to talk to Blare and see how his mind is."

Hamilton called Rogers and invited him down to the television studio ahead of the Saturday TV taping of their wrestling program.

"So he came into the little studio I had, and I told him, 'I want to do a deal in the next couple weeks where I put the Bahamas belt on you, and I want to take you to the Bahamas as my Bahamas champion,'" said Hamilton. "We held a tournament to put the belt on 'Soul Train' Garmon, but after he won it, Blare challenged him and then beat him on the third try."

In addition to Garmon and Rogers, Hamilton stated that Brad Armstrong also wrestled for him as the Bahamas champions during that era. He also considered returning to the Bahamas with Puerto Rican wrestler Joe Don Smith as his

Bahamas champion facing Doug Furnas, but Furnas opted to wrestle in Japan instead.

The only other wrestling event of note to take place in the Bahamas during the 1990s was entirely fictitious, and was stated to have occurred on February 7th of 1991. The South Atlantic Pro Wrestling promotion cited Nassau as the location for a phantom title change that put the South Atlantic Pro Wrestling Heavyweight Championship on Vince Torelli, who would soon be a world-famous mixed martial artist under his real name, Ken Shamrock.

Undoubtedly, the remote nature of Nassau relative to the North Carolina area where South Atlantic Pro Wrestling's shows were typically held made it an attractive location for a championship to spuriously change hands. It also enabled the Bahamas to join other nations as sites where wrestling championships had misleadingly changed hands. This includes Brazil as the location of the WWF's tournament to crown the first Intercontinental Heavyweight Champion, and Egypt as the location where Leilani Kai and Judy Martin secured the WWF Women's Tag Team Championship from Velvet McIntyre and Desiree Petersen.

Just because wrestling shows were no longer physically taking place in the Bahamas with any regularity, that doesn't mean wrestling couldn't be viewed there by way of cable television. This would spark interest in a new generation of Bahamian wrestling fans, some of whom would begin to make inquiries to see if they could transform professional wrestling fandom into professional wrestling careers.

## Eighteen: Now or Never

Years before Kahagas became the first wrestler to capture the North American, National and World championships of one of the post-territorial iterations of the National Wrestling Alliance, he was simply Paul Antone of Sebring, Florida.

"I was 18 when I first tried to get into the wrestling business in Orlando," Antone said. "It was all so secretive back then, so I couldn't make any headway. Later on, I was living back home in Sebring, and it was one of those times in my life when I figured, if I was ever going to make the effort to become a pro wrestler, that was the time to do it."

Driving down the highway, Antone experienced a moment of clearly divine intervention when he glanced off to the side of the road and spotted a familiar face that he had only ever seen inside of a wrestling ring.

"I looked over and saw Tyree Pride literally sitting on a forklift in the middle of the highway doing construction," Antone laughed. "He was running a road crew. I swerved around and parked in a Red Lobster parking lot, and then I went up to Tyree and introduced myself. We wound up talking in the Red Lobster parking lot for an hour and a half. He told me he didn't have a wrestling ring he could train guys in anymore, but if I could find a ring to train in, he would come and help me."

One year later, Antone procured a wrestling ring from Sheriff Howard Godwin, a trainee of Eddie Graham's who formerly wrestled as "Tommy Horn."

"I rebuilt the ring and got it ready," explained Antone. "Tyree came out to work with me and showed me the basics. Tyree was very critiquish in terms of the realism of wrestling. One thing I learned about him is, even to this day, he never smartened his real wife up to the business. His son is in his late 20s and probably would have been in the wrestling business a lot earlier if he'd been smartened up to the business. Tyree was very kayfabe. He took everything very seriously and didn't pull any punches. If something you did during training didn't look good, he'd tell you it sucked."

Years later, in 2003, Antone found himself flying into Abaco as a member of a crew of wrestlers who had agreed to work for Tyree Pride's personal wrestling promotion. With Kevin Sullivan, The Barbarian, The Warlord, Luna Vachon and Gangrel all wrestling on the show, it was essentially an all-star tour with several wrestlers who had worked for WCW and the WWF during what became the Monday Night Wars era.

"We flew in on Bahamasair, with no air conditioning on the plane, so it was burning hot," remembered Antone. "Once we landed, we loaded ourselves in the back of a pickup truck, and the promoter paraded us around town to promote the show and make the people who lived there aware of us. Then we pulled into a small 10-room hotel, and we got out to get our rooms."

When it got close to showtime, that's when Antone claims that things got far more interesting.

"I learned that when you're dealing with people from the islands, it can be tough to get your money," explained Antone. "At one point, we were sitting around with our bags packed, and we didn't know if we were driving to the show to wrestle, or if we were going to be driving to the airport to get on a plane and get out of there. The last thing we wanted was to be stuck in a small town on a remote island where people were rioting because we no-showed the event."

As the wrestlers sat around and waited for word on where they were heading, Luna Vachon said something that Antone would never forget.

"Luna said, 'This shit is never gonna change,'" Antone recalled. "She said, 'If the promoters don't pay; we don't wrestle. Be ready to grab your bag and get the fuck out of here.'"

Fortunately, the promoter delivered the guaranteed money, and the show proceeded as scheduled. However, Antone noticed a few tell-tale signs that the promoter was trying to recoup his expenses after prepaying the wrestlers.

"We had the ring set up at an outdoor tennis court or basketball court with a fence and tarp around it," Antone laughed. "The promoter took a sharpie and marked out the old prices on the poster and wrote in new ones. Before it said '$20 ringside,' but it was scratched off and now said '$80.'"

Pride's effort to present a low-key wrestling event in Abaco is representative of what attempts to run professional wrestling shows in the Bahamas had devolved into during the 2000s. Also, with easy cable television access finally reaching the Bahamas in 1992, Bahamians had as many small-screen entertainment options at their disposal as anyone else, and it took far more than a mere announcement that wrestling had arrived on an island to attract a sea of fans to an event.

As a result of these advancements, access to standard cable television packages also meant that Bahamian wrestling fans were able to watch wrestling presented by the World Wrestling Federation and World Championship Wrestling during the heart of The Monday Night War era, thereby upping the ante for the level of live wrestling action that would be regarded as worth leaving a cozy household in order to view.

As a case in point, Omar Amir Francis fell in love with professional wrestling the very first time he ever watched it in a form presented to him on a World Wrestling Federation match on the USA Network. Yet, due to the strict nature of the household Francis was raised in on the eastern end of New Providence Island, any watching of wrestling was prohibited despite the constant chatter about it in his school's classrooms.

"I would go to school, and all of the kids whose parents weren't as strict would always say things like, 'Did you see the Undertaker and Kane at *Summerslam*?!'" said Francis. "Everyone's conversations revolved around whatever happened at the pay-per-view or *Monday Night Raw*, and I was left to sit there and say, 'Oh Lord. What the hell?' I couldn't say anything because I hadn't seen it at all."

Francis was finally granted the golden opportunity to watch some wrestling action firsthand when the television was left unguarded at his grandmother's Fox Hill residence, and no one else was in the house.

"I told myself that it was now or never," recalls Francis. "I ran into her room, I grabbed the remote, and I turned on *Monday Night Raw*. The first wrestling I ever saw involved 'Stone Cold' Steve Austin and Val Venis on *Monday Night Raw*. I watched that show and I've been hooked ever since."

Once Francis and his brother grew slightly older and the family acquired cable television, his father relented and finally permitted his sons to watch wrestling. Francis and his brother would turn every viewing of wrestling into a special occasion. They would sit down in front of the TV with toaster strudels and ice cream and watch hours of wrestling action at a time.

While wrestling excited Francis, he maintained no such fondness for schoolwork. Although he was an inarguably bright student who attended the private St. Anne's High School in Fox Hill, Francis' grades suffered due to his inattention to his studies. The shortfall was such that his father – who was laboring diligently to keep five different children enrolled in private schools – ultimately became fed up with paying high tuition rates for subpar performances.

"We would go through little periods where he would try things to motivate me, and they never really worked," conceded Francis. "We came to a point where he said he wasn't going to continue to spend money to put me in private school if I was just going to continue to get low grades. One day he said, 'I'm taking you out of St. Annes. You're going to this school that just opened on Joe Farrington Road. I'm going to send you there because it's a lot cheaper and we'll see what you decide to do.'"

The school in question was a start-up school called Galilee that was founded and operated based on the promise that it could rehabilitate students that no other schools were willing to tolerate.

"They would take the students that no other schools wanted – not just from private schools, but from public schools also," claimed Francis. "I told my dad, 'You're sending me to this school to *die!* These kids are *nuts!*' Public school in the Bahamas is rough. I'm coming from a private school where things are a lot more mellow. Public schools on the island are a little dicey. People are getting stabbed and robbed after school."

Having been filtered into a collection of similarly unmotivated peers, Francis also found his classes led by teachers who didn't even make halfhearted efforts to instruct their classes. For the bulk of the school year, students availed themselves of the television and the Nintendo 64 video game system that one of the students had brought to school and hooked up in the classroom. From the time school began to the moment it ended, Francis and his classmates would spend their day consumed by video games.

"Me being a kid and not liking school, I enjoyed it at the time, because here we are playing video games, getting decent grades, and literally not doing anything," laughed Francis. "I went to Galilee for maybe two years, and then I wound up leaving the school. The woman who ran the place accused me of something that wasn't true, and then told my dad that I'd risen up and confronted her. Bahamian children challenging the accounts of adults is pretty much un-tolerated. In that setting, it wasn't appropriate for me to disagree with something she'd said. My dad wound up sending me to a public school after that."

At this point, Francis was now enrolled at Doris Johnson High School on Prince Charles Street, and he was so unmotivated to attend his classes that he would catch the jitney bus home from school immediately after being dropped off. One day, his dad came home early and caught him, and dragged him straight back to the school. This day would culminate in an episode that would leave Francis without *any* academic institutions to attend.

"A prefect – who is basically a hall monitor – was patrolling and caught me in the classroom lying there with my head down during lunch time," said Francis. "She came in and told me I couldn't be in there. I told her that I wasn't feeling well and that I would just stay in there resting until lunch was over. She asked me to leave a few more times, and when I wouldn't go, she went and got the headmaster. She was polite about it, but I'm sure I was rude to her by the end of the conversation."

The same headmaster who had welcomed Francis back to the school following his episode of truancy entered the classroom, and he wasn't in a particularly charitable mood toward Francis following their interaction earlier in the day. The two exchanged words, and then Francis was forcibly extracted from the classroom.

"He literally grabbed me by the back of my pants and started to yank me out of the classroom," stated Francis. "I remember we got to where the railings were. I grabbed onto the railing, and I asked him, 'Why are you pulling me like this?!' In response, he slapped my hand off the railing and continued to pull me by the back of my pants all the way down the stairs and to the office."

Once the pair reached the office, the situation was further escalated. The headmaster explained to the staff members in the office how rude Francis had been, and that his disobedience and intransigence were in need of correction.

"At the time, it was still customary for headmasters to beat students," said Francis. "The headmaster said, 'Put your hands on this table. I'm about to beat you with this stick.' I told him there was no way in hell I was doing that. That's when he looked at me, then he glanced over at the other two teachers in the room. Then he picked up the stick and swung with it and hit me on my head. I immediately punched him in the face, and the two of us began exchanging blows right in the middle of the office. The physical education teacher and the principal broke us up, called my father, and then they concocted a lie and said that I attacked the headmaster unprovoked. So then they expelled me."

The embarrassed and disappointed father of Francis
then conceded that it appeared his son was finished with
school, and that he would need to get a job and start working.

Even though he wasn't even 15 years old at the time,
Francis acquired employment as a salesman at the Nassau
Glass company on Mackey Street. Fortunately, Francis spent
the next two years attending night school and earned his high
school diploma through a tiny school in Fox Hill. That's also
when Francis began modeling.

"I had a friend of mine who wanted to get into the
acting business," said Francis. "We would do parkour with him
and some other guys who were amazing gymnasts. One of
them is so good that he actually got hired by Cirque du Soleil.
Another one of them even worked in *Avengers: Infinity War* and
*Black Panther*. We did parkour everywhere, but the way the
buildings in Nassau are made isn't really conducive to parkour.
We just did the best we could, but it was more that we were
training for stunt work and learning how to tumble. We would
train at NassauNastics with Coach Ramsay. We would also film
little skits, and do it wherever we could."

Francis' friends were members of a dance studio that
was owned by OilinSha Coakley, who also owned a modeling
agency. This was around the time that several scenes for the
James Bond film *Casino Royale* were being filmed around
Nassau. Francis was introduced to Coakley, and he was soon
brought into the fold as one of Coakley's models.

This arrangement afforded Francis the opportunity to
leave the island and travel to several foreign locations, and he
even won the Supermodel of the Bahamas competition one
year. However, the heart of Francis was already set on
becoming a professional wrestler.

"By that time, I'd gotten so into wrestling that I was
totally obsessed with it," said Francis. "But we couldn't access
the pay-per-views at all. There was this guy who had a video
store and he would pirate the pay-per-views and burn them
onto DVDs that you'd have to buy. Every time there was a
pay-per-view event, I would run to him and buy the DVD so I

could watch the pay-per-view. My dad finally asked me one day, 'Are you gonna do something other than watch this wrestling? What do you want to do with your life?' That's when I told him I wanted to be a wrestler, and Dad said, 'Then you'd better get to it.'"

True to his word, Francis began lifting weights to bulk himself up, and sought out a place where he could learn something about wrestling. While he had acquired a new job working at the rock-climbing wall at the famed Atlantis Resort on Paradise Island, he also found an American who was teaching Greco-Roman wrestling classes just on the other side of the bridge in Nassau.

It was the closest thing Francis could find in the Bahamas that correlated with wrestling training in any way. It also helped him to cope with the daily frustrations of working in the tourism industry within an area of the Atlantis resort that catered to the ultra-rich.

"The rock wall was right beneath 'The Cove,'" described Francis. "It was a super expensive hotel where the rooms were thousands of dollars per night. We got some very interesting characters on the rock wall. I would get asked some of the most stupid and occasionally racist questions that you could possibly imagine. I think a lot of foreigners come there with a certain perception of island people or Black people in general. Sometimes it's very subtle in the way they'll treat you, or act, or their tone. They'll ask questions like if we lived in huts on the island. Very condescending things like that. They would insinuate that I wasn't talking the way I truly would because I sounded 'White.'"

Francis would eventually get fed up with his employment at the Atlantis Resort and begin working for Coca-Cola as a technician. At this stage, a plan had been fully formed in his mind that would result in him leaving the Bahamas to fully pursue a professional wrestling career.

"I knew I needed to find a wrestling school. That meant I had no choice other than to get off the island," affirmed Francis. "There were really no other steps to take. I'd watched the documentary *Beyond the Mat*, and that kind of put me on the right track. By the time I'd started working at Coca-Cola, I'd concocted a plan to escape Nassau. That was the final steppingstone before my departure. My goal was to save up enough money to make it over to the U.S., which in my mind was $10,000."

Upon typing a query for the nearest wrestling school into the Google search engine, Francis settled on the wrestling school owned and operated by The Dudley Boyz in Orlando, Florida.

For Dudley Boyz member D-Von Dudley, whose real name is Devon Hughes, the creation of his wrestling school the Team 3D Academy was born out of absolute necessity.

"One of the reasons I opened up the wrestling school in the first place is because when Bubba and I left the WWE in July of 2005, we were pretty much on the indie circuit for a little bit," explained Hughes. "We were sort of traveling around and began noticing that the future of pro wrestling was in trouble because people were brought in the wrong way. They weren't being taught right."

Hughes attributed the paucity of quality wrestling instruction to the number of schools being led by individuals with zero high-level wrestling experience.

"How do you go to someone who says they have a wrestling school, but they've never been anywhere?" asked Hughes. "They've never been to where you want to be. They can't teach you how to get there when they've never been there themselves. That's why we've had the success rate we've had for the simple fact that we *actually* know what it takes to get there."

The Dudley Boyz had been widely heralded as being potentially the most successful wrestling tag team of their generation, and had captured most of the major tag team championships worth owning during their career as a tandem. Francis had certainly seen many of their matches, and the duo's name carried considerable weight and credibility along with it.

"I called them up and I made an inquiry with the strength-and-conditioning coach Dan Carr," said Francis. "I told him I was planning to move there in a year, and that I'd be coming soon. His response was tantamount to, 'Yeah… okay kid. Sure you are.' I'm sure they got a lot of calls from people who say they want to become wrestlers, and nothing ever comes of it in the majority of those cases. That includes plenty of international students who say they're going to come over and never make it there. They may hear what you say, but they're always going to wait and see what you actually do."

Feeling fed up with being relegated to an island that is only 21 miles long and seven miles wide, the 23-year-old Francis finally succeeded in saving the $10,000 he felt was essential to sustain him in the United States long enough to see if wrestling was a legitimate career option for him.

"I told my dad that I was heading off to wrestling school in Orlando, and he told me that my room probably wasn't going to be waiting for me if I ever decided to come back," laughed Francis. "My mother drove me to the airport and said goodbye to me, and then I left. Of all the people I told I was leaving the Bahamas, I'm sure none of them thought I was seriously going to become a wrestler."

Francis didn't attribute their lack of belief in his future success to his preferred career choice.

"It's not that it was just because I wanted to become a wrestler; people attempt to leave the Bahamas all the time, and a lot of them end up right back there," said Francis. "It's not a place like Cuba or Haiti where people are scrambling to get out and come to the U.S., but everyone knows there are more opportunities in the U.S. in general. Still, they probably thought I'd be gone for a month or two, until I ran out of money, and then I'd be on a flight back home the very next day after that."

Francis was finally on his way to a brand-new country to learn to be a professional wrestler. He was about to get a crash course in the business from two of the most respected tag team wrestlers of all time, and he would also see the extremes he would have to go to if he wanted to make his wrestling dreams a reality.

## Nineteen: Tommy Bahama

Ironically, the flight of Omar Francis from Nassau to Florida took him to Tampa, following a similar path taken by dozens of wrestlers who competed for the NWA's Florida office between 1960 and 1987, and then for Florida Championship Wrestling from 1988 to 1991.

Upon reaching Tampa, Francis promptly had some tattoo work done, and then he drove to Orlando and checked into a budget motel directly across the street from Team 3D Academy. Francis marched his 180-pound frame through the front door of the wrestling school at around 8:00 p.m., and ran smack into the school's strength-and-conditioning coach Dan Carr, who Francis had spoken with on the phone one year prior.

"Dan acknowledged that he remembered our conversation, and then he started sizing me up," said Francis. "Then he finally said, 'Yeah, yeah, if we put about 40 pounds on you, I can see you making it in this business.' I told him I was up for the challenge, and he said he'd see me the next day for training. When I came in, I handed over a $750 deposit and $250 for my first month. A full year of training was $3,000."

School owner Devon "D-Von Dudley" Hughes also had a favorable first impression of Francis.

"I thought he had potential," admitted Hughes. "He had a good look to him. He had a great body; that's something that the wrestling business is always looking for. He also had charisma, but we needed to get that charisma out of him."

Francis joined a beginner's class of roughly nine other students, including two men from Australia, one Iranian, and one Israeli student. As "rugrats," the students were not allowed in the wrestling ring. Instead, they all began their training on the rug – the literal carpet of the school – and spent the day learning how to chain wrestle. They were also initiates of the intense strength-and-conditioning test known as "The Dudley Dozen."

The Dudley Dozen required every student to grasp a straight weight bar holding a specific percentage of the trainee's body weight, which was usually about one-third of their weight. While holding onto the bar, trainees had to perform a set number of repetitions of 12 different exercises flawlessly, and in under five minutes.

"It's quite excruciating and not easy at all," described Francis. "Your bragging rights in that gym are based on how fast you can complete the Dudley Dozen, and if you don't complete them within the allotted time of five minutes, then you weren't allowed into the advanced class. It would be very difficult for someone to pass it the very first time unless you were in incredible shape. A world-class athlete like Kurt Angle in his prime wouldn't have a problem with it, but most people just walking in off the street wouldn't be able to do it. Honestly, I was in great shape at the time, and I didn't pass it the first time; I think my time was close to six minutes."

The beginner's classes were held four times a week beginning at 12:00 p.m. until sometime in the late afternoon, and they were overseen directly by Hughes. Once trainees graduated to the advanced class, that's when their instruction would be managed by Mark LoMonaco, best known as Bubba Ray Dudley.

A clear line of separation was made between advanced students and beginners, the latter of whom were not even allowed in the building while advanced classes were in session. Francis chalked this up to part of the initiation format of wrestling, and the fact that there are unwritten rules to the wrestling industry that required following. He was not particularly enamored with the early stages of the beginner's classes.

"The chain wrestling was tedious," observed Francis. "I don't know what I envisioned, but I didn't envision what I was getting. Everyone wants to get in the ring and start off with dropkicks and body slams, and it takes time. Everything is so gradual. I wasn't disappointed; I was very much up to the challenge of earning the right to do what I wanted to do at the school. There were a few people there who didn't look like they were in particularly good shape, but most people start out not looking in great shape, and then they build themselves up to their full potential."

Hughes explained that the nature of his school's training regimen can rapidly expose those who are ill-prepared for the rigors of a 21$^{st}$ century wrestling ring.

"Nowadays, you have to be a complete package to do this job," explained Hughes. "Before it was different. You had people who weren't athletes before who made it into the business and became successful. Some guys who didn't have size or anything like that actually became big stars. We had one person who signed up and thought he was going to be a big star, and we asked him to do one push-up, and he couldn't do it. You can tell who's an athlete and who isn't. If you can't do one push-up, you have no business being in the ring."

While the initial stages of his squared circle training were plodding and deliberate, Francis was not disappointed with his selection of an instructor.

"Devon was a very fair and nice guy," said Francis. "Despite the fiery persona he displayed during wrestling, it was not very easy to piss Devon off. His disposition is fairly sunny most of the time, but I've also seen him when his mood is not quite so sunny. If people intentionally messed around, or screwed around with the school, that would quickly set him off. He didn't take kindly to people doing things that he perceived to be disrespectful to his wrestling school."

Following his week of staying in the hotel across the street from the Academy, Francis moved into a residence at a nearby trailer park that housed several wrestlers. It was a convenient 10-minute walk away from the wrestling school. Francis also purchased a pillow and a sheet from the nearby Walmart, and he spent his nights sleeping on the floor.

Coincidentally, while Francis may have been sleeping on the carpet of his new domicile, he finally graduated from chain wrestling on the carpet of the Team 3D Academy to taking bumps in the ring, which was essentially the practice of learning how to land safely on the wrestling mat.

"Devon explained that we were going to be starting 'Bump Week,' which consisted of pretty much nothing other than running the ropes and bumping," said Francis. "You would run the ropes, take a back bump, and then get up and do it again. We did that *all week long*. The point of it was to exhaust us and blow us up. That week was intolerable. My back was torn up from the ropes, and my elbows were raw from hitting the mat because I didn't know how to bump properly. I would drag myself back to the trailer and sleep until the next day."

Francis found that taking bumps in real life was far more difficult than professional wrestlers working at the highest level had made it appear on television.

"That first bump I took shocked my system," said Francis. "Granted, if you don't do it correctly, it hurts even more. After a couple, you're telling yourself that the bumping isn't that bad, but once you get tired, then you get sloppy. You're landing on your elbow, or other parts of the anatomy you're not supposed to land on. Or you'd hit your head because you forgot to tuck your chin. It just gradually gets worse and worse. By the time you're done, you're in incredible pain."

Rather than getting better, the subsequent days of the week became even harder.

"The second day was one of the worst days of my life," laughed Francis. "I had all those bruises from the day before, along with scabs on my elbow that got reopened by the second set of bumps. It was *really* bad."

From Hughes' perspective, Bump Week is not only a vital conditioning series, but it's also designed to weed out those who believed a career in professional wrestling wasn't going to take a toll on their bodies.

"A *lot* of people give up during Bump Week," confirmed Hughes. "We've had people cry. Bumping is not easy. Within a five-minute span, you're probably going to take between 50 and 60 bumps. And then you have to stand in a squat position for two minutes after that. It's brutal. So Omar had to pretty much pick his tongue up off the floor, as well as his body, and then come in the next day and do the same thing. I think I put him through that for a week straight."

As Francis continued with his wrestling education and the physical toll mounted, he saw people quit their training at the Team 3D Academy, left, right and center. Some students would come in on the first day and pay for the entire year, only to depart from the school after two weeks of training and never return. Others would come for only one day and decide that they'd had enough. Still others would invest a full six months to a year, only to disappear and never be heard from again.

"Wrestling recycles people *every* day. Every single day, people get sucked in and spat back out," stated Francis. "There was one kid who was there from Colombia who wanted to be a wrestler. He was a little, short, chubby kid. He paid the full rent on an expensive timeshare place right next to the school. Once training began, he decided the physical training was too much for him, so he spent the rest of the year not going to the school; he lingered at the timeshare and ate pizza all day long."

As wasteful of both resources and an opportunity as this may have seemed, Francis understood why training at Team 3D Academy could be uncomfortable, especially given the disposition of strength-and-conditioning coach Dan Carr.

"Dan Carr was very intense. He has now had three heart attacks, but back when I started Dan was a monster who wanted his pound of flesh from everyone," recalled Francis. "He was intent on destroying you and building you back up. A lot of people took that the wrong way. Dan operated by the motto 'Strongest; longest.' You've got to be the strongest for the longest or you're not going to last. He was an extreme guy for his entire career, and he pushed people. Many of them didn't like it. They couldn't handle Dan, and they would quit. I certainly had my issues with Dan, but I never quit."

One particular quarrel Francis had with Carr centered around the time Francis injured his knee and was incapable of training up to the lofty standards set by the Academy's relentless strength-and-conditioning coach. Once Francis had nursed the injury for two weeks and was still trying to train through his convalescent period, Carr insisted on needling Francis until he finally lashed out.

"I had to tell him, 'Look… I can't do this right now. I'm hurt!'" said Francis. "He said something along the lines of, 'You island piece of shit! You lazy motherfucker! You act like you can't do anything anymore!' I told him I didn't care what he said, and that I wasn't about to get injured any worse than I already was just to make him happy. That was the one day I walked out of the school and went home. I still came back the next day."

Hughes explained how Carr was simply imposing the athlete-focused structure of the Team 3D training model on Francis.

"We train our students like athletes," said Hughes. "A lot of the people that come into pro wrestling aren't athletes. You have a lot of people who watch it on TV and think they can do it, find a wrestling school, and all of a sudden they jump in. My thing is, you need to be somewhat of an athlete to do this if you want to get anywhere in this business, and you need to have some type of organized sports in your repertoire, whether it be football, basketball, or something like that, and one thing that would definitely help would be amateur wrestling. You need to know what it's like to be in that type of setting. A lot of people who aren't from that type of setting end up here just to pay our bills pretty much."

In addition to improving his conditioning, Francis was also devoted to packing on as much size as he could in order to become physically stronger and present himself as a more imposing figure in the ring. This required more than simply lifting weights, but also far more food consumption than he was comfortable with. He had to take eating to extreme levels to pack on sufficient muscle mass.

"I started eating as much as I could," said Francis. "To try to get as many calories in my body as I possibly could, I started blending my food since it was so hard for me to eat that much. I would get two cans of tuna, two cups of oatmeal, and then add some peanut butter. Then I'd toss all of it in a blender every morning and drink that before I even went to class. It may sound gross, but it doesn't taste as bad as it might sound once you get used to it. It also helped that food is a lot cheaper in the U.S. than it is in the Bahamas."

After Bump Week, Francis and his classmates began learning wrestling moves. Hughes demonstrated how to administer body slams, hip tosses, arm drags, dropkicks, and other wrestling moves that are considered basic in the modern era. The trainees were also taught to "sell," which required them to communicate and embellish the perceived damage they were receiving from each maneuver for the sake of a viewing audience.

Not only was the learning of moves a welcome break from rope-running and bumping for their own sake, but the successful and logical execution of every move in a wrestling match was required of every student before they could graduate to the advanced class. Along with wrestling moves, Hughes also advised his students with respect to how they should conduct themselves outside of the ring.

"Devon made sure that he also taught us wrestling etiquette," said Francis. "It was nothing as specific as not looking veterans in the eye or not shaking hands too stiffly. I've met the people who give the really limp handshake – the worker's handshake – but I never did. Devon was more involved in teaching us how to navigate the dos and don'ts of the business. There are people who will run straight to the booker to tell the booker it was their opponent's fault if the match doesn't go as planned. Devon was quick to teach us not to be a snitch, and not to go running around trying to lay blame on other people, because that sort of thing will get you heat with the other workers."

Regrettably, Francis was unable to complete the full beginner's class before his tourist visa expired. This underscored the significance of what had always been a looming barrier to native-born Bahamians who not only wished to train to become professional wrestlers, but who also wished to remain in the United States and pursue full-time wrestling careers.

The isolated nature of the Bahamas and its lack of wrestling opportunities made high-level pro wrestling careers essentially impossible to acquire if Bahamian wrestlers remained at home. The next barrier was imposed by the limited time that Bahamians are permitted to remain in the United States as non-residents or non-citizens.

Francis left Team 3D Academy while telling the Dudleys that he would return one day, citing that he did not want to return to the Bahamas where the only labor he was qualified to do would pay him $5 an hour, and where a gallon of milk cost $8 at the time. Without the resources to go back and forth between countries, Francis moved to Jacksonville and managed to secure work for himself as a security guard at a strip club in Jacksonville, which was a rather rough environment.

"This club was built almost as a shrine to the local rapper who had once owned it," said Francis. "When he got killed, his brother took over the club, and it was the kind of place where if you messed around, they would drag you out back and beat the shit out of you. In those cases, I was expected to join in on the beatings, and I *did*. It's not that I liked doing it, but sometimes the people who were getting beaten kind of deserved it. Also, the owner told us straight up that if we were working on the security team and a fight happened, and we did nothing, ran away, or didn't participate in some way in breaking up the fight, once the ass kicking was over, *we* were going to get beaten up next."

While working at the club to make ends meet, Francis researched his options for remaining in the country and continuing his professional wrestling dream. He quickly learned that he could acquire American citizenship in only three months if he enlisted in the U.S. military.

"That was my path to being able to stay in the country to train," said Francis. "It was a difficult decision because I knew it was going to take a few years away from my wrestling goals, and I also knew the military was going to beat up my body, but in the grand scheme of things, I needed to be able to stay here, and what better way to do that than to serve the country, earn my citizenship and then return to wrestling? So that's what I did."

After meeting with a recruiter and signing up for military service, Francis learned that some alumni of Team 3D Academy would be making an appearance for the nearby USCW wrestling promotion in Jacksonville. Without having anything else to do that evening, Francis attended the show and ran straight into the wrestling promoter.

"He asked me if I was a worker, and I told him I wasn't really a worker, but I kind of was," laughed Francis. "Then he told me that he had room for me on the show that night. In that moment, visions of my dead body lying in the mountains of Afghanistan flashed before my eyes. I didn't want to die while never having had an opportunity to wrestle in a real match, so I told myself I might as well do this just in case. I had the match, and my name was 'Tommy Bahama' for my debut. The guy I wrestled, Chasyn Rance, was a really good veteran, and the match wasn't bad at all. Even though I was super green, he led me through the match. I was pleasantly surprised that it went as well as it did."

Francis had hoped that his appearance on the wrestling show would remain a secret. Technically, he wasn't supposed to appear at any shows prior to receiving the blessing of the Dudleys, at least not until he'd made it far enough through the advanced class. Wrestling at a show without the blessing of the Dudleys all but ensured that a wrestler would be disavowed and would never be claimed by the Dudleys as a graduate of their school.

Unluckily for Francis, the promoter of the event put his name and photo front and center on the flier for the event, which made it very easy for Francis to be identified and ratted out to the Dudleys.

Without knowing what would be said about him in the wake of his departure from Team 3D Academy, Francis spent the next three years as property of the United States government. It began when he was shuttled off to basic training at Fort Benning in Georgia. Over the course of three-and-a-half months of basic training, much of the size that Francis had worked diligently to pack onto his frame from the time he'd arrived at Team 3D Academy was quickly whittled away, which alarmed him.

"I did everything I possibly could to try to retain my size," said Francis. "I ate a lot of chicken pesto pasta. That was my MRE of choice. If I got something else in my MRE, I would try to barter with someone who had chicken pesto pasta, because that was the MRE that had the most protein in it. I would also barter for peanut butter and hoard it, since some of the MREs came with little packets of peanut butter as well. I needed the fats and the protein to keep my size on. I would steal peanut butter from the cafeteria, and there was a little section in the roof above my bunk, and I would hide the packets up there. When we would go on our camping trips, I would take all the peanut butter I'd amassed, put it in my rucksack, bring it back and hide it. I *always* had more food than I was supposed to."

In the end, it didn't matter. Francis lost all 30 of the pounds he had gained while attending wrestling school, along with a further 10 pounds. At the conclusion of boot camp, he weighed a very lean 170 pounds. It wasn't until boot camp concluded and Francis reported to his base in Tacoma, Washington that he was able to rapidly pack all of his muscular bulk back onto his frame.

Francis' weekdays were devoted to drilling with his striker unit in the remote areas of Washington. On the weekends, he secured a gig as a security guard at a nightclub in Tacoma, which was far more laid back than the club than the club that he'd worked at in Jacksonville. Unfortunately, that's also where he picked up a very unhealthy habit.

"The act of smoking physically relaxed me," said Francis. "All the inhaling and exhaling made it feel almost like yoga in a sense. It will give you a slight buzz, but the more you smoke, the more nicotine you need to feel that buzz. When I was in the military, everything I did helped to facilitate my smoking habit. Whether we were going off to the field for three months, or if I was working security and just lying in one spot for hours at a time, literally the only thing I could do to occupy myself was smoke, and that's how it started."

While Francis was gone, two different wrestling companies would make direct appeals to professional wrestling fans of the Bahamas, with results that were simultaneously compelling and disheartening. A "Bahamian" would also make his debut for World Wrestling Entertainment, but not in a form that most Bahamians would regard as a practical depiction of an islander.

## Twenty: A Million Excuses

The Bahamas that Omar Francis had left behind was in the process of tightening its connections with major sports organizations from across the world. The Atlantis Resort on Paradise Island had initiated a chain of events that would see it become the annual site of one of the most prominent early-season NCAA basketball tournaments, "The Battle 4 Atlantis." The capability of the Imperial Ballroom of Atlantis to be transformed into the Imperial *Arena* would also enable it to host the training camp of the Miami Heat as they prepared to defend their NBA championship.

While the training of Francis had taken a multi-year detour in the midst of his efforts to become the first native Bahamian pro wrestler of his generation to succeed in the United States, NWA president Howard Brody brought his NWA Ring Warrior promotion from Florida to Nassau in 2012, marking the first good-faith attempt in quite some time to rejuvenate the Bahamas as a wrestling hotbed.

By the time 2012 rolled around, the National Wrestling Alliance had been reduced to a shell of its former self, with independent wrestling companies of varying quality levels in different areas of the United States acquiring NWA membership and the right to brand themselves as NWA-affiliated wrestling promotions.

Howard Brody's Ring Warriors promotion was inarguably on the higher end of the quality spectrum for that particular iteration of the NWA. Also, while it can be difficult to account for every wrestling show held in the Bahamas by a fly-by-night promotion, Brody's effort was certainly the first by an NWA-affiliated member promotion in roughly 25 years.

"I had a general idea that Nassau might be a good market for us," said Brody. "Then we were contacted out of the blue by Sportsradio 103, the local Bahamian sports station. Dan Ferguson was the head guy there at the time. We worked out a deal where they bought the show and paid us our guaranteed amount. All we had to do was go down there and perform."

The Bahamas of 2012 was vastly different from the island nation that the NWA had last frequented in 1987. The Bahamian population had increased by 40 percent during that time to well north of 350,000. The Bahamas was also experiencing athletic success on the world stage with far greater regularity.

In particular, the track-and-field athletes of the Bahamas had established themselves as being among the best in the world, both in a per-capita sense, and in an absolute sense. The nation's track-and-field athletes had medaled in every Olympics since 1992, and elevated the Bahamas to the status of being the nation in receipt of more Olympic medals than any country with a population below one million.

Before getting everything assembled for the return of NWA wrestling to Nassau, Brody set out to determine if any sort of wrestling-friendly infrastructure existed in the area. To accomplish that, he sent Pablo Marquez, a veteran wrestler and wrestling trainer, to see if there was even a suitable wrestling ring anywhere on New Providence Island.

"I remember being flown out there a month before the show and checking out the ring that these guys said they had," said Marquez. "It was in horrible condition, and I had to tell Howard the ring wasn't any good."

Later on, Marquez would also be among the first wrestlers to arrive in Nassau for the week of the actual show. For an entire week, he sat in the Sportsradio 103 studio and did everything he could to raise the collective ire of the Bahamians who listened to him.

"I was talking a *lot* of trash!" exclaimed Marquez. "I was supposed to wrestle some guy who we were billing as Bahamian. What I said those couple days in the studios was played over and over. I was talking trash about my opponent and about the Bahamian people."

As Brody continued to put the show together, he had the idea of bringing in Tyree Pride, who was now nearing his mid 60s. It just so happened that Brody's NWA National Heavyweight Champion at that very moment was Kahagas – Paul Antone – the star pupil of Pride.

"You've just got to ask him," Antone said. "That's what I told Howard."

The conversation was short, and it secured the main event for NWA Ring Warriors' first ever wrestling event in the Bahamas.

"Kahagas got Tyree on the phone, and Tyree said he would do it," Brody said. "The only thing was, Tyree doesn't really trust a whole lot of people, and the only way he would do a match is if he was wrestling Kahagas. So that's why one of our main events was Kahagas against Tyree Pride for the NWA National Heavyweight Championship."

Another championship would be at stake that night. On the flight from Florida to Nassau, Chance Prophet of West Virginia was informed that he would be given an opportunity to become the first wrestler in at least 25 years to win a Bahamas championship sanctioned by some version of the National Wrestling Alliance.

"They just told me I'd be wrestling for the Bahamian title, and that I would be going over," explained Prophet. "I considered it an honor. We try not to mark out – or be too excited – for belts, but it was my first international championship. I'd held the national title, but due to geographic constraints, I generally defended it on the East Coast. I was just thankful to be working in front of a non-U.S. crowd. Since I'd been in wrestling, I'd had friends who wrestled in companies in Florida and Georgia who would make trips down to wrestle in Puerto Rico and the Dominican Republic. I was just excited to be wrestling in front of a crowd that wasn't inundated with all of the independent wrestling we had in America."

Another wrestler making the trip who was very familiar with the idea of wrestling in the Bahamas was Wes Brisco of the legendary Brisco wrestling family. Wes is the son of Gerald Brisco and the nephew of Jack Brisco, who wrestled in many Nassau Stadium matches during the early stages of his career.

After settling into his hotel room, Chance Prophet was ushered over to the Sportsradio 103 studio, where he said he was asked to do and say a few things that made him uncomfortable.

"Because of my persona, we had some voodoo priests who asked to come and bless me," said Prophet. "I wasn't inclined to have that done because of my Christian beliefs, so I flat out told them, 'What's in me will not mix well with what you have. Thanks for the support, though.' I was a heel anyway, so I just told them I didn't want their blessing."

When Antone and Pride arrived at Lynden Pindling Airport, Antone got a glimpse of what it was like for a wrestler to be the certified hero of an island nation.

"We weren't even off the tarmac, and people were already chanting 'Tyree Pride!'" Antone said. "You could see it and feel it all the way through the airport. It was 20 years since the last time Tyree wrestled in Nassau. The people knew he was coming, and they knew who he was. It was cool to see that happen for a guy who was a mentor. Tyree was smiling and saying, 'Yeah, that's right!' It's no exaggeration to say he was like the Hulk Hogan of the Bahamas."

On the day of the show, a key item was missing when it was time for the Kendal G.L. Isaacs National Gymnasium to open its doors and let the fans in.

"We had our own ring shipped, but it never got there in time for the show," explained Marquez. "We had to use a boxing ring instead."

After finally locating and securing a ring, the doors were opened, and Marquez stepped through the doors for his opening match with JT Flash.

"I was told my match was the first match in the Bahamas in about 20 years," stated Marquez. "I talked trash about the Bahamian people all week, but when I walked out there, I got a very positive reaction from the crowd. They were just happy to see wrestling, and everything we did got a big reaction. It was like wrestling in Puerto Rico when the people still believed in it. Even something as little as a punch or a hip toss got a great reaction from the crowd."

As the evening progressed, Chance Prophet stepped into the ring with "The Giant Titan" Michael Jarvi and won the NWA Ring Warriors Bahamas Heavyweight Championship. Tyree Pride then presented Prophet with an exact replica of the original Bahamas championship belt which was worn by Sweet Brown Sugar, Jimmy Garvin, Rufus Jones, Angelo Mosca and Dusty Rhodes.

"It was an extremely packed house filled with people who were excited that we'd brought wrestling back," described

Prophet. "When they brought Tyree Pride back, it was ridiculous. You would have thought Jesus had walked into the coliseum the way everyone wanted to meet him."

For Antone, it was a privilege to work a match in the Bahamas with the island legend who had helped his career to such a great degree.

"When Tyree came out, the crowd popped like a bomb had gone off!" Antone said. "Even though that Florida wrestling era Tyree was a part of is a thing of the past, being able to wrestle Tyree in Nassau made me feel for a brief moment like I was a part of it."

**Tyree Pride battles Kahagas (Courtesy of Howard Brody)**

The wrestlers retreated to Paradise Island once the event was over and began to partake in recreational activities, including gambling.

"By the time I got to the casino at Atlantis, Wes Brisco had already won $300 on a single roll at the craps table," Prophet said.

"Yeah, that was a nice moment," laughed Brisco.

In the morning, as the wrestlers arrived at the airport, someone was missing from their group.

"I actually woke up late, on the beach, with two girls," Brisco said. "It had definitely been a fun night. The boys were all looking for me, and when I caught up to them, I was literally running into the airport trying to get my things all together and making sure I had all my clothes on."

The first wrestling event in Nassau seemed to have been an unqualified success according to all parties involved in the show, and plans were made to present a second show just a few months later.

"We wanted to make it bigger the second time," said Brody. "We realized how much money the radio station must have been making off the event, so we wanted to fully partner with them. They gave us a breakdown of how much everything cost, and we agreed to split it."

This time, Brody called in the big guns. He brought in Dustin Rhodes, who by now had progressed well beyond his formative years in the PWF and had been a major WWE superstar as "Goldust," along with Leon "Vader" White, a worldwide super-heavyweight wrestling star who had held the world heavyweight championships in many of the most prominent international wrestling companies at one point.

Chance Prophet would also defend his newly won Bahamas title. However, Pablo Marquez would not be making the return trip to Nassau.

"I had a falling out with Howard Brody, and we were on really bad terms by the time the second show went down," Marquez explained.

Another wrestler who would not be returning to Nassau was Titan, whom Prophet had been booked to lose his Bahamas championship to that evening.

"Paul Jones said, 'We'll put the title on you, and on the next show we'll give it to Titan, and that way we'll leave them happy,'" explained Prophet. "That's how it was supposed to work, but it just didn't happen. Titan had an issue with his passport and couldn't go, so I wound up working with The Beast."

Veteran wrestler and wrestling trainer J.B. Cool opened the show this time, and he claims to have tailored his look to appeal to the fans.

"I came out with black, gold and aqua tights, since those are the colors of the Bahamian flag," said Cool. "I also had the ring announcer introduce me as 'The Bahamian Bad Boy.'"

When told that Cool, a non-Bahamian, asked to be introduced as "The Bahamian Bad Boy" when presented to a Bahamian audience, actual Bahamian wrestler Omar Francis simply laughed and said, "I *hope* they booed him!"

In addition, Cool said he looked at the matches on the card, realized there were no highflyers anywhere on the show, and decided to construct a fast-paced, high-energy opening match to give the fans something they would not be seeing elsewhere on the card.

The night unfolded as planned before the eyes of the fans. Yet, in the locker room, things were not running half as smoothly. Vader, who could make a legitimate argument for being the best and most convincing super-heavyweight wrestler in history, was also well known for being moody and sensitive at times. Regrettably, this was one of those occasions.

"Vader was not happy with his placement on the card," said Prophet. "He was pouting in the locker room, so Goldust had to encourage him to suck it up because they were in the Bahamas and there was no need to pout, and to just go out there. The pouting was because he was working with Bruce Santee, who is a solid worker, and one of the best talents I've ever shared the ring with. But for some reason, Vader was dead set against going out there and working with Bruce in a singles match. Goldust came up with the resolution that they would work together in a tag team match."

In Prophet's mind, this pouting made no sense coming from a man who once shoved his own eye back into its socket in the middle of a Japanese wrestling ring and then finished his match with Stan Hansen.

"This was *Vader*, the toughest guy in wrestling, and he was sitting in a locker room in the Bahamas complaining about being in a singles match with someone he didn't think was worthy of him," said Prophet. "After he got it out of his system, he went out in the ring and performed, and he was awesome. The kids and the people in the crowd enjoyed it. But that was the standout moment of the show from my standpoint; Vader just wasn't happy."

Eventually, two of the matches on the show were merged, and Goldust and Vader teamed up to defeat Bruce Santee and Chavis in the main event of the second show.

At the conclusion of the event, J.B. Cool was approached by a young Bahamian who worked for Sportsradio 103, who introduced himself as Tomeko Whylly.

"He asked me if I wanted to come over to the islands and teach a pro wrestling seminar," Cool said. "I told him I would work with him in whatever he wanted to do."

In the meantime, any plans for a potential "Battle in the Bahamas 3" were indefinitely put on hold.

"Our partners never gave us the money," claimed Brody. "Then they never wired the money. Then they came up with a million excuses. The bottom line is, they *never* paid us what they were supposed to pay us. We lost $20,000 on that show."

Nearly one year later, on July 19th of 2013, Whylly began emailing J.B. Cool in an attempt to arrange a training seminar in Nassau. Cool had been training wrestlers in Florida for several years, and his experience working in Mexico, Germany and Japan made him adept at teaching an array of different wrestling styles.

"Tomeko said he wanted me to come in and help with some training, and we went back and forth through email for a long time to set it up," Cool said.

The two soon agreed on an initial date in August for the seminar, but that date quickly fell through. Along the way, Pablo Marquez was also contacted to be involved in the event.

"The radio station contacted me about doing a show and seminar over there, but nothing ever came of it," Marquez said.

At Whylly's request, Cool says he designed a flier for a seminar which was to take place on August 30$^{th}$. The flier came emblazoned with the logo of the new wrestling promotion that Whylly was attempting to establish: Nassau Wrestling Entertainment.

From there, Cool described a situation where communication ultimately broke down between the two, and the seminar never took place. Then, Whylly contacted Cool again out of the blue several months later with plans to come to the U.S. to train.

"I told him how much money it would cost him to train with me for those several months," Cool said. "It was $1,500, and he would need to find a place to stay here in Florida. He didn't want to have to quit his job to come train with me. I told him we all have to make sacrifices to make it in this business."

As this was going on, Nassau Wrestling Entertainment began to promote itself locally, staging exhibition matches between Triple Ace and Violent T during local boxing events, with Whylly playing the role of face-painted wrestler Triple Ace. Videos of the confrontations were uploaded to YouTube, and were soon followed by a slickly edited music video hailing the arrival of Nassau Wrestling Entertainment. However, Nassau Wrestling Entertainment lay dormant after that, and no NWE-branded events appear to have been held since that point.

"I'm glad to hear Tomeko tried to get something going," said Francis. "He just didn't have the resources and the training to do it properly. But he tried, which is very commendable. That's the issue I faced when I was looking to get into wrestling. No one was training wrestlers anywhere in the Bahamas. There were no schools. There were no shows that I knew of. For Tomeko to try so hard to get it done that he was willing to do it in a boxing gym, or in a boxing ring, my hat goes off to him for doing what he needed to do. He obviously wanted very much to get something started."

The following year, the Bahamas received its first representation in a major wrestling company when Adam Rose of Musha Cay, Bahamas made his debut in NXT – the developmental brand of World Wrestling Entertainment – before being advanced to the main roster on *WWE Raw*.

The Adam Rose character was actually South African wrestler Raymond Leppan, and Musha Cay was popularly known for being the glamorous private island owned by magician David Copperfield. Rose would be regularly escorted to the wrestling ring by a slew of purported clubgoers, before prancing around during his matches, and then dancing his way back down the aisle along with his entourage once his matches reached their conclusion.

Leppan's gimmick was for entertainment purposes and was never intended to be a practical representation of the Bahamas or Bahamians, but it still stands as the first time a wrestler with a supposed residence located somewhere in the Bahama Islands was introduced on WWE programming.

Back in Washington, the time was beginning to tick toward the inevitable conclusion of Francis' mandatory commitment to the U.S. Army, at which point an authentic Bahamian wrestler might be free to continue the pursuit of this dream.

Francis was about to see if he could make good on the promises that he'd made to everyone who would listen to him, and also to himself: That he could overcome the odds and make a name for himself as a pro wrestler if all of the restrictions that made such a thing difficult for a native of a small island nation had been stripped away.

## Twenty-One: Promising the World

Despite his fears that he would die in battle without ever getting to wrestle, Omar Francis fulfilled his entire obligation to the U.S. Army without ever being placed in an active combat setting. Ironically, the full three years elapsed without Francis ever having been deployed overseas, let alone seeing action on a battlefield.

"I had bought a 2005 Mustang GT for myself," said Francis. "The day that I got my papers and got discharged in 2015, I took all my stuff out of my barracks. Everything that I couldn't fit into my Mustang, I tossed it away in a trash can. I drove out of Joint Base JBLM, and I was headed straight to Florida, back to Team 3D Academy in Orlando. It took me a week to get there from Washington to Florida all by myself."

The reason the journey back to Florida took so long was partially owed to the desire of Francis to view areas of the U.S. that he had never seen before, and also because Francis was still unaccustomed to driving for long distances. For someone who grew up on an island that is only 21 miles long, days of driving that stretched on for hundreds of miles felt like an eternity.

"When you live in the Bahamas and someone calls you and says they're 15 minutes away, it's like they're on the other side of the earth, and you don't feel like you can drive that far to come get them," explained Francis. "That's an *eternity* in Nassau. For me at that point, an hour was a serious drive. Five hours was a *journey*. I'd drive five hours and then stop in whatever town or state I was in. I stopped everywhere I could."

The most memorable moment for Francis during his return trip to Florida occurred when he was driving through Montana and almost hit a horse. From there, he decided to stop in a small town called Broadus with a population of just over 400 people.

"I remember I pulled up and the town seemed like it was 30 years in the past," said Francis. "The tumbleweeds were blowing down the street. I looked around and thought, 'Where the hell am I?' It was only 8:00 p.m., but the town's gas station was closed. I needed gas, and I couldn't risk driving further because I didn't know how far away the next gas station was. The last thing I wanted to do was run out of gas in the middle of a desolate road in Montana, so I went to the only hotel in town. When I got to the door, there was a note on it. The note said, 'If you're looking for a room, come find Shirley at the bar.'"

Francis made the trek across town to the local bar. When he opened the door, all eyes turned toward him, and it became clear to him that Broadus, Montana had probably not hosted too many Bahamians before.

"It was the first and only time since living in the U.S. that I'd fully felt my race," said Francis. "When I walked in the bar, it was clear that everyone was wondering what the hell this Black dude was doing in there. I asked for Shirley, and this tiny middle-aged lady popped out and walked me over to the hotel to get checked in. I had to pay $100 for the room for that night, which seemed like an insane amount given the room's quality. It had this murky carpet smell, like the carpet had been made wet by something only very recently. There was also nothing in the room except for a bed and a fly swatter."

To somewhat allay his fears and paranoia that something terrible might happen to him in the middle of the night, Francis backed his car up to the room so that he could drive straight out of the parking lot, and then pushed the bed right up to the door. Thankfully, Francis woke up the next morning without a scratch, and then hopped into his car and continued his journey back to Florida.

Upon walking back through the doors of the Team 3D Academy for the first time in more than three years, Francis was met with a somewhat rude welcome by Team 3D alumnus Mike Parrow, who had returned to the Academy to prepare for a WWE tryout match. Parrow informed Francis that both D-Von and Dan had been made aware that he had violated the school's policy and had a match before he departed for the military.

"When Devon came into the building and saw me, he honestly smiled," said Francis. "He'd always liked me, and he was both happy and surprised. People make a lot of promises in wrestling and rarely keep them. We went into the office and I explained to him why I'd done the show."

**Amir with Bubba Ray Dudley and Team 3D Academy Classmates**

Hughes admitted to being shocked by the sight of Francis back in his building.

"Did I think there was a chance he would come back? Yes," admitted Hughes. "Do people tell me all the time that they need to take some time off because of their job and then never come back? Yes. A lot of people don't come back, but he was one of the guys that did. When he did come back, I took him seriously."

Of course, there was still the matter of the one match that Francis participated in prior to receiving the blessing of the Dudley Boyz.

"Here's the deal: When you come to our school, we want to make sure that when you go out there, you're a good representation of what we taught you," said Hughes. "And if you're not able to do that, then you're not able to wrestle, or at least not use our name to say you did come from our school. We were finding some people who were doing that, and we were getting feedback from other people who were saying, '*You* came from D-Von and Bubba's school? Oh my God.' So that looked bad on us. I chewed Omar's ass out in our office and told him don't ever do that again, and he never did it again."

After finding a new place to live in Poinciana, Florida, Francis resumed his training, having saved up enough money by living bill-free in the military to focus solely on concluding his wrestling education. He quickly brushed up on his ring skills, but the worst of the habits he picked up during his military service caused immediate setbacks in the advancement of his training.

"Because of the chain smoking I'd picked up in the military, my cardio had taken a major hit," admitted Francis. "When I was in the army, we were running every day. Smoking and running every day are going to keep your lungs, liver and kidneys healthy. I had a downtime of about a week or two before I resumed training, and I wasn't running enough to counteract the amount of smoking I was doing. I was at the point where I was so addicted to cigarettes that I would get in the ring, we would do our drills, and then when we were supposed to be breaking for lunch to eat, I was running off to my car to smoke."

After one such smoking break, Omar reentered the building to find Devon waiting patiently for him in the ring.

"He told me that if I was going to do this seriously, I would need to stop smoking right away," said Francis. "He said if I didn't have good cardio, I couldn't wrestle. I stopped smoking that very same day. The withdrawal wasn't too bad. What it ultimately came down to is the fact that I wanted wrestling more than I wanted cigarettes. It wasn't that hard for me. I made up my mind that cigarettes were done, and I moved on from them. It also saved me a lot of money, because I was smoking two packs of cigarettes a day, which was costing me $16 every day. Fortunately, I haven't touched them since."

Hughes confessed to intentionally making Francis as uncomfortable as possible to help him see how incompatible his breaktime cigarette addiction was with an in-ring wrestling career.

"You're already breathing heavy, unable to move and unable to wrestle if you're tired in the ring from all of the activity that you're doing," illustrated Hughes. "Imagine that, and then add smoking to it. I either caught him smoking or smelled it on him, but once I knew he started smoking, I made it a point to blow him up in the ring to the point where he couldn't walk out on his own. He got the message that day. If I'm not mistaken, I believe he went and threw up outside."

With his smoking days immediately behind him, Francis returned to peak ring shape in one month's time, and he breezed into the advanced class three months after his conditioning returned to him. That's when responsibility for training him was transferred over to Bubba Ray Dudley, which involved a focus on interview work, and in-ring psychology.

"Bubba is a completely different animal from Devon. Bubba *terrifies* people," said Francis. "When Bubba walked into Team 3D, it was like a monster movie. When the monster is near, the air gets cold and dry; that's what it's like when Bubba walks in. Everyone is horrified. They don't know what to do or what to say. They don't know what *Bubba* is going to do or say either. But they do know that if they displease Bubba, he will verbally tear them apart, and sometimes physically. Fortunately, I never had a single run-in with Bubba, but he tore into people constantly."

The advanced classes primarily addressed the logic of professional wrestling matches. Whenever his students did something that made no logical sense with respect to what had been happening in a match, Bubba would question them in front of everyone.

"If you don't have a good enough reason for why you did something, Bubba would explain to you why you're a fool, and why you should never make that mistake again," said Francis. "Bubba is a very loud New Yorker. He's so smart, and the way he explains things to you… he may not even be trying to verbally eviscerate you, but he can, and he will. It would definitely have you not wanting to make that same mistake again. You never wanted Bubba to talk to you like you're a fool after it had already happened to you once."

The same year Francis was being elevated to the highest training levels at the Team 3D Academy, there was the sudden announcement of an upcoming wrestling show in Nassau made by Gladiator Championship Wrestling. In the June 5th, 2015 edition of *The Nassau Tribune*, GCW owner Nick Cara stated his initial intention to put on an event at the Melia Nassau Beach Resort during the July celebration of Bahamian independence.

"We have an event that we put on in every state in the United States and we also go to Europe," Cara told *The Tribune*. "But this is the first time that we are doing an event in the islands, so we decided to start the promotion now."

The announcement also mentioned the involvement of former WWE and ECW star Al Snow, along with Total Nonstop Action wrestler Hernandez. Snow was a world-famous wrestler, having emerged from his Body Slammers pro wrestling gym in Lima, Ohio to become a mainstay with the WWE during the height of its popularity.

While less well known than Snow, Hernandez had been featured on television for the better part of a decade with TNA Wrestling, and more recently with the El Rey Network's Lucha Underground promotion.

"When I first heard about the show, I reached out to Cara online to see if I could be involved with it," Francis said. "We went back and forth for a little while, but communication eventually just fell by the wayside."

One week later, Cara returned to Nassau along with Len Davies and the local organizers from Solar Verde Bahamas Limited. The group met with V. Alfred Gray, the Bahamian Minister of Agriculture, and Dr. Daniel Johnson, the Bahamas

Minister of Youth, Sports and Culture. It was also during this
visit that Cara introduced Tomeko Whylly – rebranded as
"Anansi" – to the Bahamian press.

**Bahamian wrestler Tomeko "Anansi" Whylly (The Nassau Tribune)**

"I'm very excited about the events that are coming up
and I want the Bahamian people to know that I need their
support," Whylly told *The Tribune*. "This is the first match that I
will be doing as a professional and I'm going to prove myself
to the world. Please be there. You don't want to miss it."

Days later, images of Anansi and other GCW wrestlers
appeared on Facebook promoting Cara's GCW energy drink,
which he cross-branded with his wrestling company. Soon a
video promoting the "Bahamas Bash" show was announced,
along with a new event date of August 29th, and a new hosting
site on South Andros Island, which may have stemmed from a
misunderstanding. With barely more than 3,500 residents at the

time, South Andros had limited potential as the location for a profitable wrestling event.

"Cara must have gotten some bad information," Francis said. "He must have asked what the biggest island was, and everyone said, 'Go to Andros! Andros is humongous!' No one told him that there's no one there on Andros to actually watch wrestling."

A couple weeks later, GCW's official press release shifted the location of the show to Arawak Cay in Nassau, and included the announcement that ECW legend Tommy Dreamer and MMA champion Shannon Ritch would be wrestling at Cara's show.

Shortly thereafter, on July 15th, *The Nassau Tribune* published a feature article about Anansi.

"I learned at an early age how tough the road is, trying to provide for my family," Anansi said to *The Tribune*. "At the age of 10, I discovered the world of professional wrestling and I started to train myself and I picked up any source of information that could help me as I wait on that day to come when I would finally get to compete on stage."

Anansi further declared his intentions to beef up for the upcoming GCW event, and stated that he might come to the ring with his face painted in the colors of the Bahamian flag.

Over the next month, the size of the match listing for the Bahamas Bash swelled as more certified wrestling superstars were added every week. Former WWE stars The Hurricane, The Boogie Man and Brodus Clay were soon announced for the show. Finally, on August 10th, Cara announced the addition of former WWE and TNA Wrestling star Bobby Lashley to the show on the GCW Facebook page.

The GCW show now had the makings of a certifiably star-studded independent wrestling event. Suddenly, citing events and factors beyond his control, Cara abruptly announced the cancellation and eventual rescheduling of Bahamas Bash through the GCW Facebook page.

Similarly, a GCW event in New York called "War of the Gladiators," during which Anansi was also supposed to make his professional debut, was scheduled for December 18th, 2015, only to have its cancellation announced by Cara three days prior due to a maintenance issue at the facility.

Undeterred, Cara forged ahead and rescheduled the War of the Gladiators for May 7th, 2016 in the Bahamas. This time, UFC Hall of Fame member and former NWA World Heavyweight Champion Dan Severn was booked for the event, along with Anansi, Shannon Ritch, Aero Boy, Hijo de Dos Cara, Savio Vega, and several others. The venue chosen for the event was Kendal Isaacs Gym, but it wound up not mattering where the event was booked, because it fell through yet again.

"Nick is one of those wrestling promoters who is full of hot air," accused Ritch. "He always promises the world but never delivers."

Ritch conceded that Cara informed him about the failure of his local Bahamian sponsors to hold up their end of the deal, but rebutted by citing another failed event Cara booked in the greater Caribbean region. The "Thunda in Guyana" show, promoted as a wrestling event headlined by Dan Severn and Shannon Ritch, was scheduled for May 27th, 2017 at the Cliff Anderson Sports Hall in Georgetown, Guyana. Just like the events GCW scheduled in the Bahamas, the Guyana wrestling show also fell through.

"These events would be great if promoted properly, but Nick tried to go too big too fast," continued Ritch. "Every one of the events he planned in the region fell through."

When the promised events of Gladiator Championship Wrestling failed to come to pass, they eliminated what appeared to have been a golden opportunity for an aspiring Bahamian pro wrestler to acquire some in-ring experience, and in front of a Bahamian audience no less.

By the time the next major wrestling event would actually reach the Bahamas, it would arrive in a wholly unexpected form. It would also feature some of the finest wrestling talent available anywhere in the world, and it would surprisingly unfold from bell-to-bell and start-to-finish without any of the wrestling action taking place on solid ground.

## Twenty-Two: On the Precipice

Back in Orlando, the Team 3D Academy had no formal graduation ceremony for Omar Francis to attend, nor did the training truly have a conclusive ending. The definitive end of the instruction period – at least if you wished to be claimed as an alumni of Team 3D Academy as you pressed onward and into an active wrestling career – occurred when Bubba granted his blessing to students. This would enable them to start wrestling at independent shows with the opening to return to brush up on skills every so often.

No matter how much a student may have paid, and no matter how long they might have spent at the school, the blessing of the Dudley Boyz was by no means guaranteed.

"Bubba had absolutely been known to withhold his blessing from people who simply didn't understand what they were doing, or who he simply deemed to be horrible in the ring, or they weren't learning and weren't improving," said Francis. "Obviously they were frustrated not to be working or not to receive the blessing after paying all of that money. Training at Team 3D carries a lot of weight to it, and part of what a student was paying for is that credibility. If you go to wrestle at an indie show and you're able to say to the promoter that you trained at Team 3D, they know you're good."

With Bubba in the process of relocating to Connecticut, Francis waited patiently for Bubba to return before he could ask him for his blessing to work publicly as an independent wrestler. Eventually, Francis grew impatient and asked for the blessing of Devon instead.

"His exact words to me were, 'Okay, Omar. I think you can brush up on a few things, but you get out there,'" said Omar. "They give you no help with your first independent show bookings. You ask to leave the nest, and then they present the world to you, and you have to jump out of that nest and fly on your own."

Confident that he would soon be working on the independent wrestling scene of Florida, Francis had already purchased his first set of ring gear even before conferring with Devon. His first set of ring attire consisted of black boots, black knee pads, and black wrestling trunks featuring the Bahamian crest on the front.

With Devon's blessing now in tow, Francis worked within his network of wrestling colleagues to see if anyone knew of a nearby opportunity that would enable him to acquire some ring experience. His friend Amy Rose advised him to come to a show in Port Richey, Florida and converse with the event's promoter.

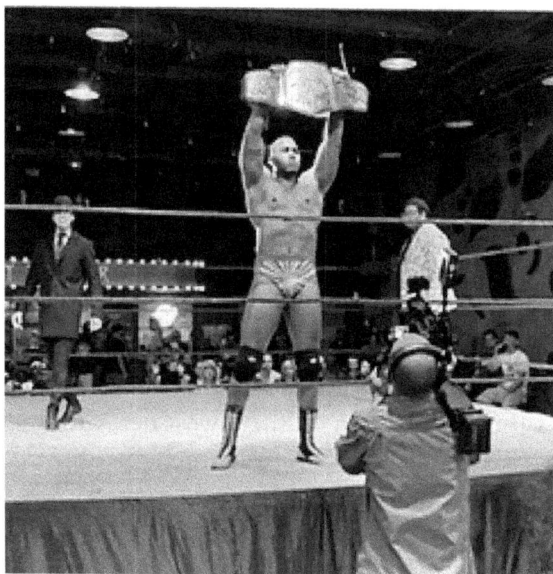

**Amir as the champion of Full Throttle Pro Wrestling**

"They would have shows in a bar, so I drove over there and helped set up the ring and then talked to Kyle Schneider. The owner of American Combat Wrestling was his dad," said Francis. "I met with them, but I didn't get on the show the first time. The next time I drove back, I went with my friend Jude Jean, 'The Haitian Sensation.' Ralph Mosca was booking the show. I talked to him and told him where I was from. He said, 'Okay, you and Haitian Sensation put a match together and show me what you've got.' J.J. and I put a nice match together and wrestled in front of him. He really liked it, and from then on I was booked on that show every week. That's how I got my start wrestling as 'Omar Amir.'"

Amir fashioned himself as a powerful, athletic wrestler, and his original trademark maneuver was a classic spinebuster. He would later adapt the move by beginning it with a body-slam-style lift, before elevating his opponent, hooking a leg and dropping him back-first to the mat, in a move that alluded to Amir's Bahamian origins when he christened it "Island Time."

Amir accepted these early independent bookings for the sake of the experience; he certainly wasn't doing it for the money.

"Every now and then I would pick up a different show, but ACW was my bread and butter for the time being," said Amir. "We were getting $5 to work on the shows, which really meant I was getting paid $5 to drive six total hours. I worked those shows consistently for about three years. As time went on, I worked at Pro Wrestling 2.0 in Orlando, Real Pro Wrestling in Port Lucie, Full Throttle Pro Wrestling, Blueprint Pro Wrestling, and FEST Wrestling in Gainesville."

The majority of these wrestling organizations represented tiers within Florida's World Wrestling Network. ACW was the organization on the lowest tier, with Full Impact Pro and Evolve Wrestling occupying the uppermost tiers. The goal of almost every wrestler competing in the WWN was to work their way onto an Evolve Wrestling event.

During his tenure in ACW, Amir rapidly improved and was elevated to higher levels of prominence in the ACW shows. Then he was paired with fellow independent wrestler Chance Auren on a tag team called "The Precipice."

"Neither of us wanted to be on a tag team together because we were both singles guys, but we were both wrestlers with a brawling-power style," said Amir. "They said they were going to put the tag team titles on us, so we figured if they're going to give us the tag team titles why not? There had been a lot of times I thought about quitting wrestling. It breaks your heart so often, when you go different places and don't get on shows or don't get any opportunities. But then when I got that feeling of not only winning a title, but also having a match that was really good, I was on top of the world that night. That was one of the best nights I've ever had. Even though ACW wasn't that big of a deal, it was incredible."

The Precipice captured the ACW World Tag Team Championship from the team of State Lines and held them for more than a year, providing Amir with his first taste of championship gold in an industry where so few who set out with a dream of setting foot in a wrestling ring ever see that moment happen. It was at this stage that Amir also got a dose of the second guessing that often happens to wrestlers who begin to make names for themselves.

"I was supposed to have a match with soon-to-be WWE star Austin Theory at the Blueprint Pro Wrestling show," explained Amir. "The match was already booked. That's when one of the bookers for WWN messaged Chance and I and asked us if we were available for a Full Impact Pro show, which is just one rung away from Evolve Wrestling. Once you're at Evolve, it's pretty much a given that you're going to get signed by a major company. They asked Auren and I if we were available for that date. If we were, we were going to drop the ACW tag belts on a Friday and win the FIP tag titles the next day."

Adhering to this plan would require Amir to cancel his match with Austin Theory, which was scheduled for the same day, potentially preventing him from capitalizing on a prime opportunity.

"I didn't know what to do," admitted Amir. "Auren and I were also managed by Skinny Vinny. This meant I had two people looking at me, and if I say I won't do the FIP show, the belts are going to someone else, and then someone else is potentially moving up and possibly getting to Evolve. I wound up canceling the booking with Austin Theory, and I kind of destroyed my relationship with that company at the same time. I can't blame them, because I had been booked, and I pulled out to work somewhere else. Instead, we went to FIP and we won the FIP World Tag Team Championship from 'The End.' That was also a great night."

The idea of being steadily featured as a tag team wrestler also grew on Amir over the course of his tenure in Full Impact Pro.

"Our FIP reign had a decent length to it," said Amir. "Chance and I began to get along very well and got very close. We started driving to shows together and got along well. He's also a Team 3D guy also. As far as our name was concerned, I think someone just had the idea of us being the pinnacle of tag team wrestling, so we said, 'Okay, we're at the very top, so we're on *the precipice*!' So that's how that came about."

**"The Precipice" – Auren and Amir, with manager Skinny Vinny**

As Amir was working his way through the independent circuit of Florida, high-level wrestling returned to the Bahamas in a sense that was largely superficial, but in a way that confirmed the nation's 21ˢᵗ century status as a convenient and accommodating island retreat.

A reasonable argument could be made that Chris Jericho is among the greatest professional wrestlers of all time, although the argument is a difficult one to make without also conceding that Chris Jericho is also one of the smartest professional wrestlers of all time. Since making his pro wrestling debut in October of 1990, Jericho wrestled more or less everywhere in the world for the better part of the next 30 years, constantly reinventing himself and turning in impressive in-ring performances throughout the duration of that time frame.

"Chris Jericho is a genius," said Amir. "He's everywhere, and he's making history every year. He's an incredible inspiration to all professional wrestlers. He knows how to do business while still protecting himself and his value."

Part and parcel to making the claim for Jericho being one of the best wrestlers of all time is the recognition of his business sense and creativity. One of his most creative business decisions resulted in the triumphant return of professional wrestling to the Bahamas, albeit in a somewhat superficial sense.

In September of 2017, "Chris Jericho's Rock N Wrestling Rager At Sea" was announced to the world as a four-day cruise from Miami to Nassau. The event was constructed to be a modern wrestling fan's oceangoing fantasy.

Far from simply being a meet-and-greet where highly respected wrestling luminaries like legendary announcer Jim Ross and world-champion-wrestler-turned-yoga-expert Diamond Dallas Page could mingle with wrestling fans, but a comprehensive slate of wrestling action featuring wrestlers from the Ring of Honor promotion was announced for the cruise as well. Prominent within the promotional materials for the show were the colors of the Bahamian flag.

The first Sea of Honor Tournament would involve 16 wrestlers and 15 total matches, with the champion of the tournament qualifying for a future shot at the ROH World Heavyweight Championship.

"I remember there was something that I saw online about the Chris Jericho cruise, and I remember thinking, 'Wow… this is pretty cool,'" said Silas Young, who was a member of the ROH roster at the time the inaugural cruise was first announced. "I'd never heard of a wrestling cruise before. Then I'd heard that they were going to be teaming up with Ring of Honor for it, and I knew that it was something I had to be a part of. I reached out to our booker Delirious directly and told him that I heard ROH was going to be part of the Chris Jericho cruise that was coming up, and that I definitely wanted to be part of it. He responded and said, 'Yeah, you're definitely going to be on it.'"

Within three months of the initial announcement of the event, the cruise's Twitter account revealed that wrestling fans from all but seven U.S. states had already booked their travel aboard the ship. Less than a week later, it was also announced that the first 400 cabins had already been sold. Throughout the year, fans were treated to constant updates about the event until an announcement that every one of the ship's cabins had been sold out was finally posted just one week before the ship's scheduled departure date.

For the participants in the wrestling matches, there were some concerns that special preemptive measures might be required before they entered a wrestling ring that was being ferried through North Atlantic waters by a cruise ship.

"I'd never been on a cruise before, so I wasn't sure what to expect going into it," said Young. "Plenty of people told me I needed to be worried about getting seasick, but to be quite honest, if I hadn't had a room that would allow me to see the water, I wouldn't even have known I was on the water. A cruise ship is like a huge cross between a mall and a hotel that happens to be on the water. It's so big that you would need to have some pretty rough water for someone to actually get sick on it."

Between the time of the cruise's announcement and the moment the ship departed for Nassau more than a year later, several events transpired to elevate the significance of the event. This included the announced participation of several wrestlers who were popular with North American wrestling fans who followed wrestling action beyond the American mainstream, which was dominated by World Wrestling Entertainment.

Among the featured stars announced for the cruise were New Japan Pro Wrestling star Kenny Omega, popular independent wrestling tag team The Young Bucks, and Cody Rhodes – the youngest son of Dusty Rhodes – who had been making waves in multiple wrestling promotions since his departure from WWE.

At the "All In" pay-per-view event in September, Cody Rhodes would replicate his father's feat of winning the NWA World Heavyweight Championship, before then winning the IWGP US title later in New Japan later in the same month.

Even though Cody would lose his world championship back to Nick Aldis one week before Jericho's cruise, the main event of Jericho's entire four-day event would feature the holders of three of New Japan Pro Wrestling's four top singles titles, one of whom was a recent NWA World Heavyweight Champion, one of whom was considered by many wrestling insiders to be the greatest wrestler in the world, and one of whom was considered by some to be among the greatest wrestlers of all time.

"There was never anything said about what the accommodations were going to be like," said Young. "Obviously we knew that we were going to be staying on the cruise ship. Typically, wrestling companies will take care of your flight and get you to the city, and you're responsible for hotels and rental cars and that sort of thing. The nice thing about working for Ring of Honor was they took care of your flights, they took care of your hotel rooms, and they usually would rent a handful of minivans and make sure everyone had a spot. So I knew we would have a room, but for a long time they would double guys up in hotel rooms because most rooms had two queen beds. On the cruise ship we wound up all getting our own little cabin. Each cabin had its own balcony, so it was a very nice setup."

**The wrestling ring on the deck of the cruise ship.**
**(Courtesy of Ethan Yerks)**

All of the matches took place on the ship's pool deck, and fans were able to stand and view the action from multiple levels of the vessel. The Sea of Honor tournament ultimately showcased the majority of the most noteworthy singles wrestlers working for Ring of Honor. Along with Silas Young, the participants were Dalton Castle, Matt Taven, Christopher Daniels, Delirious, Marty Scurll, Rhett Titus, Flip Gordon, Mark Briscoe, Will Ferrara, Adam Page, Frankie Kazarian, Cheeseburger, Beer City Bruiser, Jay Briscoe, and Kenny King.

With a victory in the tournament, the winner would earn a future shot at the ROH World Heavyweight Championship, held at that moment by Jay Lethal.

"Wrestling on the ship was wild," remembered Young. "Typically when you're in the ring, you see the fans, you get that reaction from the crowd, and you have the few seconds where you walk out and might think to yourself, 'Holy shit; I'm in Madison Square Garden and there's 18,000 to 20,000 people here; this is amazing.' But after that it just turns into a regular wrestling match because you're concentrating on what you're doing. I remember a couple times wrestling on the cruise and looking out and not just seeing the fans, but seeing the ocean for as far as your eyes could see. It was definitely a very unique experience."

Adam Page agreed that the setting was cool, but one of his matches aboard the ship became even more memorable due to the presence of an uninvited guest who materialized in the audience.

"Mark Briscoe and I were about halfway through our match, the referee said to him, 'Mark, grab a hold. There's a bird,'" laughed Page. "I never saw it until after the fact, but we were out in the middle of the ocean somewhere, and a seagull or some other type of bird landed in the crowd. People were trying to get out of its way or pick it up, or whatever. When there's a live animal in the crowd, there's not much wrestling you can do that's going to distract people from that."

When the cruise ship finally arrived in Nassau, several of the wrestlers were able to go ashore and enjoy their tropical surroundings.

"When we were docked, I went out and went to the beach with everyone else who wanted to go see the island," said Young. "I remember a few guys talking about going to the Atlantis Hotel, and there was something on a private island that I remember people talking about going to. A lot of wives and girlfriends accompanied wrestlers on this trip, so it was like a vacation with a little bit of wrestling thrown in. I just went to the beach with Kenny King, Rhett Titus, Will Ferrara and a handful of other guys. We just hung out, swam, drank and walked around a bit."

Meanwhile, Adam Page spent the day with Kenny Omega, the Young Bucks and Marty Scurll at the Atlantis Resort, which included a trip down the Rapids River, and a lot of footage being captured for the groups "Being the Elite" YouTube series.

"We knew when the next episode came out, we would be docked, and it would be Halloween, so we did a Halloween special from the ship," said Page. "Cody, Kenny, the Bucks, Marty, Flip, Brian Cage, and a handful of others, we spent almost the entire time that trip filming the Halloween special of BTE. I did a lot of the editing for the episode. This meant I slept for four hours the first night, maybe three hours the second night, and then I didn't sleep at all during either of the last two nights because of how late we stayed up editing everything.

The presence of so many wrestlers did not escape the notice of the Bahamians who watched them disembark from the cruise ship.

"There were a few guys at the dock waiting for us; it was easy to tell that the cruise ships bring in a lot of business," said Young. "There were a lot of people advertising scooters, bout tours and jet skis. We talked to a couple guys who asked us, 'What are you guys here for? Are you guys fighters or something?' When we told them we were here for wrestling they said, 'Yeah, we knew it was something like that!' We quickly picked up on the fact that tourism is a huge industry there and probably brings in a lot of money for the Bahamas."

After wrestlers and fans alike had returned to the ship, it pulled out of Nassau's harbor shortly before sunset and the wrestling continued. In the finals of the Sea of Honor tournament, Flip Gordon defeated Jay Briscoe to win what was undoubtedly the most meaningful singles contest to take place within hailing distance of the Bahamas in nearly 30 years.

"It was so much different from anything I've ever done," said Gordon, during a recap interview with Wrestling Inc. "The crowds were absolutely thunderous from first match to last match, every single show… every single concert. It was just phenomenal from top to bottom."

Gordon added that he was undefeated when afloat in international waters, having won all five of his matches during the cruise.

Later in the event, Jericho and the Young Bucks were defeated by Rhodes, Omega and Scurll in the six-man tag team main event that concluded the wrestling action that took place aboard the cruise ship. Fittingly, Rhodes and his team emerged for their match wearing tie-dyed tank tops with the words "Nassau, Bahamas" prominently printed on them. Omega picked up the win for his team after delivering his One Winged Angel finishing maneuver to Matt Jackson.

The next day was unexpectedly significant to the landscape of 21st-century wrestling.

Collectively, Cody Rhodes, The Young Bucks and Kenny Omega had begun referring to themselves as "The Elite." During an open-mic session on board the cruise ship, the four of them announced their solidarity from a business perspective, and laid the foundation for what would eventually culminate in the formation of the All Elite Wrestling company, which would represent the first respectable competition to World Wrestling Entertainment in nearly 20 years.

Consequently, the first major wrestling event held on Bahamian waters was historically relevant to the professional wrestling industry, even if none of the wrestling technically took place on Bahamian soil.

"I don't think Jericho and his team factored the Bahamians' ability to view the show into their plans because I don't think anyone views the islands as a market anymore," said Amir. "It probably never dawned on them. They probably figured they'd just stop in Nassau for the benefit of the fans that were already on the ship. I don't think they realize how many wrestling fans there are in Nassau, even though so much time has passed since it was a regular touring stop."

According to Amir, the level of wrestling talent aboard the first Jericho Cruise precisely represented the caliber of wrestling that 21st century Bahamian wrestling fans would have been longing to see.

"Bahamians are very critical," said Amir. "They don't just want anything. It's going to have to be a quality event. We see stars in the Bahamas all the time now. No one cares about a star being there. Bahamians don't swarm them or bother them. A star's mere presence isn't enough to draw a crowd in the Bahamas; it takes their talent. If performers are talented, Bahamians are happy to pay to watch them perform."

One of the contributing factors to Bahamians' raised expectations and growing nonchalance in the presence of stars had been due to the regularity with which the Bahamas was now churning out stars of its own. Olympic Champion Shaunae Miller had become one of the most recognizable stars in track-and-field, and Bahamian basketball players Deandre Ayton and Buddy Hield were two of the young up-and-coming stars in the NBA.

Meanwhile, Bahamian American Klay Thompson had developed into a multi-time All-Star and NBA Champion, and baseball player Jazz Chisholm was on a path that would see him become the first Bahamian named to an MLB All-Star team.

Back in Florida, Amir was coping with intense career disappointment. His tag team The Precipice was on the cusp of rising to the zenith of the World Wrestling Network with Evolve Pro Wrestling, only for the company to be purchased by the WWE.

"We were on the precipice – so to speak – of being brought up to Evolve when that happened," joked Amir. "Everything we had been doing sort of collapsed in on itself, and I was left wondering where we would go from there. I wound up going to a Ring of Honor tryout, and they invited a few of us to move up to Baltimore and train at the Ring of Honor dojo for free. Myself and a couple other Team 3D Academy graduates were offered positions in the dojo, and we got together, found a place in Baltimore, and moved up there from Florida."

That's where Amir found himself in 2019, attending the equivalent of a wrestling finishing school hosted by one of the most respected wrestling companies amongst impassioned fans, and being trained by industry veterans Will Ferrara, Jonathan Gresham and Joey Mercury. In addition to attending training sessions, Amir and his fellow dojo enrollees were responsible for setting up and breaking down the ring before and after ROH events. Occasionally, they would get to showcase their skills during dark matches at the beginnings of live shows.

Early in the new year, Nassau was once again visited by a cruise ship carrying wrestlers and wrestling fans alike in January of 2020. This time, the roster positions for the wrestling events at Chris Jericho's Rock 'N' Wrestling Rager at Sea were filled entirely by talent from the All Elite Wrestling roster. The four-night event also included a huge slate of special guests that included Diamond Dallas Page.

"It was a killer, non-stop wrestling fan's dream," reported Page. "A lot of the boys had some serious fun doing whatever they wanted in that ring, and the crowd loved it."

Once again, a cruise ship filled with some of the best professional wrestling talent in the world touched New Providence Island, but no matches were held on the island despite the ship letting passengers off less than two miles from where so many legendary in-ring battles once raged.

The ship was filled with many repeat passengers from the inaugural cruise, which made for a more relaxing atmosphere.

"The first time around it was a little chaotic in the sense that you and the fans are all stuck together on a ship," recalled Adam Page. "You can't avoid each other, which is a strange dynamic on days one and two since people are freaking out as you're walking by to try to go and get breakfast. On the second cruise, it was a little more laid back, probably because many of those fans had been on the first cruise and by the second one they were kind of used to it. When you're a performer on the ship, you're walking through and everyone is ogling you and yelling stuff at you, it's kind of hard to relax for four days."

This time Page wasn't spending his time focused on editing a YouTube series, nor would he disembark from the ship when it reached Nassau. Instead, he devoted his attention to the planning of the AEW World Tag Team Championship match between the team of himself and Kenny Omega challenging the "SoCal Uncensored" team of Frankie Kazarian and Scorpio Sky.

**Kenny Omega and Adam Page celebrate their victory in Nassau (Courtesy of Will Byington/All Elite Wrestling)**

With their victory, Omega and Page completed the first title change of a major wrestling promotion with a global audience to ever take place in the Bahamas.

"It was very cool just to have that setting for an episode of *Dynamite* that is seemingly live from a ship in the ocean docked in the Bahamas," said Page. "Being able to look out, see the ocean and see the sky, with the wind blowing in your hair, it was just an incredible moment. It felt good to have that moment in such a different type of setting."

Although the moment was historic, the intricacies of producing a major wrestling show aboard a cruise ship required some additional steps to be taken following the match.

"That night was very chaotic because we did the title match, and then immediately had to go film an interview right after, so we were running around trying to find the right location on the ship where the wind was right," said Page. "We also needed to have two separate planes flying two separate tapes of the episode back to the U.S. to make sure it got there so that it could be aired the following night on Wednesday."

In Baltimore, things were looking good for Omar Amir's chances of making some Bahamian wrestling history of his own, and that's precisely when the COVID-19 pandemic struck.

"Gresham was talking about putting a faction together called 'The Foundation,'" said Amir. "It was supposed to be like a New Japan Young Lions group, where he stripped us all of our gimmicks, and everyone in the group would be guaranteed to have the best match on any card we were ever put on. He wanted me to be a part of that, but as all of that was being brought to fruition, the COVID-19 pandemic hit, the dojo closed, everything shut down, and that was it."

Feeling frustrated, Amir moved back to Florida to ride out the pandemic that defined 2020, while back in Nassau, the pandemic also derailed efforts by at least one independent wrestling company to establish momentum locally.

Later in the year, Amir decided to pay a two-week visit to a friend who was living in Kentucky. As luck would have it, he also knew a wrestler working for Ohio Valley Wrestling at the time – the organization that had once directly funneled promising developmental talent to World Wrestling Entertainment and the Total Nonstop Action wrestling companies at different points of its existence.

"I was staying with one of the OVW referees, and I just happened to be there right as they were lifting the COVID-19 restrictions," recounted Amir. "Indiana seemed to have lifted their restrictions before any place else in the area. OVW was having a show in Indiana, and the guy told me OVW was having a show in Jeffersonville, Indiana on September 1st of

2020, and that maybe I should go and see if they could put me on the card."

After being paired with a wrestler named Gustavo on his first night in OVW, Amir quickly secured a job with the promotion just as the COVID-19 restrictions were being lifted throughout Kentucky.

"Al Snow was convinced we should give Omar more opportunities," said OVW wrestler and booker Adam Revolver. "He was physically impressive. We were able to see a lot of the stuff he could do, including the physical execution of moves. His wind was also there, so that's always important. Omar would hang in there physically with any of the most physically talented people we had. And after meeting him, he had a great attitude."

"Once I realized I could work every week in OVW, I realized I had no reason to go back to Florida, and I stayed," added Amir. "I was only supposed to come up for two weeks, but I never left."

And that's how 60 years of Bahamian professional wrestling history reached its end, with the most promising Bahamian wrestling prospect in history vying to stand out amongst his peers in the American Midwest, and with one of the most well-funded pro wrestling companies in history coming tantalizingly close to making a Bahamian landfall year after, but with the wrestling ring remaining securely on the ship's upper deck each time.

# Epilogue

As the Bahamas enters an era beyond its first 60 years of professional wrestling history, things have truly come full circle. In January of 2021, Omar Amir Francis successfully captured the heavyweight championship of Ohio Valley Wrestling – a championship held at different times by some of the most popular wrestling stars of the early 21$^{st}$ century.

**Omar Amir as the OVW Heavyweight Champion**

When he did so, Amir etched his name on a list that includes the recognizable names of luminaries like John Cena, Dave Batista, Randy Orton and CM Punk. He also undeniably ascended to the loftiest heights that any Bahamian pro wrestler had ever reached before.

"It was definitely pretty surreal, especially given all the names that have held that title," said Amir. "Doing something like that had always been on my dream bucket list, but I never actually saw myself living in Louisville, Kentucky, and I never saw myself working for OVW. When it happened, it was amazing. It's impossible to find the words to describe it."

Despite the significance of the decision to put the OVW Heavyweight Championship around Amir's waist, it was a booking decision that caught him completely off guard.

"I had only been there a few months," said Amir. "I'd had a couple match-of-the-week honors under my belt, but I didn't really think that much of it. So the day that the 'Nightmare Rumble' came around, I looked at the list of the entrants and the eliminations, and I saw my name at the bottom, and I said, 'Am I winning this?!' The whole day, people were coming up to me and congratulating me, and I was surprised because I hadn't been there very long, but I guess Al Snow and Adam Revolver saw something in me that I didn't even see in myself."

Revolver stated that booking Amir to win the OVW championship was a natural outcome of feeding additional opportunities to people who keep capitalizing on them.

"When you give someone the ball and they run with it, you like to see how far they can get with it," said Revolver. "Omar came in, and he was already where we would want someone to be at the end of a couple years with us. We kept giving him opportunities, and he kept taking advantage of them."

With his achievement, Amir also etched his name alongside those of some of the most accomplished graduates of the Team 3D Academy.

"I'm proud of Omar," expressed Devon Hughes. "I'm glad he has done what he's done. We've produced so many people in WWE, whether it's NXT or the main roster. Things like that, I'm very proud of. To add Omar to the mix is great. The more people we can pump out of our school to get them to where they need to be, to follow their dreams, to help them get a job, to make money and support their families, that's phenomenal, and I will continue to do that as long as I'm still breathing."

Bahamian Rhapsody

At the same time, 2021 marked another year where All Elite Wrestling flirted with Bahamian soil. Another cruise ship full of wrestling talent made a wrestling-themed voyage to the Bahamas – this time to Grand Bahama Island. The guests aboard the ship enjoyed tremendous entertainment and wrestling action, but once again no matches were visible to the eyes of a Bahamian audience, and the docking location of the ship wasn't conducive to land-based touring for the passengers who made the trip.

"I got to mingle with fans, watch some great wrestling, play fun games, listen to incredible music, and eat amazing food," said wrestling superstar and Olympic gold medalist Kurt Angle, who was guest of honor aboard the cruise ship. "I did not get off the ship because you had to drive 45 minutes to get to the other side of the island to get to anything worth seeing."

"Hopefully one day soon they'll take the ring off the ship and bring it down to the Bahamian people," added former NWA Bahamas titleholder Jimmy Garvin. "It's already there, and I'm sure the Bahamians would appreciate an opportunity to see the wrestlers do their thing."

Ideally, if such an event was to occur, it would take place at a major modern venue like the Imperial Arena at the Atlantis Resort.

"It would be great to have a show at a place like Atlantis," said AEW wrestler Adam Page. "It never crossed my mind. I would definitely love to do something like that. Logistically, it can be difficult to do remote locations like that, but if the numbers make sense to do it on a cruise ship, I don't think doing a show in the Bahamas is outside the realm of possibilities. I would *definitely* love to do it."

While Francis continues to capture professional wrestling championships, all while adorned in aquamarine, black and gold, his pro wrestling ascendance is representative of an era when Bahamian athletic success on the world stage has become the rule rather than the exception. It also marks a critical turning point, underscored by recognition of the fact that most prominent U.S. wrestling companies no longer travel to the Bahamas in an entertainment capacity, but at least one Bahamian has taken it upon himself to serve as a symbolic response from a nation that was once running over with passionate wrestling fans.

As an allegorical turning of the tables, Francis has offered himself up as one of his country's best, and now travels across the United States and entertains American audiences. In the culmination of a Bahamian dream that was first dared to be imagined by some of the most "Sensational" Bahamian people, and that is spiritually linked with the "American Dream," 60 years of Bahamian wrestling history has concluded with the Bahamas serving as an exporter of wrestling talent from amongst its citizens, and looking forward, upward and onward to the day when it can send and receive even more.

# Afterword

The Bahamas was a very special place to me. During my wrestling career, I lived in the Bahamas for many months, and I made dear friends there, on every island from Nassau and Eleuthera to Current Island, Spanish Wells, the Cat Cays, and every place in between during my fishing and diving trips. In the process, I visited places that most of my friends back in the United States had never even heard of.

The Bahamas was an absolutely magical place to wrestle, and not everyone had the appreciation for it that they should have. I was proud to wrestle in the Bahamas for three different organizations, including Eddie Graham's Championship Wrestling from Florida when it was part of the National Wrestling Alliance, Steve Keirn's Florida Championship Wrestling, and World Championship Wrestling.

For all three companies, I wrestled in Nassau Stadium against Tyree Pride, who truly was "The Pride of the Caribbean." I'll never forget the matches I had against him in front of so many passionate wrestling fans.

But if there's one thing I want you to take away from this book, it's this: I'm the last, undefeated, undisputed NWA Bahamas Heavyweight Champion. I've got the belt to prove it, and don't you ever forget it!

Sincerely,

"The Taskmaster" Kevin Sullivan

## AUTHOR'S ACKNOWLEDGEMENTS

The creation of this book would have been impossible without the cooperation of so many people, beginning with all of the wrestlers, referees, managers, historians, writers, and everyone else who agreed to be interviewed, whether they contributed one hour, or one sentence. This book exists with the sole intention of preserving Bahamian wrestling history, and your selfless willingness to share your knowledge and experiences is what has made this possible.

To the editorial staff at *The Nassau Tribune* and *The Nassau Guardian*, thank you so much for granting me permission to share so many of the images contained in this book. It makes a world of difference in the finished product.

Thank you to all my Bahamian family members by blood or marriage for putting up with me, especially the Capron, Evans, Lightbourne, Chea and Johnson families. Extra special thanks is reserved for George Capron, David Capron and Anthony Capron for facilitating my wrestling hobby in one fashion or another, and also for being tremendous uncles.

Mom and Dad, I love you both. Thanks for having me. And Mom – Pauline Capron Douglass – thank you for being a lifelong example of sustained Bahamian brilliance. No one would have expected anything less from a former class president at *The* Government High School.

Teisha Lightbourne Douglass – a true Bahamian national treasure – thank you for seeing something worthwhile in a guy from Southfield, Michigan. I love you so much.

Philippians 4:13: "I can do all things through Christ who strengthens me."

Regards,

Ian C. Douglass

Bahamian Rhapsody

**CREDITS**

**Author**
Ian C. Douglass

**Cover Art**
Marc W. Leitzel

**Foreword**
Steve Keirn

**Afterword**
Kevin Sullivan

**University of Florida Research Assistants**
Andrea Summer Bias        Kristin Conwill
Lauren Justice            Maggie Silva

**Additional Aid**
Anthony Capron        Brian Blair
Oliver Lee Bateman    John Cosper
Dave Millican         Greg Oliver
Ken Bevan             Bodine Johnson
Jon Schneider         Ronald Overs III
Erik Love             Natasha Lightbourne
Peter Lederberg   Peter W. Deveaux-Isaacs Sr.
Howard Baum           Frederick Sturrup
Barry Rose            Steve Keirn
Anquin Cooper         Pauline Douglass

**Major Photo Permissions**
The Nassau Guardian        The Nassau Tribune
All Elite Wrestling

**Interviewees**
Arnsel Johnson, Omar Amir Francis, Brian Blair, Buggsy McGraw,
Dory Funk Jr., Steve Keirn, Kevin Sullivan, Tyree Pride, Reggie
Parks, Don Muraco, Jimmy Garvin, Brian Knobbs, Butch Reed,
Rocky Johnson, Mike Rotunda, Duke Droese, Silas Young, Rusty
Brooks, Scott McGhee, Bill Alfonso, Bruce Owens, Jerry Grey,
Howard Brody, Chance Prophet, Howard Baum, Wes Brisco, J.B.
Cool, Pablo Marquez, D-Von Dudley, Sherri Lee, Black Bart,
Kahagas, Larry Hamilton, Bob Roop, Bobby Wales, Shannon Ritch,
Ricky Santana, Princess Victoria, Barry Rose, Anthony Pinder, Jim
Cornette, Kurt Angle, Diamond Dallas Page, Tom Archdeacon,
Adam Page, Adam Revolver, Sweet Daddy Siki, Joe Malenko

306

**Omar Amir**
**OVW Heavyweight Champion**

# About the Author

Ian Douglass has been a contributing writer for *Men's Health Magazine*, *The Ringer*, *Splice Today*, and *MEL Magazine*, and has had his material curated into the New American History project at the University of Richmond. He has also been a content contributor to *Popular Science Magazine*, *Fixed Ops Magazine*, *The Pro Wrestling Post*, *Pro Wrestling Stories*, The International Pro Wrestling Hall of Fame, and The Bahamas Historical Society.

In addition to writing, Ian was also an on-air reporter for the NBC News affiliate in Flint, Michigan. He is a graduate of the University of Michigan in Ann Arbor, earned a master's degree from Northwestern University's Medill School of Journalism, attended the Specs Howard School of Media Arts, and completed the Executive MBA program at the Quantic School of Business and Technology.

Between 2016 and 2021, Ian co-authored the autobiographies of professional wrestlers Dan Severn, Dylan "Hornswoggle" Postl (along with Ross Owen Williams), Buggsy McGraw and Brian Blair, with multiple books earning "Best Wrestling Book – Finalist" honors from *The Wrestling Observer*.

Coincidentally, Ian has also served as a volunteer firefighter with the Bahama Volunteer Fire Department of Durham County, North Carolina.

www.ingramcontent.com/pod-product-compliance
Lightning Source LLC
Chambersburg PA
CBHW071407090426
42737CB00011B/1386